Religion in America

ADVISORY EDITOR

Edwin S. Gaustad

SELECTED WRITINGS

OF

ISAAC MAYER WISE

David Philipson
and
Louis Grossman

ARNO PRESS & THE NEW YORK TIMES
New York 1969

Reprint edition 1969 by Arno Press, Inc.

*

Library of Congress Catalog Card No. 71-83433

*

Reprinted from a copy in the
Hebrew Union College Library

*

Manufactured in the United States of America

Selected Writings
of
Isaac M. Wise

(Aet. 60.)

Isaac M. Wise

Selected Writings
of
Isaac M. Wise

WITH

A BIOGRAPHY

BY THE EDITORS

David Philipson and Louis Grossmann

Published under the auspices of
THE ALUMNAL ASSOCIATION OF
THE HEBREW UNION COLLEGE

CINCINNATI
THE ROBERT CLARKE COMPANY
1900

PREFACE.

At a meeting of the Alumnal Association of the
Hebrew Union College, held at Richmond, Va., in
the month of December, 1898, it was resolved that
the alumni celebrate the eightieth birthday of their
teacher, the President of the Hebrew Union College, by publishing a volume of selections from his
writings. The task of editing the book was intrusted to the two members of the alumni who are
resident in Cincinnati. They were also requested
to write a biography of the master as an introduction to the volume.

It was hoped that the book would appear on the
day of the celebration, March 14, 1899. A number
of untoward circumstances, however, prevented
this. In the meantime, the great leader has been
called to his eternal rest. This volume, therefore,
assumes the form of a tribute to the memory of
their beloved teacher from his disciples, the graduates of the College.

The first part of the biography (pp. 1–58) is
from the pen of David Philipson, and Louis Grossmann has written the second part (pp. 59–111).

·The editors have the consent of Prof. Dr. M. Mielziner to print his appreciation of Dr. Wise's life and work. They feel that this is the most fitting close to the biography.

In making their selections from the mass of material written by Dr. Wise during his long career, the editors have been guided by the purpose of giving permanent form to such productions as contain his characteristic thoughts. Three of the papers included, "Moses, the Man and Statesman," "The Wandering Jew," and "Paul and the Mystics." were lectures delivered in various parts of the country; the essay on "The Law" was published in "The Hebrew Review," the organ of the Rabbinical Literary Association, now out of print. All the remaining selections are taken from the columns of "The American Israelite," the weekly paper which Dr. Wise edited for over forty-five years.

The editors take this opportunity of thanking their colleagues of the alumni for the confidence shown them by intrusting them with the work of preparing this volume, in which they have attempted to include the leading thoughts of the man who was the most potent factor in the history of Judaism in America.

CINCINNATI, *May, 1900.*

TABLE OF CONTENTS.

(v)

SELECTIONS.

LIST OF ILLUSTRATIONS.

CHAPTER I.

It is well known that the medical profession has numbered many Jews in its ranks at all times. Up to the close of the eighteenth century, it was the only higher calling open to the Jews of Europe, excepting, of course, the rabbinical and pedagogical offices within Jewry itself. Therefore, the great medical schools, especially those of southern Europe, counted numbers of Jews among the students. One of the most noted of these schools was that of Salerno in southern Italy. Among the students attending there in the middle of the eighteenth century was a young man by the name of Leo, who had come all the way from western Bohemia. Upon finishing his studies he returned to his native land, and was called by his co-religionists, Doctor, also by its Hebrew equivalent, "chakham," the wise man. This term was later germanized into Weis, which became the family name. This Leo became Kurarzt at the famous watering place, Marienbad; however, as no Jews were permitted to live there, he settled in the village Durmaul, near by, but practiced his profession in the health resort. His son Isaiah followed in the father's footsteps, and also adopted medicine as a profession ; he too went to Italy to study, not to Salerno however, but to the nearer Padua. Upon his return to his native land he settled in Durmaul likewise; he practiced his profession by day, but devoted his evenings to studying the volumes of Hebrew lore. His son Leo received Talmudical and rabbinical training at the hands of the father and became a schoolmaster; he settled in the village of Steingrub and performed the duties that fell to the lot of the public religious functionary of a small Jewish community in those days, reading the prayers at the services, teaching the children, and the like.

This village of Steingrub lay on the Bohemian-Saxon-Bavarian frontier, being one mile distant from the Saxon and three miles from the Bavarian line; hence it was rather cosmopolitan if such a term can be applied to so small a place; the different elements of the population, Catholic and Jewish, German and Bohemian, lived on amicable terms. Here on the third day of Nisan, corresponding with the twenty-ninth day of March, in the year 1819, there was born to this schoolmaster, Leo Weis and his wife Regina, their first son, but second child, Isaac Mayer; the couple had seven children, three sons and four daughters, and was wretchedly poor, the father's earnings scarcely sufficing to provide the bare necessaries of life.

The father conducted a school for the Jewish children of the village in his house; the child Isaac began to attend this school at the age of four; he received private instruction from his father besides; when he was six years old he commenced the study of the Talmud; at the end of three years, increasing cares prevented the father from giving the boy that special attention which his talents merited, and his eager thirst for knowledge required. He was

now, at the age of nine, sent to his grandfather, the
Doctor Isaiah mentioned above.   In the daytime he
visited the Jewish school or cheder; here nothing
but the Talmud was studied day in, day out, except
on Friday afternoon when the Pentateuch with the
Targum or Aramaic translation and the commentary
of Rashi formed the theme of instruction. At night
his grandfather instructed him in the Talmud and
allied subjects; at ten the boy was invariably sent
to bed, but the grandfather sat up till midnight
poring over huge tomes. These midnight vigils
excited the boy's curiosity, especially as he had
noted a large wooden box which was never opened in
his presence, but from which he had seen his grandfather take books when the child was supposed to
be abed and asleep ; the mysterious box was meddled
with and one day yielded to manipulation; it was
found to be filled with cabalistic works with the
mysticism of which the physician occupied himself
in the still hours of the night.

When the boy was twelve years old his grandfather died. He was now thrown upon his own resources. His father was burdened with a large
family and was too poor to do anything for him. He
had already determined upon a professional career.
The great center of Jewish learning in Bohemia was
Prague, the capital city ; Prague had long been a
Jewish metropolis, it had a large Jewish population,
many schools and synagogues and rabbis of note ;
it was the magnet that attracted the Bohemian
Jewish youth who were desirous of receiving a
rabbinical education.

With his bundle in his hand and twenty-seven

kreutzer in his pocket the ambitious boy set out on
the long journey afoot ; on the way he stopped at
the town of Mies, where dwelt a cousin who gave
him five florins, and in the city of Pilsen he looked
up an uncle, an artillery officer, who encouraged
him in his laudable undertaking and gave him ten
florins as an earnest of his good will. As soon as
he arrived at the capital he attended the session of
the Beth Hammidrash * situated next door to the
celebrated synagogue, the alt-neu-schul. †

But how was he to obtain the means of subsist-
ence? Fortunately he had relations in the city who
showed him frequent kindnesses. Rabbi Bezalel
Ronsperg, who had been dayan ‡ in the Jewish
community of Prague before his death, was an
uncle of his mother ; his widow was still living;
she welcomed the boy to her house, where he
took his meals occasionally. A fortunate circumstance which had an unlikely beginning, brought
him the patronagè of a rich and liberal man
by the name of Moses Fischel. Like many rich
Jews, the ambition of this man was to have a
learned son-in-law. Therefore, when a certain
youth who was represented to be a young man of
great parts asked for the hand of his daughter, the
consent was readily given. In such a case it was
usually the custom that on the Sabbath afternoon
preceding the wedding, the bridegroom gave an example of his Talmudical learning and his casuistical

* School.
† See the author's " Old European Jewries " (Philadelphia,
1894), p. 104.
‡ Judge.

powers before an assembly invited for the purpose. Young Wise and several companions in passing by a synagogue on a Sabbath afternoon and hearing the familiar accents expounding a Talmudical subject, entered the building. In a spirit of youthful exuberance they tried to confuse the speaker by a number of questions. The groom who was really an ignoramus, but had learned his lesson by rote, grew embarrassed, stammered and finally was forced to acknowledge his inability to answer the questions. Fischel, chagrined beyond measure, accosted the interrupters angrily, and losing all self control boxed the ears of Wise, the chief offender. The next morning, to the boy's great surprise, for he was but thirteen years of age at the time, the rich, respected, influential Moses Fischel called at his lodging place and humbly apologized for his hasty action. So great was the respect of the Jews of those days for learning that when Fischel, upon inquiry, discovered that these youths were among the most promising students in the Beth Hammidrash, he begged pardon for the insult offered. The action speaks for itself and requires no commentary. The rich man insisted upon the student's becoming a frequent guest at his house for meals ; and the generous sum of money that he found invariably beneath his plate went far towards enabling him to pursue his studies.

He studied at the Beth Hammidrash in Prague between two and three years. Only Hebrew lore was imparted here. The youth was so fortunate, however, as to form the acquaintance of Prof. Moses Koref, a teacher of mathematics in the Normal

School of Prague.   Koref took a fancy to the keen-witted lad and offered to give him private instruction in the evening, in arithmetic, algebra, and geometry.   This was the first taste he had of non-Talmudical studies.

From the Beth Hammidrash he went to the yeshibah * of Rabbi Loeb Glogau, also known as Loeb Schlesinger, the district rabbi (Kreisrabbiner) of the Braun district; he remained a year here. Thereupon he attended, also for a year, the main rabbinical school of Prague, the yeshibah of Samuel Freund, the rabbi of the so-called Zigenner Schul, the greatest Talmudical scholar of his age.

The most celebrated yeshibah in Bohemia at this time was that of Jenikau, presided over by Rabbi Aaron Kornfeld, a man of great learning and wealth.   This yeshibah had in 1835, the year that Wise entered it, one hundred and fifty scholars. He remained here for two years, until the new governmental edict was issued in 1837, to the effect that no one could enter upon the rabbinical office thereafter unless he had taken the prescribed courses at the gymnasium and university.   The old edict had been much more lenient, and had required only that the candidate should be declared to have sufficient rabbinical learning by a Beth Din † composed of acknowledged authorities in rabbinical lore. One morning, shortly after the promulgation of the new edict, Rabbi Aaron entered the yeshibah, and without uttering a word sat down upon the ground

* High school of Jewish learning.
† Court of learned men, usually three in number at least.

and acted as though mourning for some great afflic-
tion that had befallen him. The impression made
upon the assembled students was deep and painful ;
they knew not what had occurred. After a time the
venerable rabbi arose and told them of the edict,
saying that it dealt the death-blow to his yeshibah.
This proved to be the case ; the yeshiboth began to
decline from that time.

While at Jenikau, Wise received his first knowledge of German literature, and that from the most
unexpected source. The local rabbi of Jenikau was
Rabbi Jonathan Altar, a bitter opponent of Rabbi
Aaron Chorin, of Arad,* one of the early reformers. Chorin was mercilessly persecuted by the
rabbis of the old school, and by none more than by
Altar. This rabbi of Jenikau had two sons who
had studied at the university. They were infected,
as were so many young Jews of that period, with
the belletristic spirit ; the German poets, Schiller,
Goethe, Herder, were the objects of their devotion ;
through these two young men, sons of the rabbi,
Wise was introduced to the masterpieces of German
literature and with their aid began the study of
pure German. They undertook privately a translation of the Machzor † wherein he assisted them.

Upon the announcement of the edict by Rabbi
Aaron Kornfeld, thirty of the students of the yeshibah, of whom Wise was one, determined to go to
Prague to enter the university there. Before this
could be done, the examinations had to be passed.

* See Leopold Loew, Gesammelte Scriften, I, 251ff.
† The Hebrew Prayer Book.

None of these young men had ever attended the gymnasium ; they were all nineteen years of age or over, too old to enroll themselves as pupils of the opening class of the gymnasium. They received a dispensation from the government excusing them from the gymnasium and permitting them to make the examination for the university without having attended the preparatory school. This meant close and severe private study in German, Latin and Greek. Besides, Wise acted as house tutor in the home of Leopold Jerusalem. At the age of nineteen he passed successfully the examinations of three classes of the gymnasium.

His studies in Prague were now interrupted by the untoward circumstance of the death of his patron, Jerusalem ; the boys who had been under his charge were sent to school and Wise was compelled to look elsewhere for his livelihood. Not succeeding in finding a similar position in Prague, he accepted a house-tutorship in the village of Grafenried, in the family of Herman Bloch, a merchant. While here he formed a profitable acquaintanceship with an assistant of the Catholic priest of Wassersuppen, a town near by. These two—the Jewish and the Catholic students—met every evening, the candidate for the priesthood giving the rabbinical student lessons in Greek and receiving in return instruction in Hebrew. At the end of a year and a half Wise returned to Prague with Joseph and Edward Bloch, the sons of his Grafenried patron, in his care ; the boys were to attend school in the metropolis. Wise registered as a regular student at the gymnasium, and after an attendance of six months passed the examination of the fourth and fifth classes.

He was now elected, teacher by the Jewish community of Ronsperg on the recommendation of Salomon Judah Rappaport, the great scholar, who was rabbi in Prague at that time. True, according to the law, no one could be appointed a teacher unless he had passed the examination for the university; but there being no Jews who had fulfilled this requirement, Wise was given the commission by the government, since he had successfully passed the five classes of the gymnasium. He remained at this post one year, and then went to Pressburg in Hungary, in order to make his final examination at the gymnasium for entrance to the university. The reason for this was that in Austria no one could graduate from the gymnasium and receive matriculation papers for the university unless he actually attended the classes of the upper gymnasium for a full year. In Hungary the law was not so strict; after six months' sojourn in Pressburg he passed his examination and obtained the coveted matriculation papers. While in the Hungarian city he attended the yeshibah of the celebrated rabbi, Moses Sopher.

Returning to Prague at the age of twenty-one, he registered at the university, which he attended for two years. He lived in the house of Rappaport; he gave instruction in various branches and copied music for a living. At the end of two years he determined to go to Vienna to attend the university there. Fortified with letters from Rappaport, Samuel Freund, M. L. Landau, the editor of the

Aruch * of Nathan of Rome, and several professors
of the university, he made his way to the Austrian
capital. Immediately upon arriving in the city he
went to the house of Isaac Noah Mannheimer, the
celebrated Jewish preacher, who received him very
kindly and insisted upon his remaining at his house
until he found permanent quarters. He arrived in
Vienna in the year 1840, and during his stay of
two years in that city he dined every Saturday at
the house of Mannheimer and every Sunday at the
house of the equally celebrated cantor, Sulzer. A
few days after his arrival he registered at the university. While pursuing his studies there he was
teacher in the family of the wealthy Herr von
Werthheimstein, in whose palatial house he lodged.
While in Vienna he wrote several novels, one of
which, ''Die Belagerung von Mailand,'' appeared in
the columns of the Bohemia, a newspaper published
in Prague. At the end of the two years he traveled through Italy with young Werthheimstein, and
shortly thereafter made a second tour of that land
as the companion and tutor of a young Christian
baron.

He returned to Prague, taking up his quarters as
before in the house of Rappaport. He now, at the
age of twenty-three, passed his rabbinical examination before the Beth Din, composed of the Rabbis
Rappaport, Freund, and Ephraim Loeb Teweles,
who conferred the Morenu † upon him. He was
well equipped for his work in life; he had received

* A Talmudical dictionary.
† The rabbinical title.

a secular education equaled by few if any Jews in
Bohemia, and his brilliant examination before the
Beth Din composed of three of the greatest rabbinical authorities of the age was testimony full and
ample of the competency of his Hebrew knowledge. Rappaport, who had always befriended him,
wrote to the officers of the Jewish congregation of
Radnitz, who were desirous of engaging a rabbi,
to the effect that he would send them an אור חדש,
a new light. Upon their expressing their willingness to hear him, Wise went there, preached
and was elected to the position at once. He
preached his inaugural sermon on October 26, 1843.
He was the first rabbi to preach in German in Radnitz ; in truth, there was but one other rabbi in the
whole country of Bohemia, outside of Prague, who
preached in German at that time. He established
a day school in Radnitz. Meeting with some opposition from the authorities—for up to this time
only the Catholics had had a school of this kind—
he circumvented the opposition by obtaining a dispensation from the minister of education in Prague
to open such a school ; the dispensation carried
with it the title of professor.

While in Radnitz he married, on June 6, 1844,
his former pupil Therese, daughter of Herman
Bloch, the Grafenried merchant in whose house he
had lived as tutor some years before.

Shortly after his assumption of office in Radnitz,
he came into friction with the government because
of his democratic and radical expressions. An order had been issued that in all houses of worship a

special service should be held on the birthday of
the Emperor Ferdinand.   Police spies were sent to
the synagogue.   Instead of preaching a fulsome
and flattering sermon, the young rabbi merely
stated that this was the birthday of the emperor,
and then proceeded to give vent to some radical
utterances.   He was summoned before the Kreis-
hauptmann (the governor of the district) in Pilsen,
the seat of government.   This functionary accosted
him with the words, "Is he not a loyal citizen?"
The question remained unanswered.   The question
was repeated twice ; as before, no answer was forth-
coming.   Finally the rabbi said, "Whom are you
addressing?   I am not a *he*."   His boldness was
not punished ; the officer addressed him now in the
second person and he gave satisfactory proofs of
his loyalty.

Another cause of friction with the government
arose from the fact that the young rabbi married
all Jewish couples who applied to him, even though
they did not possess the "familiantrecht."   In Bohemia, as in some other countries of Europe, the in-
human law was in force to the effect that only a certain number of Jewish families could dwell in a
town.   Those who enjoyed this privilege possessed
what was known as the "familiantrecht," the authorization to found a household.   Hence, if a young
man wished to marry he had to wait until a vacancy
was created by the death of a holder of this privilege.   There were always a great number on the
waiting list to receive the authorization.   Many,
however, did not wait, but married according to

Jewish rites.* The marriages were not recognized by the state; the wives had to be registered as cooks and housekeepers, and the children of these unions were illegitimate in the eyes of the law. Wise, being a governmental functionary, committed a misdemeanor (in truth, it was a penal offense) in marrying such couples as had not the authorization. Summoned before the district governor at Pilsen, he declaimed against the iniquity of that regulation, and declared that he would continue to marry those people, and would rather go to prison than refuse to do so. He was summoned to Prague before Count Furstenberg, a member of the imperial council and the referee for Jewish affairs, who questioned him and asked, among other things, why the Jews had so many illegitimate children. The rabbi explained to him the iniquitous regulation. The count promised to direct his efforts toward having it repealed; and in truth shortly thereafter the barbarous restriction disappeared from the statute books.

He also came into conflict with his rabbinical superior. Bohemia was divided into twelve districts, each of which was presided over by a district rabbi. The local rabbis had to obtain permission from him to perform any local function, such as officiating at marriages, funerals and the like. The rabbi of Radnitz did not ask for this permission, but did not come into open conflict with his superior until he granted a divorce to a woman, a relation of

* See Kompert's touching tale, "Ohne Bewilligung," in Gesammete Schriften, I, 238.

the district rabbi, Abraham Kafka, who for some
personal reason had refused to give the bill of divorce.   The district rabbi summoned him before
the district court, but Wise was acquitted.   This
rabbi now sought to make matters as unpleasant as
possible.   Wise had published a small hymn- and
prayer-book ; he had omitted a prayer for the emperor ; this was made the basis for another sum-
mons before the district court.

Because of all this unpleasantness, and on account of political chicanery, he determined to leave
the country.   His ideas were radical.   He felt, too,
that he would be hampered in teaching and preaching Judaism as he conceived it.   He had attended as
a visitor, not as a delegate, the rabbinical conference
at Frankfort in 1844, and he returned to his post
with strong sympathies and predilections for the
reform movement ; furthermore, his political lean-
ings were all toward democracy.   He had picked
up in a book store in Prague several volumes of the
Federal Farmer, an American publication ; he had
also read Fenimore Cooper's novels in the original :
he had a fair knowledge of the English language.
His eyes were directed toward the United States,
the land where he could indulge his democratic
sympathies and live in a free religious atmosphere.
At the time he was contemplating this step a friend
tried to induce him to go with him to France, as that
country was the freest in Europe.   France, however, was not far enough advanced for him, nothing
but the United States would satisfy him ; "I had
the American fever," as he once expressed himself
to the writer.   When he had made all his prepara-

tions to leave, he applied for a passport to Count
Furstenberg, which this official refused with the
remark, "Do you think we opened schools for you
to take your learning to America?" Nothing was
left for him to do but to attempt to leave without
the passport. He succeeded in crossing the frontier
into Saxony; at Leipzig he found a well-intentioned
officer who supplied him with the necessary papers.
While in Leipzig he sought out the noted scholars
there. Once, when in the company of Berthold
Auerbach, Julius Fuerst and Franz Delitzsch, the
conversation turned on Austrian affairs. A movement was then on foot to erect a statue in Vienna
to Joseph II., the liberal-minded emperor who had
been the first ruler of Europe to take steps toward
the emancipation of the Jews. Turning to Auerbach, Fuerst asked: "Dr. Auerbach, what Biblical
verse would you suggest for this statue?" Quick
as a flash Auerbach answered: "Joseph recognized
his brethren but they did not know him" (Gen.
xliii, 8).

Instead of proceeding directly to Bremen, where
he was to embark for New York, the young rabbi
spent several weeks traveling in Germany, chiefly
with the object of meeting some of the men prominent in Jewish life. In Breslau he met Abraham
Geiger, the foremost Jewish reformer; in Magde-
burg he spent some time with Ludwig Philippson,
perhaps the most widely known Jew in Germany
owing to his organ, "Die Allgemeine Zeitung des
Judenthums;" in Frankfort he associated with
Leopold Stein, the poet rabbi; in Berlin with
Sachs, the eloquent preacher; there he also met

Bernstein, Stern, and the other leaders of the reform movement which was just then agitating Berlin and culminated in the formation of the "Juedische Reformgeminde" in 1847.

Several days before the Feast of Weeks he arrived at Bremerhaven. While there he was requested to preach on the holiday at Bremerle, a
town near by. A day later he set sail for the
promised land, and after a voyage of sixty-three
days landed in New York on the 23d day of July,
1846, with his wife and child. He set foot upon
this soil animated by high ideals and aspirations.
The germs of greatness lay within him, it required
only the occasion to develop them ; the conditions
of Jewish life in the United States offered the opportunity—he rose to it. The man and the opportunity met, and the man has so impressed his personality upon the development of Jewish life during
the past half century, that without detracting from
the fame rightfully attaching to any of the other
great leaders, it may indeed be said that he stands
easily first among American Jews for what he has
accomplished. *Per aspera ad astra;* the difficulties
were many, but he triumphed ; he aspired and he
achieved. The following pages will attempt to re-
count briefly the story of this 'aspiration and this
achievement.

CHAPTER II.

EARLY DAYS IN AMERICA—JEWISH CONDITIONS.

In the years 1874–75 the subject of this sketch, published a series of interesting reminiscences of his early life in America in the columns of his newspaper, "Die Deborah." The writer has been compelled to draw upon these reminiscences occasionally, for in them the thoughts and plans of the newly-arrived rabbi are indicated clearly. What his expectations in coming to America were is graphically outlined in a vivid description of a dream that he dreamt shortly before his arrival, and to which he has often referred in later years as symbolical of the hopes he harbored. It is given here in his own words, as a fitting introduction to the tale of his future struggles:

"On the 20th of July the captain informed me that we were about fifty miles out at sea opposite Boston, and that if the wind continued favorable we would be in New York ere long. It was late at night when he imparted this information. I was sitting solitary and alone, and surrendered myself entirely to my emotions. How foolish and daring it is, thought I, to have left home, friends, position and future prospects, to emigrate to a strange land, without means or expectations! My imagination now played upon the possibilities hidden in the lap of the veiled future. While meditating, I dropped off to sleep and dreamed the following unforgettable dream :

"I dreamed that a great storm, which drove the ship toward the land, had arisen. Every one trembled, feared, prayed; the inky waves rose mountain high and broke into seething masses, only to give way to other watery heights. Convulsively I embraced wife and child and spoke words of calm and comfort. It then appeared to me as though a high, steep, rocky mountain hurried toward us and threatened to crush us. 'Here we must land, or we sink,' cried the captain, with quaking voice. Scarcely had these words been uttered, ere the ribs of the ship, which had been hurled on the rock, cracked. I took a daring leap and stood on the rock with wife and child. The ocean still roared ; a wave seized the ship and cast it far out into the seething waters ; in a few moments it was swallowed up in the night and disappeared from my gaze. So then, here we were on a rugged rock ; at our feet the waters, agitated by the wild storm, raged ; above and about us rose forbidding rocks, while the darkness added its terrors. Finally, after a long interval, morning dawned, and revealed the dangerous situation. 'However steep this mountain appears, we must ascend it,' said I to my wife. I took my child in one arm, tremblingly my wife clung to the other, and then, 'forward, in God's name.' It seemed to me as though an inner voice called : 'Up, up ; above there is help.' With difficulty we clambered from rock to rock, higher and higher, constantly, untiringly. Then, as though the measure of woes was not yet full, hollow-eyed, ghostly, grinning dwarfs and tiny poodles, with large, hollow, puffed-out heads, came toward us on the narrow path, opposed our further progress and mocked me mercilessly. I brushed them aside, but for every ten that I pushed away a hundred arose from out the bare rock. They came, too, in the shape of night owls, and deafened me with their cries. They sizzed about me like angry wasps and stung me; they placed themselves like stupid blocks in my path; in short, they did everything to harass me and prevent my further progress. My wife at my side wept bitterly, the child in my arms cried for fright, but my courage, strength and confidence grew. I begged, implored, avoided, circumvented them, but all to no avail. Then I marched straight through the crowd of dwarfs, paid no attention to their ravings, pushed them aside to the right and the left, until finally, weary and perspiring, we reached the summit of the mountain. Arriving there, I saw the most beautiful and glorious landscape, the richest, most fertile meadows, but I sank fainting. Thereupon I awoke and found that it was all a dream; but I have often thought of that dream." *

The dream requires no interpretation; he who runs may read and understand. It was a true indication of the life that lay before him.

A rapid survey of the conditions of Jewish life in this country in the year 1846 is necessary in order to comprehend clearly the story to be told in these pages. The Jews were settled in larger or

* Reminiscences, Deborah, Vol. XXIII, No. 1.

smaller numbers in various cities. There was a
small native element, whose ancestors had come to
the country during the preceding century or earlier.
These constituted the so-called Portuguese Jews,
and were considered the aristocracy of Jewry.
They had formed congregations in Newport, New
York, Philadelphia, Richmond, Charleston, Savannah and New Orleans, and worshiped according to
the Sephardic ritual. These American-born Jews
were for the most part highly cultivated, and held
themselves aloof from their brethren in faith who
had lately emigrated to the country from Germany,
Poland, and other European lands. The great German immigration dated from about the year 1830.
The Jews who came to America from Europe
emanated mostly from small towns and villages,
where they had lived the cramped and oppressed
life to which the Jews were subjected everywhere.
Naturally, the great majority settled in the cities
on the eastern seaboard, although a considerable
number had drifted westward even during the early
years, so that in the fifth decade of the century
there were larger or smaller communities in Albany,
Syracuse, Buffalo, Rochester, Pittsburg, Cleveland,
Cincinnati, Louisville, Chicago, St. Louis and other
places. The animating hope that lured these pio-
neers of the Jewish communities was an improvement of their material condition. America meant
for them opportunity. There was an outlook for
better things, as far as worldly fortunes went. But
as regards religious matters, they merely trans-
planted the expression of Judaism as they had
known it at home, and continued here the local

German or Polish customs. When congregations were formed—and to the credit of the early Jewish settlers be it said that as soon as a sufficient number had gathered in any place, they associated themselves into a congregation for religious worship—these were organized on traditional lines. The same abuses that had led to the inauguration of reform in Germany, existed here.

In 1846 Jewish religious life in America was not such as to fill the breast of the new-comer with high hopes. When he entered the synagogue there was that same indecorum with which he had been but too familiar abroad. Faint beginnings there were of reform ; the congregation of Charleston, S. C., had taken the first steps, and beside this there were two small congregations that had been organized as reformed congregations—the Har Sinai, of Baltimore, in 1842, and the Emanuel, of New York, in 1844. But with these exceptions, orthodoxy held complete sway. There were but -few men of light and leading at the head of the congregations, of which there were not yet very many. The metropolis had nine ; Philadelphia three, and Baltimore three. There were about twenty-five others from Boston in the East to Cincinnati in the West, from Cleveland in the North to New Orleans in the South. There was no communal spirit among the Jews whatsoever. They had no public institutions beside their synagogues. The public religious instruction of the young was almost entirely neglected. In 1838 Rebecca Gratz had organized in the city of Philadelphia the first religious school,

or Sunday-school, as it was called; in the year
whereof we write there were Jewish schools in but
seven cities of the country, viz : in New York, Philadelphia, Baltimore, Richmond, Charleston, Albany,
and Cincinnati. There was but one Jewish publication, The Occident, edited by Rev. Isaac Lesser, of
Philadelphia. The first Jewish Publication Society,
organized in Philadelphia in 1845, was maintaining
its existence with great difficulty. The prospects
did not appear very bright. But the man whose indomitable energy was to change all this had arrived
upon the scene, and it was not long ere the enliven-
ing effect of a real leader made itself felt and a new
chapter in the history of Judaism in America was
opened.

The feeling that dominated the young immigrant
during the early days of his sojourn in New York
was that now he was a free man, and no longer a
Bohemian *Shutz-jude*. He was fully appreciative
of the change, and gloried in the opportunity for
free development. In Europe he had experienced
all the petty restrictions, the intolerable interfer-
ences, of government in the affairs of religion and
conscience ; not one step, be it ever so trivial, could
be taken at variance with the established order of
things, unless some functionary was at hand to call
the daring innovator to account. The position of
the Jew and Judaism was particularly annoying to
a man of independent spirit ; the mediæval conditions still held sway ; the Jew was only tolerated,
or worse ; Judaism itself, in the Austrian communities, had lost all creative vigor. What bliss a man
of Wise's temperament must have experienced at

the change can be imagined. No impertinent inter-
ference any longer on the part of government in religious affairs; complete separation of church and
state; one religion equal to every other before the
law. If there was much in the status of Judaism
itself that was disheartening, if he found but little
improvement in Jewish conditions, if he was disil-
lusionized in his hope of meeting with a progressive
spirit among his co-religionists, he consoled himself
with the thought that all this was voluntary, that
the state did not compel these things, and that
changes could be wrought from within if desired,
without fear of prohibitions emanating from the
civil power. He breathed the atmosphere of freedom; he was in a blessed land where he rested
under no disability because he was a Jew; he was
at liberty to work out his own future as his powers
enabled him, and so, God willing, he would.

He had come to the New World with a number
of letters of introduction in his possession. The
first that he delivered were addressed to two Jewish
physicians. When in the course of conversation
they learned that he intended to follow the rabbinical calling, they advised him strongly against it.
They pictured the affairs of the synagogue in dark
colors; they described their co-religionists in any
but flattering terms, and counseled him to have
nothing to do with them, but to devote himself to
peddling or to learning a trade. Thoroughly disheartened by this pessimistic portrayal, he returned
to his lodgings, looked through his remaining letters, and determined to present but one other, and
that to a man whom he felt was able to advise him

intelligently. The relationship between him and Dr. Max Lilienthal was so close during the next thirty-five years, up to the very day of the latter's death in 1882, that the occasion of their first meeting is of more than ordinary interest. Dr. Lilienthal had arrived in New York in 1845 from Russia, where he had labored in the cause of the education of the Jews of that empire. He was the first German rabbi who had enjoyed a university education to come to this country. At this time there were three German Jewish congregations in New York City, beside the Emmanuel congregation already mentioned. These three congregations had, shortly after his arrival, elected Dr. Lilienthal as their rabbi, with the understanding that he was to preach in a different synagogue each Sabbath. Of all people in New York, this man was, without doubt, best acquainted with Jewish religious affairs. His counsel had best be sought. "In the morning I went to Eldridge street, stopped at a small house and rang the bell timidly. A man in a dressing-gown, with a black velvet cap on his head, opened the door.

"'I would like to speak to Dr. Lilienthal.'

"'I am he; step in.'

"We stepped into the back room which was his library. 'I came from Bohemia; here is a letter from Dr. W.—your school friend, and here are some of my papers.' Dr. Lilienthal read the letter and the first of the twelve papers I had given him when he went to the door and called. 'Wife, bring coffee and cigars. I have received a guest;' turning to me he gave me a friendly and hearty Shalom

Alechem. 'Hold up your head! courage!' cried he, 'you are the man, we need you.' " *

Thus began the intimacy that lasted through so many years. Lilienthal spoke the first encouraging words to the aspiring young idealist, and strange to say their labors were intertwined ever after. A brief digression will be pardoned here to sketch hurriedly their united and reciprocal working. As will be recounted shortly, Wise's first opportunity for public service was owing to Lilienthal. And on the other hand when the latter temporarily abandoned the rabbinical profession to devote himself entirely to the education of the young, it was Wise who, having assumed charge of the B'ne Jeshurun congregation in Cincinnati in 1854, advised the B'ne Israel congregation of that same city to call Dr. Lilienthal to their pulpit; in 1855 Lilienthal arrived in Cincinnati and for the ensuing twenty-seven years the two great Jewish leaders toiled hand in hand. As co-editors of the Israelite and Deborah in the early years they lent their high gifts to the instruction of the people. Wise was seconded and supported earnestly by Lilienthal in his untiring efforts at bringing about the Union of American Hebrew Congregations and founding the Hebrew Union College. Both devoted their talents and gave their services to the college without stint in the struggling years of infancy. In all good works for Judaism and humanity they were at one. And who, that was present at the service held in memory of Max Lilienthal can ever forget the pathetic incident

* Reminiscences, Deborah, Vol. XXVIII., No. 2.

that took place when in speaking of his friend,
Isaac M. Wise could scarcely proceed, and, with
stifled voice and streaming eye, struggled with his
emotions.   This beautiful friendship will ever stand
in the annals of Judaism in America as a noble expression of intertwined effort in the common cause
of religious progress, educational effort and communal labors.   It is a precious memory to be cherished forever.

But now to the interrupted thread of our story.
Much cheered by Lilienthal's friendly reception and
encouraged by his advice, Wise determined to take
up the work for which he had prepared himself.
In his visit to the synagogue he saw and heard
much that dissatisfied him ; the ignorance of Jewish
lore on the part of men who posed as leaders was
appalling ; but for all that his choice was made, his
work in life marked out.   The first public function
he performed in this country was the dedication of
the synagogue at New Haven.   Dr. Lilienthal had
been requested to come, but being unable to respond
to the invitation, he asked Wise whether he wished
to go in his place.   The offer was most welcome.
Upon his return Lilienthal informed him that, if he
so desired, he could go to Syracuse on a similar
mission ; the new synagogue there was to be dedicated on the Friday preceding Rosh Hashana.   On
his journey to Syracuse he stopped at Albany over
the Sabbath and preached there ; the officers of the
congregation asked him to return to officiate during
the holidays.   This he did and made so profound
an impression on the congregation by his sermon on
the New Year's Day that he was informed that if

he would apply for the position he would be elected without a doubt. He refused on the ground that he would never apply for a position. He intimated, however, that if the congregation would elect him he would accept the position. He left for New York on the following day and upon his arrival found a telegram awaiting him which announced his election as rabbi of the Bethel congregation of Albany. He returned to that city in time to preach on the Day of Atonement, and remained there. He was now located permanently and ready to begin active work in his chosen field of labor.

CHAPTER III.

The eight years of Isaac M. Wise's ministra-
tion in Albany may be considered the crucial period
of his existence. It was during this time that he
conceived the projects which he carried to such
successful issue later. But it was also his storm
and stress period. Time and again he was beset
by doubts as to whether he should continue in the
work. The obstacles were so many, the difficulties
so great. Friends importuned him frequently to
devote his talents to a more grateful field ; at one
time he was asked by William H. Seward whether
he would not accept a chair in a college of which he
was trustee : again, through the recommendation
of friends, he was offered a position in the Library
of Congress by President Fillmore, and again he was
strongly advised to enter the legal profession. But
the doubts passed and despite obstacle and difficulty he remained true to the cause in which he had
enlisted.

When he came to Albany he found affairs in a
chaotic condition, as they were everywhere. "Two-
thirds of all the Israelites of Albany and of America
before 1848 were uneducated and uncultured. Their
Judaism consisted in a number of inherited customs
and observances ; the less these were understood
the holier were they considered. Everyone made

things as easy and as convenient as possible in
practice ; people did not observe the Sabbath, they
ate Trefa * and did not lay T'fillin † away from home,
but at home and in the synagogue everything had
to be conducted in the most orthodox fashion, *i. e.*,
in the manner in which everyone had seen it in his
early home. Moreover the people came from all
lands, everyone had his own Minhagim ‡ and everyone wanted to have these Minhagim observed generally. Hence arose a Babel-like confusion.''‖ He
went to work earnestly to effect changes for the
better. The great part that he was to play in
American Jewish education began with the school
which he established immediately upon coming to
Albany in the fall of 1846. He took steps also to
improve the public service and to remove the abuses
that had crept into it. He induced the congregation to introduce a mixed choir at once. The
Jewish prayer book had become over-burdened
with liturgical poetry, much of which was meaningless accretion, and did not aid in fostering the spirit
of devotion. The rabbi began his reform of the
services by excising the piutim, kinnoth and se-
liehoth § from the ritual. The disorder attendant
upon the sale of mitzwoth ¶ soon became a memory
owing to his energetic activity.

* Forbidden food.   † The phylacteries.   ‡ Customs.
‖ Deborah, Vol. XXIII, No, 9, p. 2.
§ Liturgical poems, lamentations and supplications.
¶ The custom used to be general in Jewish houses of worship, and still holds in orthodox synagogues, to sell to the
highest bidder certain religious functions connected with
the public worship.

Although this was individual work in an individual congregation yet it was part of a larger plan
which he was maturing in conjunction with a few
other kindred spirits. This plan had been suggested
by Dr. Lilienthal. It was the establishment of a
Beth Din, an advisory council for the congregations
of the country without hierarchical assumption.
Lilienthal had advocated the measure in a sermon in
1846 ; he had named Wise, Felsenheld and Kohlmeyer as the members of the Beth Din, at the head
of which Lilienthal himself was to stand. It was
the first attempt at co-operation in the history of
Judaism in America. The preliminary work to be
done by the Beth Din was the preparation of books
for use in school and synagogue. Lilienthal undertook the preparation of a Jewish history for use in
schools ; Felsenheld, the catechism ; Kohlmeyer, a
Hebrew grammar, and Wise was appointed to re-
vise the ritual and present a plan for a Minhag
America. This was in line with his practical
labors in his congregation during that winter. The
Beth Din was to meet in the spring of 1847, after
Passover, when each member was to submit his
work. Wise went to New York with his manuscript prepared. In the published report of the
meeting it is stated that "Rabbi Wise proposed a
Minhag America for divine service. He had been
charged with such a work because experience
teaches that in most places different congregations
are set up, and the strength of the Israelites is divided because every emigrant brings his own Minhag from his home, and the German will not give
way to the Polish, nor he to the English, nor the

latter to the Portuguese Jew. Such a cause for dissension would be obviated by a Minhag America, which would promote the harmonious development of the young congregations. The project of the Minhag as introduced by Dr. Wise treats of the Tefillah according to the DIN, upon scientific principles and the demands of the times, and shows plainly that the new Minhag must be based on those three pillars to be entirely satisfactory."*

He read his manuscript to the meeting, and a resolution to lay the matter over till the next meeting in order to give the other members time to consider the suggestions was passed. However, no other meeting of the Beth Din was held, and the plan of a Minhag America, a union prayer-book for all the congregations of the country slumbered until it was revived nine years later at the Cleveland Rabbinical Conference. The suggestion made at this meeting in 1847 found its triumphant realization in the adoption of the Union Prayer-Book by the Central Conference of American Rabbis in 1894, well nigh half a century after it was first broached. Much disappointed at the fact that the Beth Din did not take active steps toward fulfilling his cherished ideas, he returned to Albany and expounded his thoughts on the ritual in a circle of friends. One of these sent a communication embodying these ideas to Isaac Leeser, the editor of the Occident. Leeser published the communication with notes.† This is worthy of record because it was the first encounter between the men who repre-

* Occident, Vol. V. 110.   † Occident, Vol. V, 106, 158.

sented the two wings of Jewish thought. Leeser
was the leader of the orthodox party ; Wise was
the rising protagonist of progressive Judaism. The
communication stated that Wise held that "we
have no reason to pray for the restoration of the
sacrifices, wherefore all prayers having allusion to
such a restoration ought to have no place in our
liturgy." Leeser annotated this remark with the
statement "we must emphatically object to any
such form of prayer, which, as proposed by Dr.
Wise, should exclude the petitions for the rebuild-
ing of the temple and the re-establishment of the
sacrifice."* A private correspondence followed, but
there was no further public discussion of the
matter.

Our rabbi's first public appearance before the general community as a defender of Judaism was very
dramatic. The societies for the conversion of the
Jews were very active. The English society had
its agents in all parts of this country. The Jew,
even as is the case to-day, was considered a fit subject for conversion, as though he were heathen.
Throughout his long career Dr. Wise has exposed
at every turn the methods of the conversionists,
and he permitted no opportunity of expressing his
opinion on the subject to pass. He performed incalculable service in exposing the rascals who have
adopted Christianity for revenue only, and have
made dupes of pious Christians. At the time
whereof we are writing the conversionist craze was
particularly rampant. A society known as the

* Occident, Vol. V, 158.

"American Society for the Melioration of the Condition of the Jews," had been formed with the express purpose of bringing them to Christianity.
The editor of The Occident had found it expedient
and necessary to publish Diaz' Letters,* a series of
letters considering from a Jewish standpoint the
claim of the Christians that their faith was superior to Judaism. All this was extremely humiliating ; the Jew was regarded as an inferior creature,
in need of the light of Christianity for his guidance
and salvation. The conversionists were active in
every community, and Dr. Wise had not been in
Albany very long before the opportunity arose to
deal them a telling blow.

One morning a notice appeared in the Albany
Argus to the effect that "The Rev. Rabbi Cohn,
from Jerusalem, a missionary of the London Society for the Improvement of the Condition of the
Jews, will speak this evening in Dr. Wykoff's
church, for the purpose of forming a branch organization for this great and holy purpose. The lower
floor will be reserved exclusively for the clergy, the
church officers and their ladies. The general public will be accommodated with seats in the gallery."
The rabbi attended the meeting. The pastor of the
church opened the exercises, speaking in the usual
stock phrases of the pitiable condition of the Jews,
and the great need there was of missionary work
among them He was about to introduce the missionary when the rabbi arose and asked for the

* Occident, I, 145, 196, 296, 393, 444, 605 ; II, 203, 300, 343,
359, 491, 598 ; III, 49, 102, 149, 202 ; IV, 46, 100, 350.

floor. This could not be refused him. It was the
first time that a Jew had spoken before a Christian
public on that subject. The large congregation,
not prepared for this unexpected episode, were all
attention.

"I surrendered myself completely to my emotions," he wrote later in describing the incident;
"I analyzed the subject from the moral standpoint;
I chastised with all the powers at my command the
covetous affectation and the hypocritical sympathy
of piety; I refused determinedly all monetary support for the Jews, because we ourselves provide
for our poor, our widows and orphans, etc., and
rear our children; there are no robbers, street-
walkers nor gamblers among us; we need no help,
and accept none. I had determined to treat the
subject also from the theological standpoint, but the
repeated applause from the gallery convinced me
that this was not necessary. I contented myself
with stating that the Jew could be converted to
Christianity neither by gold nor persuasion, neither
by force nor persecution; but that I considered it
unnecessary to do so at any length at present.
I then moved that the meeting adjourn *sine
die.*" *

This was done, and never again during his stay
in Albany were active propaganda made toward
this end. He had met the conversionists on their
own ground and routed them. This was the beginning of his public service for his co-religionists.
His voice and pen have never failed when there

* "Reminiscences," Deborah, Vol. XXIII, No. 8.

has been need of a word for Judaism or the Jews during the half century of his untiring activity.

In his own congregation, in the meantime, troubles were brewing. The reforms he introduced naturally encountered opposition, and his fearlessness in denouncing evil practices from the pulpit made him personal enemies. He had a large following of devoted friends, but his opponents were ever active in annoying him. At one time in the year 1848 he had determined to leave Albany, but when the decisive moment came his opponents joined with his friends in urging him to remain, and he yielded to their importunities. However, it was not long before the waters were again disturbed. The introduction of the ceremony of confirmation for boys *and girls* aroused vigorous protest. The step taken by the rabbi toward having English and German hymns sung during the service widened the breach. The strained relations between the progressive minister and his followers on the one hand and the more conservative element in the congregation on the other, were brought to a final rupture by a union of circumstances which must now be narrated briefly.

In the spring of 1850, the rabbi, whose health had not been very robust, was advised by his friend and physician, Dr. Joseph Loewi, to rest from his labors for a space. He visited New York, where he sojourned with Dr. Lilienthal, who informed him of his purpose to abandon the ministry and devote himself altogether to the cause of education. In Philadelphia he called upon Isaac Leeser, who read him specimen pages of his English translation

of the Bible upon which he was then at work;
from both these men he received interesting information about Dr. J. M. Raphall, who had arrived from Birmingham, England, in October, 1849,
and had taken charge of the B'ne Jeshumen congregation, New York. Raphall had achieved a
reputation both as writer and speaker; he had published a work on the history of the Jews, and had
delivered lectures on Hebrew poetry. Wise had
not yet met him, but an interesting encounter between the two men was to take place during this
trip. From Philadelphia the Albany rabbi continued his journey to Washington, where he met
his friend, William H. Seward, Daniel Webster and
other men of national prominence. Seward took
him to the White House to meet the President,
General Taylor, which visit was promptly announced
by the newspapers under the caption, "The First
Rabbi to Visit a President." He remained in
Washington eight days. It was there that Seward
offered to use his good offices in procuring him a
chair in the college of which he was trustee.

While in Washington he received an official invitation to preach before the reformed congregation
of Charlestion, S. C. He telegraphed his acceptance* notably as his attention had been called to
the fact that Dr. Raphall was just then engaged in
attacking the reform movement publicly in that
very city. One or the other spoke nearly every

* This was the sermon on the subject "The Effect of Biblical Theology" which was published in the Occident, Vol.
VII, p. 217.

day in defense of his stand point. The controversy aroused much attention, but it was to have a remarkable ending. Before Wise's arrival in Charleston, Raphall and Poznanski, the ministers of the reformed congregation, had agreed to hold a public debate. Wise attended this meeting as an auditor. During the course of the debate Raphall turned from his opponent and addressing Wise personally, asked him, Do you believe in the coming of the Messiah? do you believe in the bodily resurrection of the dead? to both of which questions the answer, no! was at once returned. * This closed the meeting. Raphall and his party rushed from the hall. But the incident was destined to become historic as will appear in due time.

During one of their conversations, Mr. Poznanski had informed Dr. Wise of his purpose of retiring from the pulpit and had hinted that if he would express his willingness the congregation would elect him as his successor. Wise gave no response, but he was not surprised when, some days after he had left Charleston, completely restored to health, he was informed that he had been elected rabbi of the congregation. He accepted and handed his resignation to the board of trustees of the congregation at Albany. Again, as before, his opponents made fair promises and in conjunction with his supporters urged him to remain; he withdrew his resignation and recalled his acceptance of the Charleston offer, a step which he had cause to regret bitterly not long thereafter.

* Occident, Vol. VIII, p. 257.

Louis Spanier who had been a friend of the rabbi for years had been elected president of the congregation. For some reason or other his friendship changed to implacable enmity. Shortly after the Charleston *rencontre*, Raphall had published a bill of excommunication against Wise and had followed this up with articles against him and reform. Spanier urged these arguments as the cause of his change of heart. Now began a series of petty annoyances. Charges and counter-charges were made by the orthodox and reformed elements in the congregation. The congregation was in a state of constant turmoil for four months. The climax came at the service on New Year's morning. The choir had sung Sulzer's hymn En Komocho when the rabbi moved to the ark to take out the scroll of the law. The president without saying a word, stepped in his way and smote him with his fist so that his cap fell from his head. Instantly there arose a terrible uproar. The congregation was wildly excited. The service for that day was over. The breach was now irrevocable.* The rabbi's friends met for service the following morning at his home. It was at this juncture that non-Jewish friends importuned him to retire from the ministry with its trials and torments and enter the legal profession. Chief Justice Wood offered to take him into partnership as soon as he would pass the examination and be admitted to the bar. He wavered, but his love for his chosen calling conquered, and he declined the flattering prop-

* Occident, Vol. VIII, p- 424; see Ibid., Vol. IX, p. 166, for the final outcome of the difficulty.

osition notably when he was called upon by the friends of reform to lead their cause, the next act in the exciting drama.

On the evening following the second New Year's Day, a friend appeared at his house and requested him to attend a meeting. He found a number of the members of the congregation assembled, who informed him that after what had passed they could no longer remain members of the Bethel congregation and that they had determined to organize a new reformed congregation on the condition that he would co-operate with them and serve as their rabbi. He consented. The Anshe Emeth congregation was organized, and the first service of the new congregation was held on the Day of Atonement. "That day was one of the most touching of my whole life. The room was crowded all day long ; a new spirit seemed to dominate all. A band of courageous and spirited champions of progressive Judaism, possessed of indescribable enthusiasm had arisen out of the defeat which we had suffered. On that Yom Kippur day I saw American Judaism arise out of its grave to go forth to ever new triumphs, and it has not deceived me in my expectations."* The new congregation consisted of seventy-seven members, fifty-six of whom had seceded from the Beth El congregation.

Let me continue in a few words the history of the young congregation. Enthusiasm ran high. A large church was bought and converted into a synagogue. The dedicatory exercises took place

* "Reminiscences," Deborah, Vol. XXIII, No. 23.

on October 3, 1850. Dr. Lilienthal delivered the oration in German. The rabbi of the congregation explained the new movement in his sermon which was spoken in English. The fourth Jewish reform congregation to be organized in the United States now had its permanent home. The congregation at once introduced family pews, the first time that this had been done in a Jewish house of worship.

Peace was now his. No more annoyances, no more wrangles, within his own immediate community. But the opponents had a clear field as far as the press was concerned. A new journal, the Asmonean, had been published in New York since 1849, by Robert Lyon ; this, as well as the Occident, espoused the cause of orthodoxy ; the progressive party had no organ. Wise felt this want greatly. He had no opportunity to give public utterance to his views and principles. An offer came to him from an unexpected source. Shortly after the organization of the new congregation he visited New York, Philadelphia and Baltimore, for the purpose of collecting funds for the congregation. On the way from Albany to New York, he met Horace Greeley, who asked him for an account of his late troubles in Albany, and, after being informed, inquired why he did not answer the charges that his opponents made in the public prints. "Because I have no organ," answered the rabbi. Greeley thereupon offered him the columns of his paper, the New York Tribune. "Write whatever you want to have the public know, and I will see to it that it will be read." The cordial offer was thank-

fully accepted, but as it chanced did not have to
be taken advantage of. After his return to Albany
from this trip, during which, by the way, through
the intervention of influential Albanians, a position
in the Library of Congress was offered him by
President Fillmore, whom he saw when in Washington, he received a letter from Robert Lyon, the
publisher of the Asmonean, offering him the editorial department of his paper. This was an opportunity as welcome as unexpected. He accepted,
and week upon week set forth his progressive ideas
and his projects for reform in undisguised fashion.
His career as an editor was begun ; his articles
were the feature of the New York weekly Jewish
journal. He now gave to the public the fruits of
his learning, thought and study. Besides his editorial articles proper he wrote learned dissertations
upon subjects such as "The Bath Kol," "The Constitution of Judaism Based on the Code of Maimonides," "The Biography of Hillel, the Precursor of
Jesus." He also published translations of important Jewish writings that had appeared in Germany,
such as the chapter on the Book of Chronicles, from
Zunz' Gottesdienstliche Vortraege der Juden,
Geiger's Diwan des Jehudah Halevi, Frankel's
Beweisfuehrung, etc. In addition, he published
extracts from the Talmud or Midrash every week.

However, he felt that journalistic writings were
but ephemeral. He determined, therefore, to devote himself to the production of some permanent
work. The history of the Middle Ages was a very
congenial subject to him, and he resolved to write
this history with particular reference to the signifi-

cance of Jewish thought and Jewish thinkers in mediæval times. But this was not to be. A number of friends who had learned of his intent to devote himself to historical studies importuned him to direct his attention to the production of a history of the Jews from the earliest times. They urged upon him the necessity of such a work from the pen of a Jewish scholar. Their arguments proved powerful enough to convince him, and he began the studies which resulted in the appearance of his first book, "The History of the Israelitish Nation from Abraham to the Present Time, Derived from the Original Sources," Volume I (Albany, 1854). The book, owing particularly to its rationalistic treatment of the Biblical miracles, aroused a storm of hostile criticism. Since this was the feature of the work that aroused the greatest attention, it is necessary to quote from the introduction the author's statement of the principles that guided him in this radical departure from approved methods. He wrote as follows:

"The difficulty which we encountered at the threshold in the writing of this volume was this: The facts preserved in scriptures are surrounded by doctrines and miracles so that it often becomes difficult to say which belongs to the province of history. The facts are sometimes but touched upon by the inspired speakers and often narrated in two or three different ways, so that it is difficult to choose. We have proceeded on the following principle: History is distinguished from religion and theology as the ideas of *knowing* and *believing*. History records what is established by the criteria of criticism to be fact, while the dogmas and doctrines of religion are based upon faith, not admitting of the rigid application of criticism. Rational theology itself can not proceed beyond a reconcilation of faith and reason. This however is insufficient in history, where evidences are required that things actually took place, where, when and how they occurred.

"The next distinction between history and religion is this : the former treats of man, the latter of God. If this be admitted, it must necessarily follow that miracles do not belong to the province of history. Miracles can be wrought by God only, and history records what men have done. The historian may believe the miracles, but he has no right to incorporate them in history. As a general thing man is always the agent or the subject of miracles ; consequently the action itself may be historical and can be adopted in history if it can be ascribed to common rational causes, while the miracle itself belongs to the province of theology. We have adopted only such facts as are able to stand the test of criticism ; miracles for which we could not find common and rational reasons were not recorded by us ; still we have attempted to find such reasons wherever we could. We did not contradict or deny the rest ; neither did we deem ourselves entitled to consider them a part of history." *.

He wrote the book from the democratic standpoint ; hence he treated the institution of the kingdom as unjustifiable and contrary to the spirit of the Mosaic law ; therefore it followed that the Messianic beliefs

* Introduction, pp. xv, xvi.

commonly held by Jews and Christians were untenable.

The work met with a most unfavorable reception in many quarters, Jewish and Christian ; the standpoint taken was too unconventional, too different from accepted views. The author was bitterly attacked ; yet he did not quail, but defended the position which he had taken upon long and studious consideration of the subject.*

Events were taking place during the time of the publication of this volume that were to effect a great change in his life. His work in Albany was coming to an end. The scene of his activity was about to be shifted. His great powers were to find a field large enough for their exercise. In Albany he had won his spurs. As preacher, as reformer, as editor, as educator, as author, as staunch defender of Judaism, he had already made himself felt. Along these lines he was to broaden, so that his career in Cincinnati, the western metropolis, one of whose Jewish congregations called him to its pulpit in the fall of 1853, was the most remarkable of any Jewish leader in the United States, not only for the length of time that it continued, but for the great and lasting good that he wrought for the Jewish cause. Strong and masterful, he was a leader in very truth, toiling unremittingly and unceasingly, so that, looking back over the years that had passed, he could in truth say, "I have achieved."

* For the controversy that raged about the book cf. Occident, Vol. XI, 613, 614; Vol. XII, 16, 23, 27, 33, 79, 315, 398, 401, 455, 549, 553.

CHAPTER IV.

THE FIRST MOVEMENT FOR A UNION OF THE JEWISH CONGREGATIONS OF THE UNITED STATES.

The importance of the matter to be set forth in this chapter is so great that it has been thought advisable to treat it by itself, even though it interrupt the chronological continuity of the narrative. Ever since he had studied the conditions of Jewish life in the United States, Dr. Wise had been impressed by the fact that the great desideratum was a union of the congregations of the country. He recognized that if Judaism was to become a force, united action on the part of the organizations that represented the faith was a prime necessity. With characteristic energy, he proceeded to carry this idea into realization. In the fall of 1848 he conducted a correspondence with Isaac Leeser in reference to the subject. The orthodox leader entered heartily into the plan and advocated it in many an article in his magazine. It was agreed that Dr. Wise should issue a call for a meeting of ministers and laymen to form a union of the congregations of the country. This document, the first appeal for united action on the part of the Jews of the country, is historical, and is therefore reproduced here. It appeared in the December number of the Occident

of the year 1848,* and was headed ''To the Ministers and Other Israelites.'' It is as follows :

''To my brother Israelites in North America, I
call in the name of my God, חזק ונתחזק בעד עמנו,
'Be firm, and let us strengthen each other in behalf
of our people.' The Rev. Editor of this periodical has
granted me the favor to give publicity to my views
about the association of Israelitish congregations in
North America, to produce one grand and sublime
end—to defend and maintain our sacred faith, to
the glory of God and for the benefit of Israel and
all mankind.

'' Brethren, though I am a stranger among you,
unknown and unimportant—though I am aware
that there are men among you much better than
myself, קטנם עבה ממתני, 'whose little finger is
thicker than my loins'—though my years are but
few in number, and among you are men gray-haired
and highly experienced—notwithstanding all this,
I make use of the Rev. Editor's permission to express publicly my views on this important subject,
because I think with Elihu, son of Barachel, the
Buzite of old, אכן רוח היא באנוש ונשמת שדי תבינם,
'Verily it is the will in man' (that renders him
able to speak and to act), 'it is the spirit of the
Almighty that gives understanding to them' (who
have a good will devoted to God and virtue)—or
if I shall express the same idea in a Talmudic form
of speech, I may say I trust בסיעתא דשמיא, 'in the
help of heaven.'

''It is one of the holy demands of our religion,

* Vol. VI, pp. 431–435.

ללכת בדרכיו, to walk in the ways of God. God is
a unity, ה' אחד, wherefore all mankind will one day
be united for one great end—to worship in truth
the Most High, to adore His holy name with humility and purity. Then will also be fulfilled,
ושמו אחד, that God's name will be one. To bring
about this sublime unity, God has selected the
people of Israel from among all nations to be the
bearers of divine truth, and to diffuse the bright
light of religion among mankind. Wherefore we
may justly say, our cause is the cause of mankind—our elevation and success are the elevation
and success of the human family—our fall is also
the fall of all society; since every one must admit
the fact that true religion is the basis of civilization.
There is perhaps not a single Israelite among my
readers who is not fully inspired with the inclina-
tion to share in the mission of his ancient people,
as the voice of God called to each individual of
Israel, without exception of either sex, or age or
spiritual abilities: 'But you shall be unto me a
kingdom of priests.' Now, in order to fulfill our
sacred mission, to send our important message to
mankind, it behooves us to be united as one man;
to be linked together by the ties of equal views
concerning religious questions—by uniformity in
our sacred customs, in our form of worship and religious education. We ought to have a uniform
system for our schools, synagogues, benevolent societies—for all our religious institutions. This we
need to have throughout the world, if we are to be
considered as the same descendants of Israel, the
same disciples of Mosheh—if we are truly to fulfill

our sacred mission. Our fathers, whilst living in the
Holy Land, were commanded to appear three times
every year at the place selected by God himself.
This commandment had not for its sole object the
prescribed sacrifices, but chiefly it was calculated to
uphold a friendly union—a religious uniformity
among all Israelites.

"Let us now direct our attention to the country
where we live and the circumstances in which we
are placed. The majority of our congregations in
this country have been established but a few years
back ; they are generally composed of the most
negative elements from all the different parts of
Europe and elsewhere ; they have been founded
and are now governed for the greater part by men
of no considerable knowledge of our religion, and
generally of no particular zeal for our common
cause. The consequence of all this is that many
congregations have no solid basis, no particular
stimulus to urge on the youth to a religious life,
and no nourishment for the spiritual Israelite.
This naturally produces an enormous amount of
indifference ; and each congregation pursues its own
way, has its own customs and mode of worship, its
own way of thinking about religious questions,
from which cause it then results that one Jew is a
stranger in the synagogue of the other Jew. It is
a pity to observe that any man who is so happy as
to have a license ((קבלה) to slaughter from some
unknown person, can become the minister of a congregation, and the teacher of the youth without
any proof of his knowledge of religion, and in the
absence of any evidence of his conduct as a Jew. I

will be silent about what is called שאֵ,ת הבֵם—I will
be silent about the דין, though our wise men teach
כל מי שאינו בקי בטיב גיטין וקדשין אל יתעסק עמהם,
'Whoever is not thoroughly acquainted with di-
vorces and marriages, shall not have anything to
do with them.' I will be silent about the whole
casuistic theology, and ask only the community at
large : 'What will become of our synagogue?—
what of our youth?' You see we have no system for
our worship, nor for our ministry and schools, and
we are therefore divided in as many fragments as
there are congregations in North America. It is
lamentable, but true, that if we do not unite ourselves betimes to devise a practicable system for the
ministry and religious education at large—if we do
not take care that better educated men fill the pulpit and the schoolmaster's chair—if we do not stim-
ulate all the congregations to establish good schools,
and to institute a reform in their synagogues on
modern Jewish principles, the house of the Lord
will be desolate, or nearly so, in less than ten years,
and the zeal of the different Christian missionaries
will be sufficient to make among us a large number
of unprincipled infidels. It needs no prophetic
spirit to read this horrible future in the present
circumstances. I lay down these lines before the
throne of history as a solemn protest against the
spirit of separate action and of indifferentism which
has taken hold on so many noble minds of our
brethren, and I proclaim before the whole world,
before the present and future, my sincere conviction
that now something must be done to defend and
maintain our sacred faith. Nor is it too late;

everything can be done if we are all united before
God.

"But who are the men that shall lay the corner-
stone to this reunion? Are not the ministers of
Israel those who must take the first step? · Is not
the spiritual welfare of Israel intrusted into their
hands? Are they not responsible for it, if coming
generations should be corrupted through their neglect? Are not included in this class the pious laymen
who sigh over the downfall of the ancient customs
and forms, without the establishment of the modern
ones? Shall we not include those learned laymen
who mourn to see how some people in their ignorance sanctify the profane but profane the holy?
Yea, it is the duty of all those to unite themselves
and work for the union of all the congregations.
I call on you in the name of our God : ' Be firm
and strengthen yourselves for the sake of our
people.' Arise, ye men of piety and wisdom, ye
shepherds, ye fathers of Israel; let us all meet
איש לא נעדר ; let us first take counsel what should
be done, and how it must be done ; let us amicably
consider what we ought to do as men and Israelites
for the spiritual welfare of the present and coming
generations ; let us earnestly deliberate on a plan to
unite all Jews to defend and maintain their sacred
religion for the promotion of the glory of God and
the bliss of Israel ! I call upon all my honored
friends, both ministers and laymen, and all who
have an interest in the promulgation of God's law :
come, let us be assembled in order to become
united ! Exercise all your influence on your friends
and acquaintances, to bring together all men of zeal

and piety, of wisdom and knowledge, to consider
what should be done for the union, welfare, and
progress of Israel. Let the place of assembly be
Philadelphia, it being nearly the center for the Jews
living in North America; and let the time of meeting be the second day of the Rosh Hodesh Iyar,
5609. I trust in God to meet in the next number
of the Occident many honorable names who will
join this meeting, and also their divers views about
it; but I particularly call on the Rev. Drs. Lilienthal, Kohlmayer, Merzbacher, the Rev. Messrs.
Isaacs and Felsenheld, not to be the last ones in
offering their views. I pray them to assist my weak
voice, and call on all Israel חזק ונתחזק בעד עמנו.
And may God, the great Father of all, unite and
bless the house of Israel! May he enlighten all
men with the shining light of truth, be gracious to
all that seek Him and merciful to all that have for-
saken Him. Amen.

"ALBANY, the ninth day of Marcheshvan, 5609,
A. M."

This stirring appeal attracted a great deal of attention. It was like a breath of the spirit upon the
dry bones. In addition to this appeal, a circular
setting forth the objects of the meeting was sent to
all the congregations of the country requesting
them to elect a delegate to the convention. The
closing paragraph of the circular stated that as
soon as twenty congregations had signified their intention of sending delegates to the meeting the
same would be held. *

* Occident, Vol. VI, pp. 581-3.

The editor of the Occident, the Rev. Isaac Leeser,
wrote a number of powerful editorials in advocacy
of the plan.* Laymen in various parts of the
country declared their enthusiastic sympathy, notably A. A. Lindo, of Cincinnati, who wrote five
lengthy communications† in support of the scheme
which he had discussed with Dr. Wise and Mr.
Leeser before the appearance of the call. The two
leading ministers of New York, Dr. Max Lilienthal
and Rev. S. M. Isaacs, ‡ declared their hearty co-
operation, as did the Revs. J. K. Gutheim and
Jacob Rosenfeld, of Cincinnati. With characteristic cordiality, Dr. Lilienthal invited his Albany
colleague to occupy the pulpit of one of the three
congregations over which he presided in order that
he might have the opportunity to explain and advocate the plan. In a German sermon preached on
March 3, 1849, from the pulpit of congregation Shaare
Shomayim, Dr. Wise set forth his views. Isaac
Leeser, who was present, was so impressed by the
sermon that he asked for the manuscript and volunteered to translate it for publication in his magazine.‖ At the close of the sermon the boards of the
three German congregations promised to lay the
matter before their congregations with their indorsement. Much elated, the rabbi returned to
Albany. The date for the convention was set for
the eleventh of June, 1849, in the city of New

* Ibid., Vol. VI, pp. 421, 529, 577; Vol. VII, p. 61.
† Ibid., Vol. VI, pp. 565, 604; Vol. VII, pp. 43, 94, 134,
203, 258.
‡ Occident, Vol. VI, p. 511.
‖ Occident, Vol. VII, p. 12.

York.   However, but one congregation of that city,
the Shaare Tefillah, of which the Rev. S. M. Isaacs
was the minister, chose a delegate.   Eight other
congregations had chosen delegates, viz: the
Mikveh Israel of Philadelphia; the Beth El of
Albany; the B'ne Yeshurun of Cincinnati; the
Nefuzoth Jehudah and the Shaare Chesed of New
Orleans; the Beth Shalom of Richmond; the
Shaare Shomayim of Mobile and the Adath
Israel of Louisville.   Owing to the opposition engendered in the New York congregations, the convention did not take place.   It was felt that unless
the congregations of the metropolis, the place where
the meeting was to be held, supported the plan en-
thusiastically and unanimously, it would not be successful.   Thus failed the first movement for a union
of the congregations of the country.   However,
though defeated, the prime mover in the matter
did not despair.   He bided his time.   In season
and out of season he continued to advocate the
necessity of union until finally persistence and per-
severance were rewarded by the formation of the
Union of American Hebrew Congregations.   The
seed planted in 1848 came to fruition after a lapse
of a quarter of a century.   "Everything can be
done, if we are all united before God," Isaac M.
Wise had written in his first call for union.   This
sentence sounds the key note of his activity and
striving; of it his life is the commentary; by that
sign he conquered.

CHAPTER V.

CINCINNATI, 1854—1855.

In August, 1853, the rabbi of the Anshe Enseth congregation of Albany, received a letter from Jacob Goodheart, of Cincinnati, asking him whether he would accept the position of rabbi of the B'ne Yeshurun congregation of that city, and upon what conditions. After due consideration he answered that if the congregation would elect him for life he would accept the position; he stated further that he would not preach a trial sermon and would not be able to enter upon his duties until after a lapse of six months. Five days later he received a telegram to the effect that he had been unanimously elected rabbi of the congregation on his own terms. He resigned his position at Albany and requested his friends to make no attempts to keep him, as he had fully determined to go to Cincinnati. His friends respected his wishes and accepted the resignation, it need not be said, with feelings of profound regret.

Toward the close of December he visited Cincinnati, where he preached several times and aroused great enthusiasm. Upon his return to Albany he resigned his editorship of the Asmonean. His hopes were now all centered in his new field of labor. He felt that in the western metropolis he would have the opportunity to work more freely

(Aet. 35.)

Isaac M. Wise

and unrestrictedly than had hitherto been the case. On the last day of Passover, April 19, 1854, he preached his farewell sermon at Albany. The following morning he departed for Cincinnati, where he delivered his inaugural sermon on April 26th. In this sermon he laid down his standpoint clearly and unreservedly. He at once began to introduce reforms, such as the excision of the piutim from the ritual, the abolition of the sale of mitzvoth, and the formation of a mixed chair for participation in the service.

During the very first month of his residence in his new home he took steps towards procuring a publisher for a newspaper, which was to be the vehicle of his views. He recognized that if he was to wield influence he required an organ. In June he issued a prospectus, which was brief and to the point. He declared that it was his purpose to conduct a journal in the interest of progressive Judaism. On July 6, 1854, the first number of the "Israelite" appeared with the motto, יהי אור "Let there be light."

Through his paper he addressed a large constituency every week, and by means of it he has exercised a most far-reaching influence and brought to bear the power of his personality upon the solution of the many questions which arose in the course of the development of Judaism in the United States. His journal was the weapon wherewith he fought the fight of his long, agitated and successful career. Always full of energy and optimism, he enlisted in every project in which he was interested the full measure of his hopeful strength. The characteristic note of his editorial activity is the unquenchable enthusiasm with which he approached every problem that presented itself in the field of Judaism and the religious life.   The anecdote which he has told of his first meeting with Salmon P. Chase, later Chief Justice of the Supreme Court of the United States, well illustrates this.   Shortly after his arrival in Cincinnati he was a guest at a banquet at which Mr. Chase was also present.   During the course of the evening Mr. Chase asked him "in what school have you been educated?" "In the school of life, like father Jacob, which I frequented for eight years in Albany," was the reply. "And you have rescued so much enthusiasm out of that school?" said Mr. Chase, "I congratulate you."

At the time of his arrival in Cincinnati the other large congregation, the B'ne Israel, was without a minister. On November 5, 1854, he was elected minister of that congregation also. For about six months he officiated as rabbi of both congregations, preaching in the one synagogue on Saturday morning and in the other on Saturday afternoon. He continued this until the B'ne Israel congregation succeeded in bringing his friend, Dr. Lilienthal, to Cincinnati as their rabbi. The close and intimate relationship between the two great leaders has been spoken of above.

The lamentable condition of the American Jewish pulpit had been a source of much concern to him ever since he had been in this country. The men of learning in the pulpit were few and far between. He felt that one of the greatest needs of Judaism was competent leaders. He began

in the very first volume of the *Israelite* the agitation
for the foundation of a college for the pursuit of
Hebrew learning and the education of rabbis.
With his indomitable energy he succeeded in interesting Cincinnatians in his plan and the Zion
Collegiate Association was formed.   In the fall of
1855 Zion College was opened, the first attempt in
this country at the conducting of an institute in the
interest of Jewish science.   The account of this
movement will be told in connection with the story
of the higher Jewish education that culminated in
the founding of the Hebrew Union College.

Isaac M. Wise was now fairly launched upon his
life's work. All the great achievements that he
carried to a successful issue he had already conceived and brought to the notice of the public.
The first practical attempts towards realizing his
ideas and ideals all failed, but what of that? he
toiled, wrote, agitated and persevered until final
success crowned his labors.   The earliest efforts at
a conference of rabbis, the Beth Din of 1847,
failed, but the tireless worker survived to see the
successful organization of that representative body
of Jewish ministers, the Central Conference of
American Rabbis; the first attempt to form a union
of congregations in 1849 did not succeed, but he
who issued the call for that first convention grew
not discouraged ; through the years he sounded the
same note and his hope was realized in the organization of the Union of American Hebrew congregations ; the first college for the education of rabbis
lived but a brief span of years, but the idea that
called it into existence died not ; it found expres-

sion in the voice and pen of its originator, and at last came into being with the opening of the Hebrew Union College.

In that year—1855—he had the threads of his activity well in hand; those threads he spun into the web of a full, useful, honored life, great in good, rich in achievement. What a faithful commentary is his career of the fine lines of the poet, for truly he was,

One who never turned his back but marched breast forward,
    Never doubted clouds would break,
Never thought, though right were worsted, wrong would
        triumph.
    Held we fall to rise, are baffled to fight better, sleep to
        wake.

CHAPTER VI.

WISE AND REFORM.

The history of Jewish Reform in the United States is yet to be written; but whatever be the point of view from which it will be regarded, one fact is certain: the historian will have to reckon with the life and doings of Isaac M. Wise. Without these his account will lack unity, and also a standard of valuation.

Isaac M. Wise declared that we must work out our reformation in this country on lines wholly our own. He was the first one to insist on an American Judaism. Believing in the continuity of Judaism, he felt that, at the same time, Judaism has greatest scope in this country. He taught Judaism as an American patriot, and not as a denominational zealot. This marks him off from all of his contemporaries. These, whether unconsciously or not, strove for alien things. German reformers like Einhorn or Hirsch, and Anglicised conservatives like Isaacs or Leeser, seemed alike incapable of naturalization. There was need of an intelligent understanding of the American conditions and of sympathy with them. Wise said as early as 1858: "We need English preachers, and we must become American Jews as speedily as possible. For the first time in many sad centuries we are given an opportunity to announce Judaism without fear and to be a part of the world. We cannot afford to continue as aliens one day longer." It was the fatal error of the

German reformers who settled here, that they failed
to realize this.

The Jewish community in this country had been
in a formative condition for at least fifty years.
There was as yet no homogeneity, which is essential for stability. The communities were of a com-
posite constituency. A large part of the misunderstanding and conflicts which pass under the name
of Reform difficulties, must be charged to the fact
that the local organizations were composed of mutually exclusive elements. The Sephardim lacked
self-assertion, the very quality that made their ancestry illustrious. They were scattered through the
East, in Newport, New York, Philadelphia, Charleston, Savannah and Richmond, and were impotent
despite their affluence and numbers. This decadent
element was a source of much reactionary influence.
It was intolerant of progress, being half conscious
that it ought to lead in accordance with its received
dignity, but also that it could not lead. They had
one or two somewhat helpful men—S. M. Isaacs
and Sabato Morais, but no person of first magnitude, and no congregation as a "Mother in Israel."
(*Asmonean*, I, No. 10, p. 78.)

Charleston was the only congregation among these
which contributed in some degree to the furtherance
of Reform in this country. It had the leaven of Reform as early as 1848; it provided for an improved
public worship, and it made an independent statement of its articles of faith. But the attempt,
under the frown of the conservative Spanish, was
soon reduced to insignificance. Only the episode
of Wise's election in 1850 and the brave words

he uttered there have saved Charleston reform from oblivion. Reform has become a force in American Judaism because of the German element, and eminently because of such Germans as constitute the leading congregations still to-day. These organized the religious and benevolent institutions of the Jews in this country.

Equity demands that we state that there was something logical and plausible, and surely honest in both conservatism and Reform; but the same equity entitles us to say that reformers like Einhorn, Chronik, Samuel Hirsch and orthodox irreconcileables, like Leeser and Morais, were tolerant of those who differed from them and had sympathy with men, not according to the measure of the sincerity of these, but according to the degree of reinforcement they believed these gave them.

It is his frank appreciation of everybody which marks off Isaac M. Wise from his otherwise not untalented contemporaries. He was at once thoughtful and fair. He could be a severe opponent, but he was never an implacable one. In the depth of his heart, he reserved a fellow-feeling for even those who offended much against him. He consented, as soon as he could, to reconciliation with those who had not scrupled to go beyond the limits of fair polemics. He forebore with the denunciations of the "*Sinai*" and forgave the onslaughts of Hirsch, whose passion was genuine but undisciplined. Isaac M. Wise had a militant manner, but only against opposition that was gratuitous and mean. Makeshifts he scorned and obstinacy he brushed aside ; but he stacked his arms as soon as

he caught glimpse of a disinterested motive.   Another point of difference between the Reform of
Wise and that of his contemporaries, both German
and American, is his democracy.   He did not propose to reconstruct American Judaism in accordance
with the "Science of Judaism," but in accordance
with the needs of the people.   "The people," he
said, "must be taken care of!"   (*Deborah*, May 14,
1896.)   "The reform idea need not be brought to
the people, that has come from its heart!"   (*Deborah*, June 4, 1896.)   Wise maintained that Reform
must proceed not from the "study of the Rabbis,"
but primarily from the heart of the community.
"They did not know," Wise says of the German-
American reformers later, "that it will not do to
impose anything on the people.   Reform grew from
a necessity within."   (*Deborah*, June 4, 1896.)
Wise did not rest in philosophy, he pursued aims,
and in summing up this period of storm and stress,
he took pride in the fact that "American Judaism has
preserved its own ideals."   (*Deborah*, June 4, 1896.)

Wise pursued no policy of mere expediency ; his
mind was constructive.   It mattered l'ttle to him
what disposition was made of statutes which had
become inoperative.   The Rabbinical law or theology or metaphysics or the Science of Judaism
were not involved half so much as the destiny of
the people.   He could truthfully say, "The voice
of the people is in our favor!"   (*Israelite*, Vol. I,
No. 5, p. 39, August 11, 1854.)   Only a month before he took formal charge of Congregation B'ne
Yeshurun, he wrote "For the Americanization of
Judaism" (*Asmonean*, March 10, 1854), and he

meant by that no mere adaptation, but a native Judaism. In Europe he was understood by Geiger and Jellinek, but in this country by none. This naturalization is being accomplished in Germany now through the constraint of Anti-Semitism. We have been spared this scandal in this country by the prevision of Isaac M. Wise.

Reform and orthodox parted on questions of expediency. The introduction of family pews and of a choral service (by men and women jointly) and the uncovering of the head and other innovations, were onerous to the Jewish puritans of those days whom Lilienthal described well, when he spoke of their "masterly inactivity" (*Israelite*, February 6, 1857). There was a demand for a revised ritual, but a ritual cannot be revised from the point of view of expediency alone, for it is the expression of the religious life. The Jewish prayer-books which were then in use seemed to hide rather than to reveal the genius of Judaism. The "*Gebetmacherei*" of that day, of which Wise says that it furnishes material for a history of liberalism (*Deborah*, May 4, 1896), laid down the following rules : "The prayer-book must imply no belief in a 'personal' Messiah, no corporeal resurrection, no return to Palestine, no restoration of the sacrificial cult, no duplication of holidays, and finally, no cabalistic notions." It was the positive side, however, which provoked differences, which sometimes seem irreconcilable. The prayer-book controversy, in fact, has a place in the history of the organization of Jewish communities rather than in Jewish theology, for the favorite prayer-books divided the

country geographically more than doctrinally. The
prayer-books of Huebsch or of Merzbacher, or of
Einhorn had their prestige through congregational
politics much more than through inner justifi-
cation. They failed equally to respond to the needs
of American Judaism. There was but one man in
the United States who saw that this matter of ritual
was a life question, and that man was Isaac M.
Wise (*Israelite*, July 20, 1866). He declared himself not for a Wise prayer-book, but for a *Minhag
America*. The Jews of America, he said, must be
brought together to form a homogeneous community.
They will persist in a restrictive theology for as
long as they are provincial. He charged the Rabbis
with a want of large views, and with retarding unifi-
cation, and, said he, "this separateness is un-Jewish,
and against the destiny of Judaism in this country."
The future of Judaism in this country depended on
the solidarity of the Jews. The prayer-book is a
means for social reconstruction; local favoritism must
yield, as much as local prejudice, to all-round necessities, and each must sacrifice his preferences for the
sake of an homogeneous Jewish people. We must establish a moral union, before we can hope to have a
final ritual. Wise did not express in his *Minhag
America* a new theology, but a renaissant Jewish
people. The prayer-book was to give not doctrine
but life, and it was to bring to an end the internecine
struggle that was going on between German Jew and
Polish Jew, Eastern Jew and Western Jew, Reform
Jew and orthodox Jew, the Jew who clings to his
favorite Rabbi and the Rabbi who holds the fort of
his congregation and pulpit. Wise had introduced

a mixed choir in Albany as early as 1850, and, at
the dedication of his new temple there, he inaugu-
rated family pews. But these changes, however
startling they were in their day, were by-play in
the constructive Reform he nursed as his ideal.
When he saw that that was practicable, he committed
himself to a pronounced American ritual with that
intrepidity he shared with all such as fling their
personality into a cause.

It is not the place here to speak fully of the Cleveland Conference of 1855. This Conference was abor-
tive ; but it showed that the discordant elements
might be eventually brought together. Wise did
not attempt to reconcile the mutually exclusive
elements, neither in the Conference nor out of it.
He rested his hope in the current of action more
than of thought. He wanted the genius of Judaism
to express itself not in the ministry alone, but also
in the people. Wise was the first who insisted on
it that, with deference to the prestige which Rabbis
may deserve for learning and piety, the voice and
conscience of the people must be respected.

There was also another point of difference between Wise and other reformers. Their radicalism
was negative, his was positive. They were progressive without a plan, their campaign for reform
was without appreciation of the laws of growth.
They held that the past is altogether bad, and that
Judaism must turn from it, otherwise Judaism
would be soon a mere reminiscence. Einhorn said :
"What has been haunting the mind so long and has
had a mere ideal existence has now seized upon
hearts, has inflamed them, and the things that have

been tolerated will be tolerated no longer, not only in spite of religion, but in the name of religion." To this Lilienthal retorted with saneness: "Unnatural leaps are of no avail in history—in history as in nature all things are confined within a process which works by degrees—opposition to this eternal law brings failure." But Einhorn persisted that the ethics of the Talmud is exclusive (engherzig), that it lacks the world-encompassing spirit of the Bible, that the letter, into which it forces everything, is its finality and that it accentuates correctness of deed, however external, and the semblance of holiness so much that it interdicts rational thought on religious law. Such "Reform" could be met by peremptory challenge alone, and Wise gave it forcibly to the *Feuerbach* of Baltimore (*Israelite II*, No. 32, 1856). Einhorn himself reduced his attack to futility by admitting that "The Talmud is one of the most important movements in the development of Judaism. It has led it safely through the calamitous epoch of Jewish history and has enriched it in many ways. In fact it must be acknowledged as a high merit of the Talmud that it has broken the inflexibility of the Biblical letter; it has, though unconsciously, reformed the Mosaic law in its most vital aspect, with respect, namely, to the demands of time within and without." * Lilienthal's fair resumé of the controversy is this: "If it is admitted that the Talmud was itself a reform, why should not the principles which justified that reform be searched for?"

* Sinai, I, 1.

(*Israelite II*, February 15, 1856.)   Wise flung himself into the controversy in his own way.   ''The
Sanhedrin,'' he said, ''was empowered, being in-
stituted by Moses and being maintained by Talmudic authority, to meet emergencies; it could
suspend Biblical laws, it could provide for new
conditions.   It could take care that the letter of the
Bible be pervaded by the creative power of life''
(*Israelite*, March 7, 1856).   ''Reform,'' he added,
''will not advance as some radicals may wish, but
it will take deeper root, and occupy a larger field
than a reform restricted to a few and separate Congregations.''   ''We convened the Conference in
Cleveland,'' he explained, ''to bring life into all
Congregations, so that the ones may not remain
stagnant while the others, reforming head over
heels, break with the history of our people''
(*Israelite*, March 7, 1856).   It is characteristic of
the statesman-like views Wise had of the conditions
that his *Minhag America* was published without his
name on the title page.   It is the first revised book
for Jewish devotion in America without an editor's
name.   Wise, who would assert himself very emphatically, contented himself with a noble self-denial
when the people's holy right was involved.   Lilienthal gave the *coup de grâce* to the opposition.   He
told the extremists, who took their cue from the
Reform Verein in Berlin and Frankfurt am Main
that ''Reform in Europe, though nearly one thousand
years old, did not take root in the community,''
and in reply to Leeser's belated attacks, he declared that reform is ''an effort to raise Judaism to
the highest efficiency,'' and that, as at the time of

Mendelssohn, reform is "a movement for the admission of Jews into the brotherhood of universal civilization."

The details of the reforms are easily recorded. In 1846 Wise introduced the first mixed choir and drilled it himself. In 1850 the scruples as to the playing of the organ on the Sabbath, vainly reinforced by the Chacham of London, were overcome. On June 13th, 1856, Wise confirmed his first class of boys and girls, and the ceremony not only gave an added significance to the Shabuoth, but became also a religious event in the Congregational life. He disposed of the custom of "calling up to the Thora," and brushed aside its commercialism, as well as its impropriety, by the very moral point that "the female sex was disfranchised by it." (*Deborah*, May 14, 1896.) He abrogated the second days of Holidays on October 2d, 1859, though the observance of the second day of Rosh Hashana lingered on until 1873. It was not until 1881 that the German language was practically crowded out of Jewish worship. "Wise's Hymn Book," published in 1868, had still to compromise with the conditions, and had a German as well as an English division. The *Minhag America* prayer book reduced the German part to a minimum. Its Seelenfeier survives because it is classic in feeling and stirs by its unique pathos. In 1873 a resolution of K. K. B. Y. made it "not unlawful to attend divine service with uncovered head," and three years afterwards the temple was made free for "the funeral of any one deceased in the family of members." Modifications of the adopted *Minhag* became necessary in the course of time, for a native American generation was being recruited into the Jewish Congregations. The years between 1880 and 1890 were years of intellectual regeneration, and Wise was not slow to respond to the new needs. A revised form of service was becoming necessary. In view of the steady organization of the Jews of this country into a Union of Congregations and their identification of interests, and the entry of an American ministry which Wise was sending out, a Union Prayer Book was a logical and moral need.

CHAPTER VII.

WISE AND THE RABBINICAL CONFERENCES.

Wise was central in the history of the American Jewish communities, but he was also the organizer of the Jewish ministry of this country. His life-long efforts in this direction culminated in the establishment of the Central Conference of American Rabbis. I may state at the outset that in the forty-five years, which constitute the history of American Conferences, Isaac M. Wise was the leading spirit, and that they owe their significance to his genius. The Philadelphia Convention of 1869 is the only one which was dominated by his opponents; but that one is the only one which was without appreciable bearing upon the development of Reform. It accentuates the fact which Wise, indeed, had declared on all occasions, that ultra-radicalism is mere petulant idealism, from which nothing helpful can ever come. In all others of the first four Conferences, and in the nine regular, and one special, sessions of the Central Conference of American Rabbis his personality was dominant.

It is not within the province of a biographer to render a verdict on what he records; his task is merely to assign the facts within the development of the career. I shall therefore describe disputes about which the reader will be perplexed; but he need not wonder so much that changes were made

as that the reformers made them in so indirect a
manner.

Isaac M. Wise did not follow the law of his
zeal; in fact, he devoted many of his best years to
paralyzing the passion of men who, in the words
of Lilienthal, strove to "lift the globe like Atlas"
(*Israelite* II, No. 41, p. 333). Wise believed in the
continuity of history and in the continuity of Jewish history especially. When Einhorn declared that
the Talmud had no standing in Judaism, he replied
"This signifies no Bible!" This trust of his in the
historical forces was tantamount to religious conviction. It is in the light of this that the declaration of the Cleveland Conference of 1855, which was
the first in America, can be appreciated.

I proceed to sketch it. From August 10th to October 15th, an appeal for a Conference appeared in
The Israelite. Its purpose, as Lilienthal put it in
a later review, was "to prepare the way for future
Synods" (*Israelite* II, No. 17, November 2, 1855).
The principles of Judaism as defined by the Conference, are as follows:

"The conference of the rabbis and congregational
delegates, assembled in Cleveland, actuated by the
earnest desire to preserve the union of Israel and
its religion by mutual understanding and union,
and convinced that the organization of a Synod is
the most efficient means to attain this sacred aim,
whose legality and utility is taught in the Bible,
Talmud and history—consider it their duty—

To convene a synod, and call upon the American
Jewish congregations in an extra circular, to send
their ministers and delegates to the said synod.

"The Conference also feels obliged to give utterance to the following points on which they unanimously agree as the leading principles of the future synods.

1. The Bible as delivered to us by our fathers and as now in our possession, is of immediate divine origin and the standard of our religion.

2. The Talmud contains the traditional, legal and logical exposition of the biblical laws which must be expounded and practiced according to the comments of the Talmud.

3. The resolutions of a synod in accordance with the above principles are legally valid.

4. Statutes and ordinances contrary to the laws of the land are invalid."

It is easy to misunderstand these declarations. The Bible is an inviolable source for Jewish doctrine and the Talmud is a tradition on the lines of it. A revision of this tradition is necessitated by the changed environment, but it must be undertaken with reverence and on the ground of its own logic. There is in this nothing we would not now-a-days assent to. Even Leeser accepted this declaration for the truth of Jewish tradition, and only after his return home did he join in the protest against the "Cleveland platform," which had been instigated in his neighborhood. Wise, ignoring the inconsistency of the Philadelphia conservative, urged: "Is it right or wrong that the Cleveland Conference refused to depart from the historical basis of Judaism pointed out by three thousand years of history?" (*Israelite* II, December 21, 1855.) Einhorn, the other extremist, also contesting the Cleveland declarations, claimed that the time had come for a radical reform not on the lines of tradition, but despite it; but Wise responded: "Radical reform has had its way in Germany, it has disintegrated German Judaism; to wit: 'splits' in Frankfurt, Mainz, Mannheim, Berlin." The Cleveland Conference has set the moral standard for all future Conferences. It expressed the conscience of American Judaism. It was unique for another feature. Wise nursed the ideal of a Synod for many years, and at Cleveland already he suggested a convocation of it. He differentiated between a conference of theologians and an assembly of representative Jews. The latter should be the organ for the communal conscience. It is not inconceivable that Judaism, which has always been democratic, will some day take up the Wisean ideal, and will cease to intrust its destiny to the ministerial profession alone.

The second Conference, Philadelphia, 1869, was the first organized opposition to Isaac M. Wise. It could not, however, sustain its hostile attitude, for at the closing session Wise was chairman, and at the Sabbath morning after its adjournment he was the Conference preacher. The resolutions adopted at these meetings dealt with the formal abrogation of laws for which, in all honesty, not a single Jew in the country had waited, and about which, when declared, nobody felt any concern. There was submitted but one really new proposition, and that by Isaac M. Wise, though it was promptly shelved. The proposition was that "Whereas, circumcision is no necessary condition for entrance upon Judaism, and the omission of the rite does not exclude any Israelite from

the community of Israel, and does not absolve him
of his duties as such, Resolved, that the circumcision of proselytes be not required as an act of
initiation." (See *"Protokolle der Rabbiner-Con-
ferenz, abgehalten zu Philadelphia, vom 3 bis zum
6 November,* 1869," New York, 1870, pp. 39–41.)
This proposition of Wise's was adopted not earlier
than 1895. Two years after the Philadelphia Conference, a meeting of Rabbis took place in Cincinnati, the radicals lurking from afar for an opportunity. This came through a chance conversation
outside of the sessions. The "personal-God" question was current at that time. It had originated
amongst Christians and had point in a decadent
scholasticism. At an unofficial gathering during
the week of the session, some one, touching upon
the subject of a personal God, had expressed
himself hastily. This casual remark was deemed
sufficient for a protest against the Conference and
to the responsible things it had done at its official
meetings. It is not clear just what the protest
meant to attack. It had been issued by Samuel
Hirsch, who, as author of an Hegelian philosophy
of the Jewish religion, cannot have meant seriously to defend the proposition that God is "personal, real, and substantiated." But Wise was compensated amply for the scandal that had been pre-
cipitated. "In the east," he says, "the incident
showed that the Rabbis are not leaders, and it induced me to abandon the hope of ever finding
sympathy with them. I stopped bothering about
them, and I resolved I would appeal to the people!"
An equally abtruse and an equally alien subject was

broached in 1880, in the Rabbinical Literary Association, which had been organized the year before. It was a discussion on "The God of Judaism and the God of Science." This controversy was as bitter as it was superficial, and it drew public attention away from the positive and clarifying thesis which Wise had presented at the same meeting. (See *Hebrew Review*, pp. 12–32, and this vol., pp. 25–152.) Wise maintained that the traditional law is to be recognized only to the extent in which it reflects the Mosaic spirit, and he declared that the elaborate Mosaic dispensation is reducible to the simple principles of the decalogue. It was the annunciation of a real truth. It was hotly contested, but it cannot be denied that the legislation of Moses does converge toward a primeval revelation, which gives to Jewish history unity as well as a divine sanction.

In 1887, a number of Rabbis convened at Pittsburg, and elected Wise as president. The Conference adopted a Declaration of Principles with enough "liberalism" in them to meet an artificial conservatism which had just then a fresh but hopeless reawakening. But this Declaration was not of a kind to enthuse Wise, for Judaism gains nothing from opportunism. It is not felicitous to put Judaism on a level with "attempts to grasp the infinite," "the consciousness of the in-dwelling of God in man," and "conceptions of the God idea spiritualized by Jewish teachers." Such phrases do not do justice to the uniqueness and the genuineness of Judaism. Nor can the statement: "We recognize in the Bible the record of the consecration of the Jewish people to its mission," be taken as an avowal of revelation. It is certainly not true that "the Rabbinical laws originated under the influence of ideals altogether foreign to our present mental and spiritual states." In *Deborah*, August 13, 1896, Wise says: "The Conference at Pittsburg did not intend to restore genuine unanimity. The prime motive in calling it together was to give support to the reformers of the East against the Rabbinists of the East."

To those who know the strenuous opposition Wise offered to the Sunday-service movement, which is largely opportunistic, it is inconceivable how Isaac M. Wise can be claimed for the Pittsburg platform, which asserts that "there is nothing in the spirit of Judaism or of its laws to prevent the introduction of Sunday services in localities where the necessity for such services appears or is felt."

It was this sort of time-serving that induced him to provide for a stable basis. In July 9, 1889, accordingly, he organized at Detroit, Michigan, the Central Conference of American Rabbis. The history of this Central Conference is the history of the best in American Judaism during the last eleven years. His annual messages to this body are replete with intense feeling and sagacity. The Conference has published a number of Year Books, which contain treatises on important subjects affecting Judaism and Jews, and its discussions have an acceptable tone of moderation. Finally, it has supplied a long-felt want for a national ritual. The Union Prayer Book, published by the Conference, may fall short in point of classicity of style, and may not reflect the genius of Judaism as a Book of Common Prayer should, but as a form of worship common to all American Congregations, it is a moral force that cannot be overestimated. Wise had held to the hope for many years that the sacred subject of prayer might be rescued from the anarchy to which it had lapsed. When the Conference was ready to take up the work of a revision of the liturgy, he declared he was willing to yield up his *Minhag America*, then the most popular Jewish Prayer Book in the country. Wise's fine acumen is manifest in what he said at the Conference session of 1896 on the subject of a proposed Union Hymn Book: "We want not only a text, but a Jewish text; not only a text for Jews and by Jews, but also a Jewish standard of the spirit."

It would he profitable to excerpt from the proceedings of the Conference the thoughts he munificently scattered in them. Each presidential address teems with suggestions for the upbuilding of Judaism and for its stability. One principle he insisted upon: Judaism is inviolable as a revelation; it is Mosaic and Sinaitic, or it is nothing. At a time when Biblical criticism, like every new science, shifts its standards and is open to the false lights of incomplete research, a check is an act of wisdom. We cannot be too grateful to the man who declined to jeopardize American Judaism and upheld its proven facts. Literary valuation is, after all, not equivalent to the verdict of history. Still he did not impose upon the Conference his views as to the authenticity of the Pentateuch or the historical

character of the revelation on Mount Sinai. He
presented these upon many occasions, but never
with any purpose to urge them; though it is well
known that he took them very seriously.

There was another principle of which he had a
similar certainty. He believed in Congregational
autonomy. Every local Jewish community, he held,
is free to arrange its household in accordance with
its own needs, and he insisted that each be given
freedom of conscience as well. It was this conviction that led the Union of American Hebrew Congregations (of which we shall speak later on) to
declare in its constitution that each Congregation
was free within its own scope, and the history of
the Union and the uninterrupted development of
American Judaism through it, prove how wise it is.
In the Conference of Rabbis, however, this toleration of differences has become indispensable. The
respect for personal convictions has enhanced, and
has not hindered, the deliberations. Wise has thus
spared American Judaism much harrassing. It had
suffered long enough from excessive individualism.
In the earlier years mere insistence was often
taken for strength, and personality was accentuated
easily in times of excitement. Wise closed in with
his opponents, not so much on the ground of dogma
as on the ground of character. On the one side
were those who were trained in German schools and
had come from a German environment; on the other
side he stood alone, in more senses than one, the
heart of a new and an 'American Judaism pulsating
within him, and conscious that his work and word
were its work and word. This feeling that he

represented the cause of the community made him both humble and assertive. When he organized the Central Conference, Wise declared it must consist of "men of national conceptions, without local prejudices, without sectionalism; also without selfish ambition or private interests" (*Year Book* for 1898–99, p. 10), or, as he expressed in his original draft: "The object (of the Conference) is to lay the foundation of a central authority of American Judaism on democratic principles, the autonomy of the Congregations, the personal and the official right of every Rabbi in office;" and it shall represent "the collective wisdom and enthusiasm, learning and practical sense." "We think that the best that can be done by the present generation for the future of Judaism in this country must be done by a solid union of its best intelligence, by the co-operation of all, by respecting each individual factor;" "the wisdom of the many is superior to the wisdom of any one;" "the elevation of the representation is synonymous with the elevation of the cause." In the *Deborah* of August 13, 1896, he describes the Central Conference thus: "Independent, self-emancipated, self-governing Judaism in accordance with the freedom and the liberalism of this country."

CHAPTER VIII.

THE UNION AND THE COLLEGE.

When on July 4, 1854, Isaac M. Wise published the first number of "*The Israelite*" and on February 9 and March 2, 1855, announced the "*Deborah*," there existed already a number of Jewish weeklies. But these were uninfluential, the *Occident* excepted, which persisted for some time. Wise had contributed to the *Occident* and *Asmonean* from Albany, and in the first year of his incumbency at Cincinnati he still edited in the latter a department of theological and philosophical subjects. Seeing that the Jewish press was of no avail for the constructive work he had in mind, he established an organ of his own, with the motto "Let there be light!" The new weekly was not to compete with its effete contemporaries. It was to oppose them. It was to speak emphatically for reform, and its purpose was to cut a way for reform into the heart of the people. After forty-six years we may say, that this object has been accomplished. Reform, however, was not an end in itself for Wise; it was a means only for the regeneration of Judaism (*Deborah*, November 5, 1896). The "*Israelite*," was as unlike the "*Sinai*" of Baltimore, which was schismatic because of the acknowledged impulsiveness of its editor. Wise had his power under control. He did not scruple to meet opponents in a free field, but he treated them not as personal enemies, and never in spite. During the journalistic fight of years he cannot be charged with a single word of vindictiveness, though it must be said that many made it a point almost of religion to contravene him.   It was not for want of fair-mindedness and forbearance on his part that the reconciliation with these was tardy. The history of "*The Israelite*" and of "*The American Israelite*," as it was later called, is conterminous with the history of American Judaism, and the organization of American Judaism runs parallel with the editorship of Isaac M. Wise.

He stirred the Jews of this country and roused them to united action.   Three causes operated up to the year 1871 to prevent affinity between American Jews. The first was incident to immigration and the coming together of such as had different antecedents.   With the exception of some few Jewish organizations, such as Congregation B'ne Yeshurun in Cincinnati and Temple Emanuel in New York, and one or two Portuguese Spanish Congregations in New York and Philadelphia, which were somewhat homogeneous, the membership of most of the Jewish settlements was exclusive of one another or at best neutralized one the other.   A second cause in the want of unanimity lay in the character of the Rabbis and laical leaders. These were without views beyond the needs of their separate localities.   Even Einhorn, whose idealism was matched by his impetuousness, was restricted within provincial lines, and did not rise to a plane of statesmanship to which he might have brought abilities of a high order. The third element that was in the way of organization lay in the fact that differences on technical matters of ritual and the like crowded out the thought as to more essential questions. But in all these lay hopeful germs of a larger life and of a sound American Judaism.

On October 10, 1872, Congregation B'ne Yeshurun appointed a committee of twelve to convoke a Conference with the Congregations of the west, south and south-west in order to form a Union of Congregations, the object of which should be: "The establishment of a Jewish Theological Faculty for the education of Jewish ministers and teachers." On March 30, 1873, the first session of representatives of all Cincinnati Congregations was held, and the first Convention, "representing Congregations west and south," took place at Melodeon Hall, Cincinnati, on July 8th of the same year—the Roll of Delegates showing that twenty-eight cities were represented. Very appropriately Isaac M. Wise closed the historic proceedings with prayer. On February 13, 1873, Henry Adler addressed a communication to Congregation B'ne Yeshurun, offering to deposit $10,000 for the endowment for a "Jewish Theological Faculty." The nucleus for the necessary funds was thus assured, the rest could be left to the awakening conscience of the Jews in this country.

It would be a mistake to suppose that the inauguration of the academic work at Cincinnati was all that Isaac M. Wise meant to achieve by his tireless agitation. Already in 1865 he had said "We shall never be silent until we have roused the Congregations of Israel to a consciousness of their duty." A college could not last long without the

moral support of the public. The logic in the organizing movement demanded that the Congregations be first brought into an alliance. Wise was
the man who could bring it about, for he had faith
in the loyalty of the Jew.

The Union of Congregations was more than
merely formal, it was to promote distinct needs.
The solidarity of the Jews of the United States
must become a forceful fact. The American Jews
were up to 1873 the only denomination without
cohesion, and it had, therefore, no acknowledged
standing. The first mallet stroke at the initial
session of the Union of American Hebrew Congregations in Cincinnati, July 8, 1873, changed this.
American Judaism awoke to self-respect and rose in
the estimation of the American people.

Discord and words had been flung about for
many years by conservatives and orthodox and reformers in an interminable warfare. In the interest
of the real Union, therefore, every question of doctrine was excluded and the absolute autonomy of
the Congregations indorsed (Proceedings of the
Cincinnati Convention in the *Proceedings of the
Union of American Hebrew Congregations*, Vol. I,
1873–79, p. 14). The local communities were to be
guaranteed an unhampered development and a
healthful life. The time had come when it was
no longer true that American Judaism is "episodic"
(*Israelite*, May 18, 1866), but it became more than
ever true that "Israel lives in its Congregations"
(*Israelite*, July 29, 1887).

The regeneration was not complete, however, until it came from within. The call of the Cincinnati

Congregations declared that "the establishment of a Jewish Theological Institute is of the highest importance and necessity," and that in it "the future advocates of our religion shall be educated." This was a reassertion of what Wise had prophetically said in 1854: "Learning saved Judaism before and it will save it again" (*Israelite II*, No. 31, p. 252).

This is the place for a sketch of an attempt Wise made towards the foundation of a college. In his call of 1848 already he speaks of the "great want of schools," and on September 8, 1854 (*Israelite I*, No. 9), he said : "We wish to see men in office who are educated for it and trained for their calling. If our schools should flourish, we must have teachers who have studied the art of instruction, and know how to apply it." At the Cleveland Conference he had submitted a project for the establishment of Zion College, in which he was supported by several Congregations.

At first he planned the foundation of boarding schools—he called them Universities—where Jewish youths, including girls, may be under Jewish influence and acquire a knowledge of Judaism. It was not a feasible but a timely scheme. The public schools, at that time, were sectarian, and Isidor Bush's plea in "*The Asmonean*," for patronage of them by Jewish parents, quite right in itself, was met by the fact that the schools were dominated by the missionary spirit. The subject had been considered at the Cleveland Conference and had been referred to a Committee, but nothing came of it.

On November 27, 1854, Wise organized a Zion

Collegiate Association, and a board of officers was elected. He himself served as Recording and Corresponding Secretary, and was succeeded by Bernhard Bettmann, whose identification with all these movements is a matter of history. The Association existed only one year, but the experiment made it manifest that the Jews of Cincinnati and those of Louisville, New York, Baltimore and Philadelphia, could co-operate. Zion College had no ulterior object to train Rabbis, but was to have provided a general Jewish culture. Wise had pleaded for the moral and religious uplift of the people and for nothing else. He addressed assemblies in Baltimore and other cities, and Temple Emanuel in New York indorsed the movement. At a meeting which he addressed there, "one hundred and twenty-five men, twenty-five ladies, and also ten youths," became members of a local Zion Collegiate Association.

"We have thrown this sacred enterprise," he said, "into the arms of the people, and we shall be greatly mistaken if the people do not support it."— "We hope that we shall at no distant day see one grand and complete Israelite College for all the states of the Union. Many petty institutions might flourish, but a University worthy of the talents, lofty conceptions and practical sense of the Jewish mind requires the support of all."

A projected consolidation of the Zion Collegiate Association and the Jewish Theological Seminary, which had been chartered in 1852, came to naught. Maimonides College of Philadelphia, which was never more than a local institution, had to close because of its fruitless sectionalism. (Proceedings

of First Council of American Hebrew Congregations, p. 63.)

These tests gave Wise an insight into the condition and convinced him that only by a union of the
congregations could his cherished hope of a Rabbinical College be realized and something be done
for American Judaism. Wise had brought home to
the Jewish public the fact that its naturalization
was going on, that a native strength was now mani-
festing itself, and that the current of the new life
was in the direction of his high-going aims. The
congregations had put up with alien teachers, and
alien methods, and alien language, and an alien
spirit long enough. They felt themselves American,
and they demanded American Rabbis and American
teachers for their American-born children. They
would tolerate no longer an incongruity between
home and synagogue, and, while they had regard
for the irreproachable men who had served to the
best of their ability, they had a duty to the new
generation.

On October 3, 1875, the Hebrew Union College
was opened, and American Judaism became a
reality. It is tempting to tell of the unique triumph
the records of the Hebrew Union College have
been to Isaac M. Wise, and to the men who have
been with him in his ideals and in his labors. But
we leave that to the verdict of history. There was
pathos in the struggle, integrity in the work, and
deep-sightedness in the purpose. Above all, Wise
and his confreres responded to the necessities of the
day. About himself he said modestly: ''I thank
the Almighty that I am deemed worthy of co-

operating in this work of Israel's resurrection "
(Report of President H. U. C., September 10,
1876, p. 319. Also Annual Report, July, 1877, p.
337).

The strife was ended, the West could afford
to cease its provoking independence and the East
its hostility and truculence. A joint report of
the Board of Delegates of American Israelites, and
of a Committee of the Union of American Hebrew
Congregations at the session in New York, February 11, 1887, agreed on establishing a Preparatory
School for the Hebrew Union College in the City
of New York, and at the Fifth Council of Mil-
waukee, July, 1878 (Report, p. 546), the Preparatory School of Temple Emanuel was declared a
preparatory school of the Hebrew Union College.
The Sixth Council of New York made the first ap-
propriation for its maintenance (Proceedings, p.
667). The school, however, lingered ineffectually
for some years and was eventually abandoned. The
center of American Judaism henceforth was uncon-
testedly in Cincinnati.

Isaac M. Wise was President of the Hebrew
Union College for twenty-five years, from the
moment of its establishment to his death. He gave
it the morale it has, and if its graduates may be said
to have brought about a renaissance in American
Judaism, it is because he gave them training and
zeal. Their careers have been inspirited by an
emulation of the example he has set them. His reports to the Board of Governors of the College
teem with avowals that the Law is sovereign and
that learning is sacred. He does not tire to reiter-

ate that the Rabbinate of the future must not slip
into routine, that it must strive to be creative. His
pains-taking lectures on the Theology of Judaism,
on the Immutability of the Law, on Jewish Philosophy, on Apologetics, and on other subjects, appeal to his pupils with force. They feel that what
he said has more than class-room significance. He
was a man such as youths with impulses and ideals
must admire and love, and he entered the lives of
his pupils in every forceful sense.

CHAPTER IX.

ISAAC M. WISE AS AN AUTHOR.

The literary labors of Isaac M. Wise were not an amiable pastime of his; they were part of his strenuous life purpose; his scholarly pursuits, too, were drawn into the current of his career. The early epoch of American Judaism was preoccupied with the problems of organization, and it would have been luxury for so agitated a character as his to spend his energy on academic refinements. All that Wise wrote partakes of his rugged nature and of his moral stamina. Isaac M. Wise is one of those rare men whose life has unity; every part of it fits into every other part.

His books may be classified into the speculative, the controversial and the historical, and they represent as many stages in Jewish thought in this country within the last fifty years. In the early 70's the alleged conflict between religion and science had been raised by some to the dignity of a dogma. On the score of it many Christians alienated themselves from the church, and some Jews affected a similar estrangement from Judaism for the same reason. It was held by some that whatever minor differences there may be between Christian and Jewish dogmatics, they were alike contradicted by the canons of science. This opposition to religion was, fortunately, short-lived, but it was virulent for a considerable time. Wise saw that this had to be

met. He proposed to make it clear that Judaism
does not contradict the valid claims of science. He
himself had "plunged into the whirlpool of philosophy," as he says in the preface of "The Cosmic God,"
and had "come out of it unharmed and invigorated."

Wise's "The Cosmic God" * is an answer to those
who harassed Judaism along with all religions, and
is a defense of faith against those who had become
enslaved by the "*Zeitgeist.*" It is the pathos of religion that it must close in with any one whom it
listeth to provoke a quarrel. "The Cosmic God"
rendered a distinct service, by setting an example
of good sense as well as courage, for it met the
skeptics on their own ground. Isaac M. Wise was
the first Rabbi in the United States who saw the
duty of the hour. Congregation B'ne Yeshurun,
on the other hand, was the only congregation in the
land which indorsed its Rabbi in his lectures on a
technically untraditional subject. It appreciated the
fact that a Rabbi's thought must not be restricted,
and that it is his distinct function to repel attacks on
what is dear and forever true to the heart of man.

The second kind of Wise's literary work also met
existing conditions. In 1868 he published "The
Origin of Christianity and a Commentary on the
Acts of the Apostles" (8vo, 535 pages); in 1874,
"The Martyrdom of Jesus of Nazareth, a Histor-
ico-Critical Treatise on the Last Chapter of the
Gospel" (134 pages); in 1883, "Judaism and Christianity, their Agreements and Disagreements"
(123 pages), and in 1889, "A Defense of Judaism *versus* Proselytizing Christianity" (129 pages).

* Cincinnati, 1876, 181 pages.

Each assigns to Judaism a definite position toward the Christian denominations, which were urging claims for conversion. "The Origin of Christianity," however, has a scholarly purpose besides that of apologetics. Wise dedicated it to the "Free Religious Association," and declares (Preface, p. iv) that he wrote it "with the utmost regard for religion and for the Bible, with due reverence for Christianity, the important factor in the history of civilization, and with a profound regard for the religious feelings of all good men." He set aright the historical value of the New Testament records. Of course, a refutation with regard to that would in consequence invalidate the canonical character of the New Testament. Wise went out of the beaten track and availed himself of the Talmudic sources. A Jewish treatment of the schism, at the time of the origin of Christianity, seems obvious nowadays, but it was not that thirty years ago. We may not subscribe to Wise's identification of Acher and Paul, and it may be that he is not altogether confirmed by recent authorities on the authorship of the gospels in his thesis that there was a lingering Judaism in both Pauline and Petrine Christianity; but this much is incontestable: Wise's analysis in the "Origin" is the first serious attempt on the part of a Jew to approach the problem in other ways than those of polemics. He was the first Rabbi who wrote on the origin of Christianity as a historian without passion. To Christians his book suggested that the Jew, too, had something to contribute, and that from the Jews might be had the genuine light upon the origin of their faith. Jews,

on the other hand, were told for the first time that
the appreciation of Christianity was also a Jewish
duty.

A translation of Adolf Wisclecenius, *Bibel für
denkende Leser* (*Israelite*, 1865), and still earlier, in
1858–59 and 1863, a number of essays on the New
Testament, in 1869 an essay in ten chapters on
"Jesus Himself," and a number of critical articles
on Bible passages which have an alleged bearing on
the Messianic doctrine of Christianity, and in 1873
"Three Lectures on Jesus, the Apostles and Paul"
(reprinted in this volume) were followed in 1874 by
the "Martyrdom of Jesus of Nazareth." In the
last Wise declared: "The crucifixion of Jesus was
not decreed by the Almighty, his martyrdom was
not necessary for the salvation of mankind, and the
dogma of vicarious atonement is immoral" (p. 12).
Wise was forced to a campaign into the heart of
Christendom through zealots and missionaries who
had swarmed over the communities of the Jews.
The fiction that the Jews had crucified Jesus had
then still the force of a doctrine, and gave sanction
to fanaticism and traditional resentment against
them. It was with a wider outlook into the future
that Wise undertook to vindicate scandalized Judaism. His book was "A Defense of Religion in
Behalf of Truth and Christianity."

"Judaism and Christianity, their Agreements and
Disagreements" is a fuller treatise on "Christian
Evidences." Judaism and Christianity are not
competitive religions, but supplementary to one
another. "Christianity in its primitive and original
form was a Jewish sect"—"The Sinaitic revelation

and the covenant were the principles of early Christianity"—"The reformation in Christendom signifies a return to the standpoint of Sinai, which is the standpoint of the entire human family" (p. 118). "The Canon Law is divine to the Christian priest and layman just as the Talmud is to the Jew, and as tradition is to the Mohammedan." "Christianity has sects—in every phase of its development—documents of its history, as it were."

The final volume, entitled "A Defense of Judaism *versus* Proselytizing Christianity," left the press on Wise's seventieth birthday in 1889. It is "a challenge accepted in self-defense." "Silence," he says, "might lead people to believe that we are under the ban of ignorance"—"it is time to defend our own!" (p. 9). "The proselytizing mania is not under the control of conscience," he declares (p. 12). The book is an effective attack on that ungenerous side of Christian practice, which cannot be endorsed except on the level of fanaticism. "When and where did God alter human nature, and when did He change His own, that He consigned any of his His creatures to damnation!" (p. 44). . Wise closed his challenge, after he had reviewed the morals of Christendom, thus: "A Jew can learn nothing from a Christian!" "The Jew is his equal in morality, he is as merciful, as benevolent, as liberal, as much a lover of peace, and as law abiding!" "Do not molest him!" (pp. 153 and 128).

In 1880 he returned to his favorite historical studies and published the "History of the Hebrews' Second Commonwealth" (386 pages), a companion to the vol-

ume he had published in Albany (See pp. 42–44 of
this book), and as a text-book for the Hebrew Union
College. It deals with the period from Zerubabel
to the Fall of Jerusalem, and he declared himself
on the origin and composition of almost every book
of the Bible, of the Apocrypha of the Old Testament, of the New Testament, on the Great Synod
and on Jewish jurisprudence. It is the only comprehensive text-book of Jewish history written by
an American Jewish author for American Jewish
students, and is also the only attempt made to treat
Jewish history as an organic whole. He comes to
the following conclusions: "1. Exodus and Leviticus were edited after the death of Moses—from the
original documents—and contain few of the editor's
additions and many omissions (perhaps also exag-
gerations) in the historical portions. They may
have been edited any time after the Conquest and
not later than the time of Deborah. 2. Numbers
was edited later, from fragments omitted by the former and parts originally belonging to Deuteronomy.
3. Genesis and Deuteronomy are the original works
of Moses, with some very few later additions in
Deuteronomy. 4. Numbers bears the imprint of
the prophet Samuel, by whom (and his school) it
must have been edited. . . . The additions to
Deuteronomy also do not reach beyond the time
of Samuel." ("Pronaos," p. 183.) He assigns
the book of Ruth (see, however, "Pronaos," pp.
120–1), Jonah, some of the Psalms, such as 19, 103,
104, 119, 127, 137, and the book of Job, to the
Medo-Persian period; the Song of Songs, Esther
and Ecclesiastes, Psalms 49, 50, 52–4, 71, 73, 74–9,

along with Daniel, the Wisdom of Jesus ben Sirach
and the Wisdom of Solomon to the Grecian period,
and, finally, Psalms 46–8, 66, 67, 71, 106, 115–119,
144, 146–150 to the Revolutionary period. We
may believe that his critical hypotheses are not yet
verified, but we must acknowledge that Wise appealed to what must remain the arbiter in every
question .of criticism, namely, the character of the
literature which reflects the temper of the time, the
soul of the people.

From November 12, 1886, to March 18, 1887,
Wise published a series of articles on "Essence of
Religion," "The Elements of Theology," "On Judaism, Abrahamism and Mosaism," "The Covenant,"
"The Sources of the Theology of Judaism," and
"The Thora of Moses." These were followed by
"Apologetics of Judaism," "That God is and
What He is," "The Theology of Moses," "Revelation, Inspiration, Prophecy," and a large number of
other essays on kindred subjects. In these he showed
that Judaism is essentially an elaboration of the
revelation on Mount Sinai, and that the Ten Commandments contain germinally the theology and
morality of the Mosaic and post-Mosaic phases of
Judaism. The series culminated in several articles
on the "Authenticity and Last Edition of the
Pentateuch," the main argument of which constitutes the closing chapter of his "Pronaos" (193
pages). This book appeared in 1891.

The "Pronaos" attacks "negative criticism," in
order to "save the records which establish Bible
truth." Wise's defense of the integrity, as well as
the primitivity, of the books of the Bible was not

like that of a conservative Christian whose faith
would collapse, if the Canonical substructure of it be
impaired, and who rejects in every sense the ascer-
tained methods of criticism, which Wise respected.
In fact, Wise acknowledged that there is a calcu-
lable good in the New School of Biblical criticism,
for—however much the critics may diverge in detail—they share in the conviction that the fountains
of Judaism are not stagnant. It was their account
of Bible history, however, which he rejected as
untenable. He resented on that account the advanced school of Kuenen and of Wellhausen as
vehemently as he protested against the moderate
criticisms of Geiger and Graetz. He refused to ally
himself with such as put suspicion on the documents
which were very sacred to him. The genius of the
Jewish faith, he felt, must be rescued from the reach
of a new skepticism, as in his "Cosmic God" he had
tried to save it from the old skepticism. Whence
comes that force of life, of adaptability, by which
the Jewish people has evidenced that it is chosen?
An act of God fixed the destiny of the race; not
man nor men of genius, not even prophets. The
divine truths and the illumination they give have
come from God himself, who is at the center of
thought as of life. The Thora is, accordingly, the
repository of the revelation of God, and the un-
alienable source (and standard) of Judaism (Pronaos, p. 12). The critics and evolutionists in religion have no such positiveness; they cannot explain Judaism except in terms of opportunism.
There are Jews, who justify Rabbinical legalism in
some such way. And there are Christians as well

as Jews, who interpret prophetism as a revulsion against nationalism. But Wise insisted that the primeval revelation is a historical force in all the chapters of Judaism alike, and that it has given to the Jewish people the hold it has in the world.

This sketch of the "Pronaos" must suffice. In Jewish-American literature it is the only answer to the critical school at a time when it was easy to pamper the taste of the mediocre with magnificent radicalism. A kind of liberalism had come into vogue which, had it not been for Wise. might have gotten a dangerous prestige. It will not be so easy from now on to divert the current of Judaism from its ancient channels.

Wise did not stop at academic presentations; it was not in his nature to break off just where a man of action begins. He translated views into policy. In 1861 already he had published the "Essence of Judaism" for his confirmands in Congregation B'ne Yeshurun. In this book he says: "The decalogue contains, expressed or implied, the whole moral law." In 1872 he published an excerpt of the "Essence of Judaism," as a Sabbath-school text-book, entitled "Judaism, Its Doctrines and Duties." This text-book went into every Sabbath-school of this country and with it the doctrine that the revelation on Mount Sinai is valid eternally. A number of Catechisms had been written under the pressure of reformatory ideas. Hirsch wrote in 1856 and introduced in this country his "Systematischer Katechismus der israelitischen Religion," and S. Adler his "Leitfaden für den israelitischen Religionsunterricht" in 1868, and Leeser published a translation of Johlson's "Lehren der mosaischen Religion," Philadelphia, 1830. But while these were in a certain degree faithful to the Jewish spirit, they were, in the main, disputational and partisan. American Judaism would have been exposed to incalculable mischief, if a tone of dispute would have been introduced into the schools. Most of the school-books that were extant were without an inner unity, some of them affected conservatism, and some suggested extremist views; all of them were flagrant violations of the principles of educational science. Wise has given us the first hint at the possibilities with regard to religious text-books. He avoided apology and polemic and was scrupulous about pedagogic form. Is it too much to hope that the religious school-books of the future will not violate the elementary laws of teaching?

In 1866, Wise prepared the second volume of "Minhag America," for Congregation B'ne Yeshurun, and it was in use throughout the country until the appearance of the second volume of the Union Prayer Book. It will be remembered mainly for the impressive Seelenfeier it contained. This beautiful piece of impassioned devotion is a classic in American-Jewish literature. Two years afterwards Wise published his "Hymns, Psalms and Prayers," "as an expression of our religious feelings, hopes and wishes in the language most acceptable and in the form most agreeable to our age" (p. 5). Minna Kleeberg, Maurice and Nathan Mayer, Isidor Kalisch and Wolf Rothenheim contributed to this volume, but he projected it as a suggestion for an American-Jewish liturgy, and in the conception of this he

was alone.   A liturgy is an essential condition for
edification, and worship is something more than text
and melody.   Many "independent" congregations
still tolerate a promiscuous service, according to the
taste of organist and singer.   Wise here again is a
pioneer, and it is to be regretted that the interval of
thirty-two years, since he introduced his "Hymns,
Songs and Prayers," has not brought us any reform
according to his conception.

All of Wise's books, the historical, the controversial, and the educational are so many avenues
along which his personality reached out.

From theology, Biblical criticism, and liturgic and
pedagogic reform, we may finally turn to romances
and novels, for such, too, Wise wrote.   Wise never
trifled; he wrote these last with as much earnestness as he wrote on Revelation and the Synod.
Jewish writers to-day ought to make use of the
wealth of moral life, of tragedy and of pathos,
that lies in the history of the Jews.   No alien
can quite succeed in getting near to the Jewish
heart.   We must return to our own hearth-
stones, and the reformation amongst us, which has
been largely formal, must now become moral.
Wise may have been premature in his novel writing, but he saw very early that there should be a
revival of pride in our beautiful history, and that
the virtues of our ancestry have a vitalizing power
such as the story of all heroism has.   Wise took
his subjects out of Jewish history and treated them
with psychological tact.   In this, too, he showed a
high order of ability.   I mention the following: "The
Convert," 1854; "The Jewish Heroine," 1854 (trans-

lated from the Spanish); "The Catastrophe at Eger,"
a narrative of the sixteenth century; "The Shoemaker's Family," 1855; "Resignation and Fidelity,
or Life and Romance," 1855; "Romance, Philosophy
and Cabalah, or the Conflagration at Frankfort o. t.
M.," a narrative of the last century, 1855; "The
Last Struggle of the Nation," 1856;* "The Combat
of the People, or Hillel and Herod," 1858; and the
"First of the Maccabees;" † and a number of others
throughout the earlier volumes of the *Israelite*.

In German he wrote: "Die Juden von Lands-
huth;" "Der Rothkopf oder des Schulmeister's
Tochter;" "Baruch und sein Ideal;" and others,
all of which he published serially in "*Die Deborah*."

*Translated into French by Rabbin Dreyfous, of Mulhouse,
and published in "*Le lien d'Israel*."

† Dramatized in Hebrew by Dr. Bliden and J. Epstein,
Jerusalem, 5654.

PLUM STREET TEMPLE.

CHAPTER X.

ISAAC M. WISE AND CONGREGATION B'NE YESHU-RUN.

Wise entered upon his Rabbinate in Congregation B'ne Yeshurun on April 26, 1854, and occupied it till his death, March 26, 1900, nearly forty-six years. His ministerial labors are as typical of his character as we have thus far found his other activities were. The Congregation was already in 1848 one of the most thoughtful in the country. It had indorsed Wise's appeal of that year by a formal resolution and by the appointment of delegates to attend the proposed convention. His words had evoked admiration, and the response given to them by the Congregation was as prompt as it was hearty. B'ne Yeshurun was a homogeneous community, without that admixture of elements which had been the cause of disturbances in other Congregations. There were sturdy men in it who had brought with them from their European homes a genuine love for Judaism and a considerable degree of culture. Above all, they had honest convictions, and appreciated that they bore grave responsibilities toward the future of Judaism in this country. It does not diminish the credit of his leadership, if we assert that Isaac M. Wise would not have achieved success, despite his acknowledged gifts, without the intelligent sympathy and the substantial assistance his Congregation gave him. His-

torical justice awards to Congregation B'ne Yeshurun a position of honor in American Judaism by
reason of its record as a "Mother in Israel."

In the latter part of 1853, Wise was invited to
come to Cincinnati and to meet the people of the
Congregation. These had watched him from the
distance, and had admired him for his strong words
in behalf of Union and Progress. They found in
him, on meeting him personally, the qualities of a
man of first caliber, and at once offered him their
pulpit and their hearts. But Wise, conscious of the
responsibilities implied in the call to the Congregation as much as to himself, deferred the negotia-
tions, so as to give time to both sides for delibera-
tion instead of yielding to impulse. After the lapse
of several months, he offered to release the Congregation from the obligations they had assumed, if they
believed that they had risked their corporate interest by his election. But the Congregation insisted
on its call, and, accordingly, he was duly installed,
April 26, 1854. Congregation B'ne Yeshurun was
evidently eager to enter with him upon the campaign of reform. It has, indeed, given him sus-
tained devotion and co-operation for fifty years, and
we know now that the pioneer members had been
far-sighted, for they had indeed secured the right
man. From the moment of his arrival in Cincinnati, B'ne Yeshurun and Isaac M. Wise were iden-
tified in every public-spirited enterprise, and their
names are linked together inseparably.

It will be my task in this chapter to narrate what
Wise did as Rabbi and the services he rendered to
his Congregation. These more local labors have

become suggestive to other Congregations and to Rabbis no less than his labors in other respects have been.   Wise was much in demand with Congregations throughout the country for this reason.   He traveled extensively, and was everywhere received with enthusiasm.   A Congregation of lesser quality might have resented the frequent interruptions of his local labors, but B'ne Yeshurun gave Wise all possible liberty and latitude.   His personality was magnetic, and he compensated readily for his absences by the irresistible force of his manhood. Besides, B'ne Yeshurun did not pursue a selfish policy, and had no disposition to restrict the ambition and the influence of its spiritual leader.   This breadth may be rare in the Congregations of our day, and was unparalleled in the earlier days, and it is for this reason, too, that we must maintain that Congregation B'ne Yeshurun is a classical prototype in Judaism.   Despite the fact that Wise spent a considerable part of his time in lecturing outside of Cincinnati, dedicating synagogues, making appeals for Union and the College, traveling about like St. Paul, whom he admired, there is not a single protest, but there are many votes of approval and encouragement, on the minutes of the Congregation.

Three Congregations paid a unique tribute to the magnetism of his personality—B'ne Israel, of Cincinnati; Adath Israel, of Louisville, Kentucky; and Anshe Chesed, of New York.   The first tendered him its call during the first year of his ministry in B'ne Yeshurun, and offered to content itself with a sermon from him on alternate weeks.   The call was declined (see also page 56), and a way, accordingly,

opened for Dr. Max Lilienthal, whose friendship with
Wise from that date was uninterrupted up to the latter's death, in 1882. The Louisville Congregation declared it would ask for no more than a sermon once a
month. This, too, was declined. But the last of the
calls, to which a number of others could be added,
might have been crucial. It was given Wise by Congregation Anshe Chesed, in 1873, when he was in his
prime and harbored great plans. This Congregation
elected him for life, and offered him lucrative emoluments, and, what was very tempting to him, great
possibilities for a Rabbinical College in the wealthy
East. His rejection of this call marks a turning
point in Wise's life, and it brought about also that
the Cincinnati community roused itself up to his
standard of earnestness and capacity for sacrifice.

On August 24, 1866, Wise dedicated the magnificent Temple of Congregation B'ne Yeshurun with
impressive ceremonies and the writer will never forget the fervor with which Wise once pointed up to
the great dome of this Temple and asked that the
sons, for whom the fathers had built it, turn their
eyes heavenward with equal piety. In a communication which Wise addressed to the Congregation at
the time when the building of the Temple was being planned, he declared it was about time "Judaism welcome the light of day and deck itself with
becoming pride!" Since that day (and many times
before) Wise officiated at the dedication of synagogues, so that it is likely that he dedicated every
Jewish house of worship in the United States west
of the Alleghenies and many in the east of them.
He witnessed not only the rearing of palatial

structures, but also the rise of Jews to self-respect and to gladness in a faith that can afford to stand in the light of the world.

We have already spoken of the point of view which Wise had in his large-scoped reform of Jewish-American affairs, and we have said that he scorned mere surface-improvements and that he strove to put the germs of life into them.   He desired to secure for the Jews such conditions as would insure growth and a healthy religious life.   His rabbinical record is replete with evidences that it was wise and practical.   He was no opportunist, and he was uncontroled by either his own whims or by the whims of others.   He had but little opposition at home as compared with the hostility he encountered elsewhere, but he was understood by those who came into touch with him, and it took a long time for others to perceive that he was prompted by singleness of purpose.   Congregation B'ne Yeshurun was spared the turmoil through which other congregations had to pass, largely because the character of its Rabbi was a guarantee that what he said and proposed to do was genuine.   Thus it came that the abrogation of a number of customs which had lost meaning was not accompanied by any disturbances of the congregational peace, and the innovations Wise made offended nobody.   It will be difficult to find a parallel in this respect.   Starting with the current orthodoxy of the old days, Congregation B'ne Yeshurun has gone through all the phases of the Reform Movement into a religious status which is the highest and the most vital. B'ne Yeshurun has uniformly reflected the spirit

of the day. When Wise made his first attempt to
give Jewish worship a modern form, and published
his Minhag America, his Congregation adopted it
forthwith, and encouraged him by requesting a second volume for the holidays. His "Hymns and
Prayers" was received with similar favor in 1868,
and when, in 1892, the Central Conference of American Rabbis edited a "Union Prayer Book," B'ne
Yeshurun accepted it upon Wise's recommendation
rather than upon any proven efficiency of it.

He introduced the right of confirmation on his
first Shabuoth in Cincinnati. Though he had confirmed boys and girls already in Albany and several before in Germany, he is original in the interpretation of confirmation. It was not to be a
sacrament, but an educational discipline. In the
Talmud Yelodim Institute, which had been established as a parochial school in 1849, he applied
this thought of his with regard to religious education. The Institute had had its origin in the failure
of the Public Schools to be just to the fair claims
that the citizenship of all faiths had equally. Until
1868 the schools were sectarian. Talmud Yelodim Institute ceased as a day school as soon as zealotry came
to an end in the Public Schools, and Congregation
B'ne Yeshurun adopted it then as a religious Sabbath School. The Institute had served substantially in the education of the Jewish youth, but religious training began to be an issue by itself. For
this the formality of Confirmation was of course,
insufficient. Wise addressed himself to this new
question with his usual acumen and industry. An-

ticipating the change, he had written in 1861 a text-book for teachers, "The Essence of Judaism," for the instruction of the youths of Congregation B'ne Yeshurun. "Catechisms," he says in this book, "offer no complete outline of Judaism and dwell more on ceremonial observances than on the spirit and essence of the religion taught in the Bible." (See Preface, page 3.)   He followed up the "Essence" with a text-book for pupils: "Judaism, Its Doctrines and Duties," dedicating it to "my young American Israelites whom I love as the offspring of a noble race and the future standard-bearers of the holiest cause." (Introduction, page 3.) A few years after he had taken hold of the Talmud Yelodim Institute, its standard became sufficiently high to permit the directors to inaugurate a department of "A Hebrew High School," in substitution for Zion College which had been closed. (*Israelite*, May 1, 1857.) His well-known advocacy of the Public Schools, in recognition of which he was for some time a member of the Board of the Cincinnati Schools and Examiner of Public School Teachers, coupled with the increased demand for specific religious instruction in Jewish doctrine and literature, went far toward bringing about this change from the parochial and daily to a religious and Sabbath School.

Wise was influential also in various directions, other than those of a ministerial kind.   Through his instrumentality, the Order of Bene Brith was enabled to establish the Jewish Orphan Asylum and Order Kesher Shel Barzel the Home for

the Aged and Infirm in Cleveland, Ohio. At
the Conference in that city, a year after he had
arrived at Cincinnati, he proposed that "a Committee be appointed to lay a plan before the
next Synod to establish a Widows' and Orphans'
Asylum in some central location of the United
States, accessible to all individuals and supported
by all congregations." In 1855, he appealed to
President Buchanan for his intercession for the en-
franchisement of the Jews in Switzerland by with-
holding his approval of a treaty proposed by that
government, and, assisted by Lilienthal and several
others, he was successful. A similar timely interview with James G. Blaine, then Secretary of State,
went far toward ameliorating the May laws of 1882,
by which Russian Jews who had become American
citizens were assured their rights in Russia. He
was a loyal democrat and evinced his fidelity to his
party in almost the last editorial he wrote. During
the days of the Emancipation Struggle, he was
nominated for the State Senatorship, but declined
it because of his distaste to the excitements of a
political campaign. It will surprise no one who
knew the intensity of his cosmopolitan nature, if
I record here the fact that he traveled with Kossuth
for some time, and had a share in that patriot's
historic appeal to the free American people. He
was the first Jewish Rabbi who officiated as Chap-
lain of a Legislature. Two of the prayers he
offered in this capacity in the State Capitol at
Albany are printed in the "*Asmonean*" of January
30, 1852. In the days of the stalwart independents

in both Church as well as of State, Wise was a friend of the most famous of them, Thurlow Weed, Horace Greeley, William H. Seward, President Fillmore, William C. Bryant, Governor Seymour, the Beechers, and later also of O. B. Frothingham, and he was Vice-President of the Free Religious Association of Boston. In short, Wise was in the current of life, and allied himself with all men and every movement for political and moral justice.

Wise's emphatic defense of the Sabbath is well known. He was an uncompromising upholder of its sanctity. He invested it not only with doctrinal importance, but made it also useful. In the winter of 1866, he began to deliver lectures on Friday evenings, and continued these till his death. He treated of profound and of current matters; he spoke of creeds as well as of practical matters. We are indebted to these courses of lectures for many of his books. It was in the pulpit, in fact, where Wise, forceful on many occasions, was circumspect at all times. His style was simple and direct, his manner natural, betokening certainty and self-con-control, and his thought was clear and methodic. He stated his text and subject without elaborate introduction, and submitted his conclusions with severe singleness of purpose. Few were more convincing than he, though it would have been easy to be more ornate. He was the first American Jewish preacher who took his sermons seriously as appeals and not as academic disquisitions. His sermons were engines of warfare into the heart of his auditors, just as his lectures were battering-rams against materialism and intolerant Christendom. The files of the "*American Israelite*" are filled with his pulpit addresses, and testify to the fact that his eloquence came from his manhood and not through art. (*Deborah*, April 2, 1896.)

I have narrated elsewhere what part Congregation B'ne Yeshurun took in the formation of the Union of American Hebrew Congregations. It gave the impulsive and took the initiative in it, and it has been its sponsor for twenty-five years. The first President of the Union and the only President of the Board of Governors of the Hebrew Union College, during the entire history of the College, and the leading men who have borne the brunt of the struggle and are bearing still the burden of the responsibilities, are men from B'ne Yeshurun. It is plain that Dr. Wise would have been impotent without the sympathy and assistance of these. Providence has done in this instance what it does so often when a great cause is at stake: it brings kindred spirits into co-operation. In the establishment and the management of the College, Wise and B'ne Yeshurun were also fellow-workers, and may share honors and gratification. When in 1873 Wise was tempted by Congregation Anshe Chesed, of New York, to remove from Cincinnati, he hoped that settlement in the metropolis would bring his projects to speedier fulfillment. But Congregation B'ne Yeshurun reassured him of its sincere support, and it has made these promises good to the fullest extent. The history of the Hebrew Union College may, indeed, be considered as running parallel with the friendship between Wise and his congregational household.

There remains one more item to speak of: Wise's journalism. From July 4, 1854, to the day of his death, Wise wielded a trenchant pen, which the enemies of reform feared and the friends of progress admired. He was a pioneer editor, who set the pace for all who follow him. He was the first rabbinical editor, and he did not restrict himself to pamphleteering. He measured his editorial duties and the scope of his "*Israelite*" by a standard taken not from his ambition, but from the right of the reading and thinking public. He treated his opponents not with frivolity and not with personalities. He himself was open to reconciliation with those who abused him. He wrote with impatience often, and with extravagance, and did not scruple to condemn with rigor; but he .never forgot the law of fairplay and of right, notwithstanding all passion.

We have reviewed the life and doings of Isaac M. Wise, and we have found him to be as versatile in gifts as he was varied in his service. He was a reformer and builder, a man of action, and craving still all his life for the teacher's chair. He was an author of philosophic work and at the same time a fluent journalist, who flung out effective but fugitive words every week. He was modest in virtue, but also assertive in truth; a veritable giant, and still the meekest of men. We leave the judgment of what he did to the Genius of History. In 1850

already he felt what that would be.*   He was then
a young man, full of zeal and ardor.   His illustrious career, which is now complete, has confirmed
his own prognostication.   He was, indeed, a prophet
with power from God, one of the classics.

On March 26, 1900, he was bedded to rest in the
Jewish Cemetery on Walnut Hills, and he sleeps
near the chapel in which he had spoken many a
word of comfort.   We carried him to his grave in
pride, and we passed away from it in tears.

"You and I remain; our path is plain—
     The rank from out of which he stepped, we fill.
His sacred cause, we 'll cherish it, maintain;
     God blessed his life: He will defend us still !" †

וייקץ והנה חלום אך /אלהים פתרונם. *
אוהבי הללוני אויבי קללוני
אין יתרון לשניהם.
אלו שגו להלל ואלו זדו לקלל.
ה' ישפט ביניהם:

*Albany, April 29, 5610, in *Asmonean*, Vol. II, No. 2, May
3, 1850; also, in *Israelite*, May 2, 1856.

† B. Bettmann, in "History of Congregation B'ne Yeshurun," 1892.

AN APPRECIATION.*

BY PROF. DR. M. MIELZINER.

"Know ye not that a prince and a great man hath fallen this day in Israel?" (2 Sam. iii. 38.) These were the lamenting words of King David after the funeral of his greatest general, whose death threw all Israel into the deepest gloom. And the very same words may be applied to him whose demise we are mourning. Dr. Isaac M. Wise was "a prince and a great man in Israel." He was a prince, a spiritual prince, a trusted leader, not only of his congregation, but an acknowledged leader in Israel also. And more than this, he was a great man, distinguished by the noblest qualities of mind and heart, which made him beloved and revered by all who knew him, by all who came in touch with him. And, therefore, his death is felt, not alone by our community of this city, but also by all Jewish congregations in this country, as was evidenced by the numerous rabbis and representatives that came from near and distant cities to show the last honor to the prince and great man that has fallen in Israel.

Eulogies in honor of the deceased great leader and teacher will soon be delivered from the pulpits of all temples and synagogues of this country. But

* Memorial Address delivered at the Hebrew Union College, March 31, 1900.

it was found to be proper that already to-day at the re-opening of our interrupted sessions a memorial service be held here in our Hebrew Union College. For who has more cause to honor the memory of the departed great leader than this college? This institution was his beloved child, which he fostered and brought up, and to which he devoted his best time and power, aye, his very last activity in life was the instruction he gave here on last Saturday just before having received the warning stroke that the end was near. I know, students, that you loved and revered him as dutiful sons do love and revere their fathers, and you have reason to lament: "We are now orphaned, for our spiritual father is no more!"

Addressing you on this occasion, it is not my intention to deliver an oration in which to review the life and work of our lamented President. For this purpose the time is too limited, and my innermost being is still too much agitated by the grief over our great loss to be able to do justice to it. I shall restrict myself to point out in a few plain words some characteristic features of the work and the merits of our departed friend and teacher.

My friends, we are told in the Talmud that when R. Jochanan ben Zaccai, the most distinguished teacher of his time, was about to die, he was surrounded by his disciples, who asked for his last admonition and blessing, and on this occasion they addressed him with the words:

נר ישראל, עמוד הימיני, פטיש החזק.

"*Thou art the light for Israel, the right-hand pillar, the powerful hammer.*"—(Talm. Berachoth 28.)

These three epithets are, indeed, very significant. They characterize the principal merits of that great master of old. And I think they designate also the principal merits of the great master whose death we are mourning.

A lamp or a light for Israel, R. Jochanan ben Zaccai was called by his disciples. That sage, as you know, flourished during and shortly after the fall of Jerusalem and the destruction of the temple by the Romans. Gloom and despair had taken hold of the minds of the remnant of Israel. With the fall of the temple and the altar Judaism seemed to be lost forever. Into this dark night of gloom and despair R. Jochanan ben Zaccai brought light. He proclaimed that Judaism was not indissolubly bound up with the sacrificial service of the temple of Jerusalem. He reminded them of the teachings of the prophets, "That works of charity and love are sacrifices more pleasing to God than the blood and fat of animals." He proclaimed that not Jerusalem, but the divine law of truth, justice, love and holiness are Israel's true sanctuary. To cultivate and diffuse this law he devoted his energies. He modified many religious laws and customs according to the changed circumstances, and thereby he infused new life and fresh energy into Judaism and became truly a light of Israel.

And the same is true of our American ben Zaccai. When, fifty years ago, he came to this country, he found the Jewish affairs here in a sad state of disorder. Our co-religionists, having come here from all corners and countries of the old world, brought with them the notions, customs and practices of the

Ghetto in former times of oppression and persecution, which could not harmonize with the spirit of
this land of liberty and freedom. The prospect of
maintaining and developing Judaism on this blessed
soil of freedom was dark and gloomy. But Dr.
Wise's endeavors were at once directed toward
bringing light into the existing darkness, order and
harmony into the prevailing disorder and imminent
dissolution.

With the motto, "Let there be light," he published a paper devoted to religious instruction and
enlightenment, which paper ever since from week
to week has spoken to the minds and hearts of our
people to the remotest parts of the country.
Through this paper as well as by the power of his
eloquent word, which resounded in almost every
synagogue and temple in the United States, and
everywhere instructed, edified and enthused large
audiences, he exercised a wonderful influence upon
our congregations, near and far, and succeeded in
rejuvenating Judaism by freeing it from notions
and practices of the Ghetto, from dead and obsolete
forms and ceremonies, and by bringing its mode of
worship and its appearance more in harmony with
modern thought and culture and with the happier
circumstances under which we are living here in
this free and enlightened country.

And also as author of several important literary
works on Jewish history, on philosophy and theology, he proved a light for Israel, as thereby he
spread knowledge of Israel's glorious history and
sublime mission and teachings, not only among our
own people, but also among our non-Jewish fellow-

citizens, and thereby secured a better understanding and estimation of the Jew and his religion.

R. Jochanan is further called by his disciples, "The right-hand pillar."

What does this mean?

In the porch of King Solomon's temple were erected, as you know, two pillars. The pillar on the right side had the name of *Jachin*, which word means "he establishes." By calling Jochanan b. Z., the right-hand pillar allusion was made to his undying merit of having established an institution which proved a mighty pillar for the support of the temple of Judaism. I do not need to tell you, my friends, to what institution I refer. When the Roman general granted the request of R. Jochanan b. Zaccai to be permitted to establish an academy at Jabneh, he could not foresee that by this Judaism would be saved; for from that academy went forth the great master minds that developed Israel's law and secured its continuation for future generations.

And so also Dr. Wise established institutions for the maintenance of Judaism in this our promised land. I shall not speak of his great merit of having, through his influence, established the Union of American Hebrew Congregations, which has proven a powerful factor of promoting the cause of Judaism, nor of his merit as founder and efficient president of the Central Conference of American Rabbis, which comprises almost all the rabbis of the United States. I only refer to his merit as founder of the Hebrew Union College for the cultivation of Jewish knowledge and literature and for the education of rabbis and spiritual leaders of

American Hebrew Congregations.   To his foresight
and wisdom, to his untiring labors and undaunted
energy we owe the existence of this college, which
some twenty years ago seemed to be an impossibility
here on American soil.   Even those who from the
beginning discouraged the undertaking of establishing it, and for a long time even antagonized it, admit now willingly its necessity, its usefulness and
its great blessing for the maintenance of Judaism in
this country, especially since graduates went forth
from this college who occupy the pulpits of some of
the largest congregations throughout the country.
He was not only the founder of this college, but
ever since its foundation until his last moment its
president and one of its most efficient professors.

You students were daily witnesses of the faithful
and self-denying devotion and fatherly care which
he, in spite of the increasing disabilities of old age,
and in spite of his other arduous labors and duties
as Rabbi of one of the largest congregations and as
editor of two religious papers, uninterruptedly bestowed upon this institution and its students and
their studies.   Verily, to him, too, applies the epithet, "The right-hand pillar."

Finally, R. Jochanan ben Zaccai's activity was
also characterized by the attribution that he was a
"strong, powerful hammer."

The same master of old who, when he once pro-
pounded to his disciples the question, "What should
man endeavor most eagerly to obtain?" gave his
approval to the answer of the one who said, "Man's
best possession is a kind and noble heart,"—the
same master who was of so kindly and gentle a dis-

position that he ever was the first to greet with
friendliness whomsoever he met, were it even a
heathen or one of the lowest social standing, the
same master was, when necessary, a strong, mighty,
crushing hammer to refute antagonistic opinions, to
combat false, sophistical arguments.   This epithet,
"mighty hammer," was probably given to him because he was the first who successfully combated
the Zadducean principles, and who knew how to refute the arguments of those who insisted upon the
literal interpretation of the law, and were opposed
to his spiritual and liberal interpretation according
to the exigencies of the changed times.

My friends, do you not here at once recognize the
prototype of the master for whom we are mourning?   Kind, gentle, yielding, almost child-like in
personal intercourse with every one, Dr. Wise
wielded a pen that was often like a mighty hammer
when it combated antagonistic opinions, or repelled
attacks from within or from without; not personal
attacks—for such he mostly ignored—but attacks
upon that which he considered right, just, true and
holy.   In former years, when he had to contend for
religious reforms, he was a mighty hammer to bat-
ter down the walls of superstition and prejudice, to
break down obsolete, dead forms, customs and ceremonies.

But, in accordance with the saying of our ancient
teachers, "Where wise men destroy, it is for the
purpose of building up," Dr. Wise used the hammer not merely to destroy, but also to build anew.
His tendencies were not destructive, but rather constructive; where he abolished antiquated useless

forms, he took care to replace them by new ones, more and better answering to their purpose, more appealing to mind and heart.

My friends, it is a Talmudical saying : "A sage who dies can not be replaced." The harmonious combination of excellent qualities and virtues found in one sage can not easily be found again in another. Also, Dr. Wise can not be replaced. "Oh, for those who are gone and can not be replaced." He can not easily be replaced in our college, neither in our community nor in American Judaism.

The last blessing that R. Jochanan b. Z. gave to his mourning disciples was: "May the fear of God (that is, true religiousness) influence all your actions."

Your master, for whom you are mourning, left you a similar blessing and admonition in that Psalm verse which, as we were informed in the funeral oration, he had selected as his life's motto, and which he himself had selected as text for his funeral sermon; it is the verse:

"Who is the man who feareth the Lord? Him shall God instruct the way that he shall choose" (Psalm xxv. 12). That is, true religiousness influences our actions, leads us the right way on which to go.

Take, my young friends, the lesson of this Bible verse to heart. Make it your life's motto. Follow in the footsteps of your departed master; take his noble virtues as your model. Thus you will prove yourselves to be his true disciples. Thus you will honor his memory.

May God in His mercy send consolation to all who mourn over the master who is no more.

May God in his mercy send the balm of consolation to the wounded hearts of those who were bound to the departed by the most tender ties of love and affection.

Let us bow to His divine will.

Amen.

(Aet. 80.)

Isaac M. Wise

LECTURES AND ESSAYS.

THE LAW.*

אין בארון רק שני לחות האבנים (I Kings, viii, 9).

Law and doctrine are the two generic terms by
which Judaism designates its original apothegms.
Law is commanded, doctrine is taught; law is obligatory, doctrine is advisory; law is established,
doctrine is accepted. Every law is based upon one
or more doctrines which it generalizes, as a law of
nature is deduced from phenomena, acknowledged
by reason or authority, or both. The doctrine is a
simple theorem. Therefore, every law suggests a
doctrine, but not every doctrine has become a law.†

According to historical exegesis, the body of
law and doctrine which constitutes Judaism is contained in the Pentateuch. There can be nothing in
Scripture which is not suggested in the Pentateuch.
All the prophets have received the substance of
their message from Mount Sinai. They have not
added an iota to the Torah, nor have they taken
anything from it. The rabbis of the Talmud express themselves to this effect. All orthodox expounders of Scriptures indorse them in the con-

* The argument of this essay was presented at the conference of the Rabbinical Literary Association at Detroit, Mich.,
July, 1880.

† Those who speak of the letter and the spirit actually
mean law and doctrine.

ception that the Pentateuch is the exclusive basis of Judaism, and the standard by which the rest of Scripture must be understood. Among the pre-Talmudical rabbis only the Pentateuch is called Scripture (תורה שיבכתב); the other books of the Bible are called the received or traditional material (קבלה).*
It was the opinion of both Rabbi Jonahan and Simon ben Lakish that in future the authority of Prophets and Hagiography will cease, but that of the five books of the Law will never cease.† This view is substantiated by a rational study of the whole Bible. The body of law and doctrine is the Pentateuch, expressed or implied. Therefore, those expounders of the Law who place themselves upon the standpoint of those critics who maintain that the five books of Moses, or portions thereof, were written by prophets after Moses, must admit that those prophets recorded in the Pentateuch the quintessence of their religious and ethical knowledge. Judaism must be studied in the Pentateuch.

The post-biblical expositions on doctrine are called *Hagada;* those on law are called *Halacha.* The *Hagada*, in its various forms, expounds, mostly homiletically, passages of the Bible, especially narratives, and is therefore called *Hagada*, which signifies that which is narrated. The *Halacha*, liter-

---

* See, for instance, that very ancient passage in *Siphri Shelach,* והנפש, Sec. 212.

† *Yerushalmi* Megillah 1. הנביאים והכתבים עתידין ליבטל וחמשת ספרי תורה אינן עתידין ליבטל; מצות בטלות לעתיד לבא. The passage in *Babli,* Niddah, 61b, refers to a future state of existence. Death absolves man from all obligations of the law.

ally the path or walk, expounds the laws of Moses,
and extends their application, either on scholastic
grounds or to meet new emergencies. The *Halacha*
relies for its authority (ראיה) only on the laws commanded after the Sinaitic revelation.* Laws established before that event, and adopted by Israel, are
supposed to have been repeated on Mount Sinai
(חזרו ונשנו בסני). Any *Halacha* not based upon
an express law of Moses is supposed to be based
upon a mere suggestion (רמז), for which rabbinical
authority only is claimed. Any *Halacha* logically
implied in a law of Moses, and derived therefrom
by any of the thirteen rules of rabbinical harmeneu-
tics, is, in the opinion of the rabbis, of authority
equal with that of the law of Moses itself, because
it is logically contained therein, except in penal
law, where it is the rule that reasoning from analogy
gives no authority to impose any fine or punishment
(אין עונשין מן הדין). In cases of doubt as to
the Mosaic permission or prohibition of an act
(ספק דאוריתא), it was considered prohibited by the
law itself, according to some casuists, or by rabbinical law, according to others. Hence the rabbis of
the Talmud maintain that they added nothing to
the laws of Moses.

They did add, however, and did take away. In
the first place, they adopted as a part of the legal
system, besides customs and enactments, also the

---

* דברי תורה מדברי קבלה לא ילפינן; אין מביאין ראיה
ממקרא שנכתב קודם מתן תורת
See Kitzur Kelale Haggemarah.

traditional laws (הלכה למושה מסני), in regard to
which all authorities agree that these are laws
which have no foundation whatever in the laws of
Moses. In the second place, the hermeneutical
rules themselves, upon which the whole structure
rests, are additions to the laws of Moses. Moses
did not ordain them as laws, not even the *Kal
Vechomer* rule; and the most conservative expounders of rabbinism claim for them the authority
of traditional law only.* In the third place, there
is a discrepancy in those hermeneutical rules themselves, a difference of opinion between Rabbis Ish-
mael and Akiba in regard to the rules of *Kelal Up' rat*
and *Ribbui Umiut;* it is therefore undecided which
of the two was handed down traditionally from
Moses to the rabbis. And yet the Talmud contains
Halachoth based on either of those conflicting
rules, one class of which, like those based on the
rule of *Semichuth*, must be additions to the laws of
Moses. In the fourth place, every Halacha constructed by any scholastic method or authority is an
addition to the laws of Moses, because the law
(Deut. xvii, 8) authorizes, besides the prophet,
only one body to expound the law, the Seventy
Elders, to which alone and exclusively the law of
לא תסור refers: "Thou shalt not depart from the
word, which they shall tell thee, to the right or to
the left." This authority, in after times, could be
claimed by the Sanhedrin alone. Moses Maimonides also admits, in the preface to his *Mishneh*

* The same might be said of all laws based on the rule of
גזירה שוה

Torah, that the above law refers only to the enactment of the Beth Din or Sanhedrin of respective generations, and not to the scholastics, who claim that they add nothing to the laws of Moses. The rabbis must have felt this point when they abolished the penalty which the law imposes (Ibid., verse 12) upon one who rebels against the decision of the Sanhedrin. It is stated in the Talmud (*Yerushalmi* Sotah, ix, 10, and elsewhere) that during the period from the death of Jose ben Joezer to the death of R. Gamliel II, the Sanhedria were lawfully authorized bodies (ששמשו פרנסות). All other bodies of that name were mere scholiasts (אשכלות), because they were not lawfully authorized (שלא שמשו פרנסות). Consequently all Halachoth fixed by any Sanhedrin between Jose ben Joezer and Rabbi Akiba might be considered as contained in the laws of Moses, because established by lawful expounders of the law. All other Halachoth, which are certainly the bulk of the rabbinical literature, must be considered additions to the laws of Moses. Where, in the sea of the Talmud, will you find those Halachoth of the lawful Sanhedria, when ever so many of the general laws of the Mishna (even סתם משנה) were construed by the individual opinions of dialecticians? But this query is foreign to my subject.

It is well known to students of the Talmud that the rabbis have taken away from the laws of Moses. They changed the penal code, and went almost to the point of abolishing capital punishment. They established the rule that women need not observe such commandatory laws as depend on any fixed

130   ISAAC M. WISE.

time. They established that other rule that all
commandments relating to the land are obligatory
in Palestine only. To say nothing of details, these
general points prove my contention. Besides, the
well-known admission of the Talmud, how in several cases, הלכה עוקבת מקרא, ''the Halacha super-
sedes Scripture,'' I can point to other passages of
the same import. In Talmud Babli (*Makkoth* 24a)
Rabbi Jose b. Chanina states that four later prophets abrogated four Mosaic decrees.* On the same
page in the Talmud is the celebrated homily of
Rabbi Simlai, which states that Moses gave six
hundred and thirteen commandments. David reduced them to eleven in Psalm xv. Isaiah reduced
them to six (xxxiii, 15), and then again to two
(lvi, 1). Then came Micah and reduced them to
three (vi, 8); Amos to one, ''Seek me and live''
(v, 6); and so also Habakkuk, ''The righteous
liveth by his faith'' (ii, 4). A similar passage occurs in *Yebamoth,* 49b, where it is reported that
Simon ben Azzai said: ''I have found a genealog-
ical (secret) scroll in Jerusalem, in which it was
written, etc., King Menasseh slew Isaiah. Raba
said that he proved the law against him and slew
him,'' etc. Then three cases are quoted, in which
Isaiah contradicts Moses.†

In the light of these quotations, we ask how
those savants understood the repeated commandments of the Bible (Deut. iv, 2 ; xii, 32), not to

* ארבעה גזירות גזר מושה רבינו על ישראל באן
ארבעה נביאים ובטלום
† משה רבך אמר וג' ואת אמר וג'

add to nor diminish from the law? We repeat this
question to the Jewish metaphysicians of the Middle
Ages, who were certainly aware of the abrogation
of quite a number of laws : How could they defend the eternity of the law (נצחיות התורה), and
make it a dogma of Judaism? Moses Maimonides,
for instance, maintained it (*Perush Ham Mishnayoth,
Chelek*) as the ninth dogma of rabbinical Judaism ;
and in his *More Nebuchim* (Part III, chapter xxxvii)
he puts a number of the laws of Moses under the
heading of להציל מטעות ע"ז—"To protect against
the errors of Paganism." Maimonides, like all
other Jews, believed in the final disappearance of
Paganism ; hence he must have believed in the
transitory nature of all laws of Moses relevant to it.

It would be vain to contend that the rabbis of the
Talmud did not mean to say that nothing must be
added to (or taken away from) the six hundred and
thirteen commandments of Moses, although Abraham Ibn Ezra, in one instance, maintains that
"Thou shalt not add," etc., refers to the laws
against Paganism, when they themselves repeatedly
tell us that any addition, even like one blessing
added to the three-fold blessing of the priests, or
even a change in the Tephilin, etc., is a violation of
that law. It is certain that the Jewish metaphysicians of the Middle Ages insisted on the eternity of
the law as a dogma, because this is a cardinal point
in rabbinical orthodoxy. How, then, is that con-
tradiction to be solved?

This question becomes still more perplexing, if
one takes the law itself before the judgment-seat of
common sense. How could any legislator impose

the obligation upon his constituency not to add to
nor diminish from the laws he prescribes for them,
when he must acknowledge that laws must be accommodated to the needs of successive ages? How
could, especially, the author of Deuteronomy utter
such a law of limitation on one page, and the law
of a supreme tribunal to decide cases not provided
for in this law, on another page? (Deut. xvii, 8.)
The problem is not solved even if we should admit
that Deuteronomy was written much later than
other parts of the Pentateuch. The difficulty is
the same, whether directed against Moses, Samuel,
Jeremiah, Ezra, or Simon the Just. Besides, it
cannot be denied that the author of Deuteronomy
intends to supplement and amend laws recorded in
other parts of the Pentateuch, and assumes the authority of Moses; consequently, his prohibition to
add or diminish refers also to the other parts of the
Pentateuch. On the contrary, such an admission
would only complicate the question still more.
How could an intelligent legislator, a thousand
years after Moses, put on record such a law of limitation, when he himself amended the laws of
Moses? Nor is the difficulty to be disposed of by
that view which interprets the injunction "Thou
shalt not add," etc., to mean interpolations and
erasures and not incorporation of new laws; for, in
the first place, Joshua did embody his covenant
with Israel בספר תורת אלהים "In the book of the
Law of God." (Joshua, xxiv, 29.) Samuel did
incorporate a royalistic constitution (משפט המלוכה),
Bassepher, "into the book" (I Samuel, x, 26),
which, orthodox critics agree, refers to the Book of

Law. A law enacted by David (I Samuel, xxx, 24–26) was added to the Pentateuch (Numbers, xxxi, 22). Rashi admits that Deut. xviii, 8, was written after the time of King Solomon. In the second place, if the law in question had been directed merely against interpolations and erasures, it would have been placed after Deuteronomy, xxxi, 9, "and Moses wrote this law and gave it to the priests," etc., and not in connection with לשמור in the first case, and תשמרו לעשות in the second, which expressly refers to the practice of the law and not to adding or taking away of a book or passage.

Since the question is not answered by any of the above hypotheses, I propose to submit a thesis which, I believe, does solve the problem. It is not new, as I will attempt to prove, but it appears to me to be true and of great importance as a hermeneutic rule to expound the law, a fundamental principle of Jewish history, a firm and positive standpoint of progressive reform. The thesis may be formulated thus:

First. The Decalogue is the Torah, in letter and spirit, the eternal law and doctrine, the exclusive and adequate source of theology and ethics, the only intelligible categoric imperative. Therefore, it is called in the Pentateuch *Had-dabar,* the word or the substance, the only true logos by which the moral world was called into existence, and which, as the Talmud states, existed before the creation of this earth; or also, *Had-debarim ha'eleh,* "these words;" or *Asereth Had-debarim,* "the ten words," and not *Asereth Ham-mitzvoth,* "the ten command-

ments," which is a misnomer; for its laws are categories, its doctrines are fundamental principles; in
its logical order it is a unit, and in its totality it
comprises the entire substance of theology and
ethics; no new category of law can be added to it
and none can be taken away from it without de-
stroying its unity and perfection.

Secondly. The body of law contained in the Pentateuch is called *Torath Mosheh*, "The Law of
Moses," which reduces to practice the fundamental
concept of the Decalogue, provides the means to
enforce it, and expounds and expands its doctrines.*

Thirdly. The Law of Moses is constituted of
(a) *Mitzvoth*, commandments with a direct object;
(b) *Chukkim*, ordinances of a ritual character
(Leviticus, ix, 8–11); and (c) *Mishpatim*, statutes
of a judicial character (Exodus, xxi);† the two
latter classes have an indirect object. The doctrines underlying these laws, and reduced to practice by them, are contained in the Decalogue, and,
like it, are eternal; while special laws are temporary applications of those doctrines to meet emergencies, and are therefore of a temporary character.

Fourthly. Inasmuch as the Mosaic doctrines were
ideally implicit in the Decalogue before they took

---

* This idea is expressed in the Talmud (Nedarim, 38a) by
R. Chama b. Chanina, thus:

לא העשיר מושה אלא מפסולתון של לוחות

† Edoth, a term used in Deuteronomy (iv, 45; vi, 17 and
20), and then in other books of the Bible, and Pikkudim,
occurring chiefly in Psalms, cannot be taken as classes of
laws, because they are not used in this sense in the Pentateuch, nor in any prose passage of Scripture.

form in special provisions, and inasmuch as the Decalogue was given to Israel through the agency of Moses ("I standing between God and between you to tell you the word of God," Deut. v, 5), every law of the Pentateuch, whenever, wherever, and by whomsoever written, may justly be termed a law of Moses, as the whole Torah may justly be styled the Law of Moses.

I offer the following proofs in support of these propositions :

I. Proofs from the Pentateuch.

The fact that the revelation of the Decalogue is presented in so elaborate and sublime a setting suggests that this revelation was regarded as the most important event in Israel's history.* The thoughtful reader of the nineteenth chapter of Exodus cannot but feel that something of importance will follow. The Decalogue is the picture ; the narrative of the revelation is its frame.

The next points to be taken into consideration are these : The Bible represents the Decalogue alone as direct revelation of God to Israel ; all other

* The revelation on the rock (Exodus, xxxiii and xxxiv), although directed to Moses only, is also surrounded with a marvelous solemnity, because it expounds the doctrine of divine mercy (כח התשובה) as announced in the Third Commandment, without which (מדת הרחמים), as the Talmud correctly remarks, the world, or rather the human family, could not exist. The laws of expiating sacrifices, the Day of Atonement included, are the Chukkim, reducing to practice this doctrine, to which the Pentateuch refers again in Numbers, xiv and xvi, and especially in Deuteronomy, iv, 29-31; vii, 9, 10; xxx, 1-10; and elsewhere.

known revelations are represented as indirect, made through Moses or the other prophets. Again, the object of the Sinaitic revelation is to establish the covenant between God and Israel (Exodus, xix, 5, 6; xxxiv, 6–9); this importance is attached to no other portion of Scripture. Therefore, the second Isaiah characterizes the Sinaitic revelation thus: "And I, this is my covenant with them, saith Jehovah; my spirit which is upon thee, and my words (the Decalogue) which I have put into thy mouth (revealed directly) shall not depart from thy mouth, and from the mouth of thy seed, and from the mouth of thy seed's seed, saith Jehovah, from now to evermore" (Isaiah, lix, 21). This certainly says that God, in order to perpetuate his covenant with his chosen people, expects that it shall never forget the directly revealed words, the Decalogue, and never swerve from the divine spirit resting upon it in consequence of that holy law.

The covenant which makes Israel a kingdom of priests and a holy nation, a covenant people and a light of the nations, according to Isaiah's statement, depends, besides the spirit, on the Decalogue exclusively. And yet Isaiah only repeated that which he found in the Pentateuch (Exodus, xxxiv, 27): "And Jehovah said to Moses, Write thee down these words (the Decalogue), for by virtue of these words I have made a covenant with thee and with Israel." And then Scripture narrates: "And he wrote on the tables the words of the covenant, the ten words."

I think no further proof is necessary to convince the Bible reader that the covenant of God with

Israel depends on the Decalogue, and no other document, commandment, revelation, doctrine, or precept. If the covenant depends on the Decalogue,
then Judaism does. The Sinaitic revelation was the
קול גדול ולא יסף, "The great voice to which he will
not add." It is all sufficient. But we·have a class
of critics who look upon Deuteronomy as a later
legislation (תורה מגלה מגלה נתנה), and to convince such I beg leave to quote from Deuteronomy
also.

In Deuteronomy likewise (ix, 9, 11, 15), the two
tables of the Decalogue are called "the tables of
the covenant," meaning those tables upon which
was engraved the law of the covenant. There, too,
this law is called (x, 4) "the ten words." The
Deuteronomist also informs us (iv, 13): "And he
(God) told you his covenant, which he commanded
you to do, even the ten words; and he wrote them
upon two tables of stone." It is the same report
of the same fact, the same lesson on the same subject, only that the Deuteronomist states the matter
more explicitly, and gives us the unmistakable dis-
tinctions characterizing the Decalogue and the law
of Moses.

In the fourth chapter (9–13) the Deuteronomist
cautions his hearers not to forget "the words which
thy eyes have seen," that day when the people of
Israel stood ·before God at Horeb, and the great
I Am spoke to them out of the fire, announcing to
them the law of ·the covenant, the ten words.
In this case there is no limitation of time or
space. אשר צוה אתכם לעשות, "Which he commanded you to do," he says—always, anywhere.

והודעתם לבניך ולבני בניך, "And thou shalt make them known to thy children and thy children's children;" he enjoins upon his hearers. Here is the divine law, the eternal law, the unalterable law, to which nothing can be added, and from which nothing can be taken away. But in the verse immediately following we are told: "And Jehovah commanded me (Moses) at that time to teach you ordinances and statutes (חקים ומשפטים), to do them *in the land* to which you are passing over to possess it." Here is indirect revelation with the limitation of space, hence also of time, to be observed *by you in the land of Canaan.* Nothing could express an idea more clearly, more directly, and more intelligibly than this passage, which says that the law of the covenant, the Decalogue, is eternal, and the law of Moses was given to Israel to be observed in the land of Canaan, subject to emendation as prescribed in the seventeenth chapter, 8–11, and the eighteenth chapter, 15–22.*

On the other hand, Moses is never represented in the Pentateuch as claiming any law to be his own production. He says: "And Jehovah commanded me at that time to teach you statutes and ordinances." The words "at that time" certainly refer to the time of the Sinaitic revelation. His laws are introduced by the words "God spoke" or

---

* In the Talmud (Nedarim, 38a) R. Jose b. Chanina expresses the idea thus: * * * לא ניתנה תורה אלא למושה ולזרעו מושה נתנה לישראל. Then R. Chisda points to Deut. iv, 5–14, to come to the conclusion: אותי צוה ואני לכם. He might have pointed also to Deut. v, 28, and vi, 1.

"said to Moses" or "commanded" or "called him," and the like. In whatever manner we may understand those solemn introductions to the various laws, they plainly suggest that Moses made no laws of his own, but embodied the doctrines of the Decalogue in laws and institutions, in order to reduce the divine theories to practice for the people of Israel in the land of Canaan. And if other legislators or legislative bodies after him did the same thing, they were justified as well in introducing their enactments with the phrase "And Jehovah spoke to Moses, saying." Hence all the results of criticism do not invalidate these statements of the Pentateuch, even if Moses had written no laws; although it cannot be doubted that the Pentateuch contains many a chapter of law which could have been written by Moses only.

May I be permitted to refer briefly to the two facts of history, that the prophets, with the exception of one case in Jeremiah, never reproved the Hebrews for the transgression of laws other than those of the Decalogue; and that the people, although they did not do "all as written in this book," as King Josiah said, were well aware of and thoroughly acquainted with the Decalogue and its doctrines? The proper distinction being made between the eternal law and the Law of Moses, it will be found that the Hebrews, in the age of the Judges and even during the kingdom of Israel, also knew the law and observed it as *the* law, the constitution and religion of Israel, with the exceptions incident to their time. It appears that the history of the prophetical period is a continuous proof that

the eternal law was considered unalterable, and the
temporary laws were set aside or amended, owing
to various circumstances, on the very principle laid
down in this essay.

II.   Proofs from Ezra and Nehemiah.

That the Hebrews in the captivity knew the eternal law as the divine law is evident from Ezekiel,
Daniel, and especially from the second Isaiah,
Zachariah, Haggai, and the Psalms of that period.
That they did not observe the whole Law of Moses
is also evident. Thus, for instance, the holidays,
with the exception of the First Day of the Seventh
Month, and perhaps the Day of Atonement,* had
been forgotten, because they were not observed.
The same, it appears from Ezekiel (xliv, 31), was
the case with the laws of forbidden food, which he
considers obligatory upon priests alone. It was not
believed that the Law of Moses must be observed
in a foreign country, or by Israel in the dispersion.
Therefore, when the exiles returned to Palestine under Zerubbabel, they knew and revered the eternal
law, rebuilt the temple, re-introduced the ancient
cult, were intensely religious and patriotic; still the
whole Law of Moses was not introduced till the time
of Ezra and Nehemiah, eighty or ninety years later.
It is useless to advance the theory that Ezra was the
author of the Pentateuch, when the Samaritans,
who were his arch-enemies, had the same Pentateuch; all the prophets and historians up to Samuel

* Compare on this subject Isaiah, lviii; Ezekiel, xl, 1; Ezra,
iii; Nehemiah, viii; and Josephus, Antiquities, I, iii, 3; and
Ezra, vi, 19–22; Nehemiah, viii, 14–17.

speak of the existence of the Law; the nineteenth Psalm has already a systematic division of the laws; the very first Psalm mentions "The Law of Jehovah," and Ezra, although a great scribe, was not a writer of such power, as is evident from his speeches in Ezra and Nehemiah.

Ezra and Nehemiah came to Palestine, the former as chief-justice and the latter as royal governor, to convert that Medo-Persian colony into a Hebrew commonwealth; consequently, the introduction of political law was necessary. The Book does not inform us that Ezra came to Palestine to teach and enforce the eternal law, which was well-known and respected; he came to introduce those portions of the Law of Moses which are called *Chukkim* and *Mishpatim* (Ezra, vii, 10, ולעשות וללמד בישראל חק ומשפט), in order to organize the body politic, with its cult and ritual, according to the Law of Moses. It was not introduced, however, without material changes. The laws of the Jubilee year were omitted entirely, the laws of taxes for the priests were radically changed, the third of a shekel was adopted in lieu of the half-shekel as the tax for the sanctuary, and quite a number of new laws were enacted and enforced, as recorded in Nehemiah and partly in the Talmud. And yet it is evident from Nehemiah, ix and x, from the spirit of opposition and skepticism against which Malachi declaims, and from Nehemiah xiii, that large numbers of the people and their rulers were not satisfied with the re-introduction of the modified Law of Moses, and did not submit to it willingly. This still appears in the closing passage of Malachi,

which, as Nachman Krochmal maintains correctly,
was added much later by the compilers of the
prophetical canon; here the Hebrews are solemnly
warned to remember the Law of Moses, which God
had commanded him at Horeb for all Israel, *Chukkim* and *Mishpatim*, referring distinctly to that
passage in Deuteronomy, "And Jehovah commanded
me at that time," etc., and to the existing opposition to those *Chukkim* and *Mishpatim*. To this
attitude is referable the radical differences between
the Hellenists and Chassidim in the second century
B. C., as well as in the building of temples on
Monnt Gerizim and in Egypt. I can think of no
theory to explain these facts, except the one advanced, viz., the distinction made and universally
acknowledged in Israel as obtaining between the
eternal law expressed and implied in the Decalogue,
and the Law of Moses in its *Chukkim* and *Mishpatim*.

It must be stated here, that my views in regard
to Ezra and Nehemiah are not new; they are substantially stated in the Talmud. In *Yerushalmi*
Shebi'ith, vi, 1, we find the following addition to
Siphri, Re'eh, Section 59: "From here (we know)
when they were exiled they were free (from the
Law of Moses). It is written (in Nehemiah),
'And all the congregation that came from the
captivity made tabernacles, and dwelt in tabernacles, the like of which the children of Israel had
not done from the days of Joshua, the son of Nun,
to that day.' Why is Joshua mentioned here? R.
Hillel, the son of Samuel B. Nachman, explains,
the righteous man in the grave is abused on account

of the honor of (another) righteous man in his time. Their coming into Palestine under Ezra is thus compared to their coming thither under Joshua. As coming into the land under Joshua they were free (of the Law of Moses), and were then obliged to observe it, so also in the time of Ezra they were free (of the Law of Moses), and were then obliged to observe it.'' * This opinion is never controverted in the Talmud. The question is, by what authority were they obliged to observe again the Law of Moses? R. Jose b. Chanina thinks the law itself contains a provision to this effect. Rabbi Eliesar, however maintains that it was done voluntarily, as he says : מאיליהן קיבלו עליהן

III. Proofs from the Talmud.

Having thus been led into the Talmud, I beg leave to quote a few passages from the rabbinical writings in support of my thesis, though I believe this is superfluous, as the proofs from the Bible may be considered sufficient. When the people of Israel lost its independence and its country, its temple and its government a second time, the Law of Moses, as in the Babylonian captivity, lost obligatory force. The same was the case with the enactments of Ezra and the Sanhedrin. This is partly affirmed in the rabbinical maxim, כל הדר בחוצה לארץ כאלו עובד ע׳ז, "Dwelling outside of the land (Palestine) is like practicing idolatry;'' because there one is not commanded

---

משגלו יהו פטורין * * * מה ביאתן בימי*
יהשוע פטורין היו ונתחייבו אף ביאתן בימי עזרא
פטורין היו ונתחייבו

to observe the Law of Moses. A broad admission
to that effect is made in *Siphri*, Ekeb, Section 43,
and quoted by Rashi to Deuteronomy, xi, 18, viz ;
"Although I exile you from the land to foreign
countries, ornament yourselves with the commandments, so that when you return they shall not be
new to you.   This is like to a king, who was angry
at his wife and sent her back to her father's house ;
he said to her 'Ornament thyself with thy jewels,
that they be not new to thee when called back,' "
etc.* This is the key-note.   Historical Judaism, in
as far as it is not contained in the Decalogue, in the
eternal law, is rabbinical, practiced on the authority
of the rabbis (דרבנן), based upon the Messianic belief, the national restoration of Israel to its own
country, and the idea of Ezra, that with the restoration the authority of the Law of Moses is re-estab-
lished.   The laws and customs, in as far as they
are not contained in the Decalogue, are observed,
"so that if you return (to Palestine) they be not
new to you."   The intelligent reader of the Talmud
can see in a moment the forced *Derashah* (ex
position of Scripture) by the ancient rabbis to
אלה החקים, Deuteronomy, xii, 1 ; *Siphri* Re'eh, 59 ;
Yerushalmi, Shebi'ith vi, 1, and *Babli* Kiddushin
37a, which is intended to make certain laws of
Moses obligatory (חובות הגוף), while the laws depending on the land of Palestine are declared inob-
ligatory.   Because they could find no passage in the

* א׳ע׳פ שאני מגלה אתכם לחוצה לארץ היו מציונים
במצות כשאתם חזרים לא יהיו לכם חדשים

Bible expressing that duty, they resorted to this forced *Derashah*.

Entirely different is the language of those ancient rabbis in regard to the Decalogue, the eternal law, whose universally obligatory character they never question and whose sufficiency they never deny; so that it was a maxim, "He who professes the Decalogue professes the entire law, and he who denies the Decalogue denies the entire law;" or also, "He who affirms Paganism denies the Decalogue, as he who rejects Paganism affirms the entire law." (*Siphri*, Shelach, 111, and Re'eh, 54.)

A cursory glance into the *Mechilta*, Bachodesh v, and elsewhere, must convince the reader that its author understood the Decalogue as I do. He distinguishes (Par. iv) the words of the Decalogue from all other parts of the Pentateuch, and says that the Holy One spoke them in one continuous utterance,* which certainly refers to the unity and perfection of the Decalogue. Then (Par. v) he asks the question, why the Decalogue was not announced at the beginning of the Pentateuch, and answers with a parable, that a king must first do something for the benefit of a nation before he gives it laws; hence he acknowledges the Decalogue as the law of the covenant. Then comes the allegory, that before he gave the law to Israel, God asked various nations to accept it, but they refused, because it contained the special laws: thou shalt not kill; thou shalt not commit adultery; thou shalt not steal. These objections, however, could be

* מלמד שאמר הק׳ב׳ה בדיבור אחד עשרת הדברות

raised to the Decalogue only, in which these laws are contained; hence he considered the Torah (מקבלים אתם את התורה) and the Decalogue identical.

Some passages of particular force must be quoted here. In the temple at Jerusalem the divine service was opened daily with a benediction, and then the Decalogue was read before the Shema (Tamid v). Maimonides remarks to this Mishna: "Because they (the ten words) are the principles of the law and its beginning." Then he points to *Yerushalmi* Berachoth i, 8. There we are informed by R. Levi that *Shema* and *Vehayah* were read daily, because the Decalogue is contained in them. Furthermore, that the ten words should be read daily also outside of the temple, and it is not done on account of the sectarians,* in order that they may not say this alone was given to Moses on Sinai. Here, it appears, it is intimated that the Decalogue only was read at the beginning of the divine service until the party which maintained that the Decalogue is the Torah had to be silenced (after the destruction of the temple); then the *Shema* was selected instead of the Decalogue, because it is supposed to be contained in it.

Chananiah, the nephew of R. Joshua b. Chananiah, said (*Yerushalmi* Shekalim vi): "Between every word of the ten there are the suggestions and letters of the law, filled like Tarshish, like the great sea." R. Simon b. Lakish (in Shir Hash-shirim Rabbah it is R. Jochanan), in commenting on this,

---

* Maimonides changes the מינים into מתנגדים.

said: "Beautifully did Hanania teach us, as in this sea there are between every two large waves many smaller ones, so there are between the words (of the ten) the suggestions and letters of the law." The picture is beautiful and the lesson true. It tells the old, old story, that the Decalogue is the Torah.

The same book reports (Megillah iii, 8) a halacha contradictory to the Mishna (ibid. iv, 1), that according to one authority he who is called to read the Torah in public, should recite the benediction before and after reading the passage of the song of the well; according to another, all the songs in the Pentateuch should be distinguished by those benedictions; but according to R. Joshua b. Levi, those benedictions should be recited only on reading the Song at the Red Sea, the Decalogue, and the imprecations in Leviticus and Deuteronomy. Of this R. Abahu says: "I have not heard this; it appears right in connection with the Decalogue;" namely, that it should be distinguished more than any other passage of the law. This halacha with Rabbi Abahu's remark has been accepted literally in *Mesecheth Sopherim* xii, 5, 6; hence it was adopted by the Geonim.

Another passage to this effect occurs in *Pesikta* de Rab Kahana (Lyck edition, 103a). R. Huna compares the Torah to the state carriage of a princess, which, when appearing in the street, is preceded and followed by men bearing swords and arms. "So is the Torah, laws precede her (Exodus, xv, 25); 'there he ordained *Chok* and *Mishpat*,' and laws follow her (ibid. xxi, 1); 'and these are the judg-

ments,' " etc. Here no doubt is left that the Decalogue is regarded as the Torah.

Ever since the Feast of Weeks has been observed, it has been called by all Israel זמן מתן תורתנו, "The time of the giving of our law." Throughout Mechilta, Pesikta, the Midrashim, in the liturgy and in the theological writings, מתן תורה, "the giving of the law," and מעמד הר סיני, "standing at Mount Sinai," are identical; hence the Decalogue must be the Torah. By the force of circumstances and the authority of progressive history and legislation, sanctioned by Moses, the ancient rabbis (Tana'im) assumed supreme authority in Israel when the Hebrew state was dissolved and its laws abrogated; they reduced to practice, in the new state of affairs, the doctrines and principles of the eternal law, expressed or implied in the Decalogue. They held semi-annual meetings at Jamnia, Usha, Tiberias, or Sepphoris, and then at Nehardea, Sura, Pumbaditha, etc., and called them Sessions of the Sanhedrin. The opinions and decisions of authorized savants replaced the oracles of the prophets. They maintained even חכם עדיף מנביא, "The savant is superior to the prophet." They based their authority to protect the eternal law among the dispersed Israelites on the old principles, and maintained that the last enacted are more precious than the ancient ones (חביבין דברי סופרים יותר מדברי תורה). They sought to preserve the historical thread of development, not only by seeking in the Pentateuch a support for every law and custom which they sanctioned or enacted, but also by adjustment to it of post-biblical enactments and opin-

ions of savants down to the schools of Beth Hillel
and Beth Shammai. Still, they could justly maintain that they did not add to, nor take away from,
the eternal law, and they did not; and, on the
other hand, they could maintain with equal justice
that the laws are enforced by the authority of the
rabbis, as they did say plainly regarding the institution of marriage : כל המקדש אדעתיה דרבנן מקדש,
"Every marriage is entered into on the authority
of the rabbis." "Thou shalt not add," etc., refers
to the eternal law alone.

IV. Proofs from the Metaphysicians.

The Jewish metaphysicians of the Middle Ages
were, with very rare exceptions, strict rabbinists
and implicit believers in the Bible. Their systems
were apologetic, their main aim was to defend
Judaism against the attacks of the prevailing
scholasticism ; they combatted philosophy wherein
it came in conflict with Jewish doctrine ; they paraphrased and spiritualized such Biblical passages as
are in apparent conflict with the canons of philosophy. With the exception, perhaps, in some instances, of Solomon Ibn Gabirol and Levi ben
Gerson, this is the method of the Jewish metaphysicians of the Middle Ages. They may safely be regarded biblically and rabbinically orthodox. When
some condemned and burned the More Nebuchim of
Moses Maimonides as a heretical book, Nacmanides,
Kimchi, and others defended it from the standpoint
of strict orthodoxy.

And yet these very metaphysicians, Abraham
Ibn Ezra included, admit that the Decalogue is the

Torah, and that the eternal law is contained therein, expressed or implied. Saadia is the first to make this statement. Among the many authorities that quote him is also Rashi to Exodus, xxiv, 12. He says: "All the six hundred and thirteen commandments are included in the Decalogue. Our master, Saadia, in his Asharoth, explains that the principle of every word (of the ten) is in the commandment depending on it." * The rabbis maintain that the Decalogue consists of six hundred and twenty letters, on account of the six hundred and thirteen Mosaic and seven rabbinical commandments which it contains.

This idea of Saadia was elaborated by Rabbi Eliezer ben Nathan, the grandfather of Rabbenu Asher, in the thirteenth century, in a book called Ma'amer Haskel (Roedelheim, 1804). This book subsumes all the commandments of the Pentateuch under the ten categories of the Decalogue. The author does not succeed in every instance in proving that a particular commandment embodied a doctrine as implied in this or that law of the Decalogue. Still he succeeds well in illustrating the main idea of Saadia, that the Decalogue is the Law.

The prince of Hebrew poets, Jehuda Halevi, was an opponent of philosophy and an uncompromising defender of rabbinical Judaism and of historical evidence, which appeared to him all-sufficient. Still, in his al-Chazari, ii, 28, he admits in plain words,

---

* With Abraham Geiger, I am not certain that the Arabic Midrash on the Decalogue, published by Wilhelm Eisenstaedter, Vienna, 1868, is identical with Saadia's Asharoth, mentioned by Rashi.

אמת היא ששורש החכמה מופקד בארון אשר הוא
במדרנת הלב והם עשרת הדברים ותולדותיהם והוא
התורה וג׳, "It is true that the foundation of all
wisdom was laid down in the ark, which represents
the heart, and that is the Decalogue and its logical
consequences, which is the Torah," etc. This is
clear language, to which David Cassel remarks
in a note: "Universally and justly the Decalogue
is acknowledged, not as the mere quintessence or
foundation, but as the sum, the totality of the entire law." (Compare Baehr, Symbolik I, p. 384.)
Abraham Sabba, in *Zeror ha-Mor* to Jethro, 78b,
edit. Venet, states: "Behold, in this Decalogue is
contained the whole law, as ancient authorities
have placed the commandments in their order, in
their books on the commandments," etc.

Joseph Albo opposed the views of Jehuda Halevi,
and still, *Ikkarim*, iii, 26, he says the same thing of
the Decalogue. So does Bachya, in his *Choboth
Hallebaboth*, i, 1. So do all of them.

But I stop here, lest I prove too much, as I verily
believe I have established my thesis. I will only
add that when these metaphysicians argue for the
eternity of the law, they mean the eternal law contained in the Decalogue, expressed or implied. I
do not refer to modern authorities, or I would
quote Leopold Stein, David Einhorn, S. L. Steinheim, and quite a number of others.

This, I believe, is the historical basis of reform,
progressive and law-abiding. The only problem to
be solved is, who shall decide for the community of
Israel which law or custom is an embodiment of a

doctrine contained in the Decalogue, which one should be preserved and which amended. For the individual, the Decalogue, conscience, and reason must decide, and guide him to salvation by righteousness.

MOSES, THE MAN AND STATESMAN

(1889).

Great men are instructive and attractive text-books, whose paragraphs are deeds. Magnificent deeds overwhelm the heart and the admiration of them captivates the mind with that superior force by which the drama exceeds the lyric poem and nature excels the finest work of art. The lives of great men are leaves in the Bible of humanity, illustrated by that unexcelled master-painter whose name is truth. In the panorama of every-day life, we observe the movement of figures, so clearly akin to ourselves that they become uninteresting, and, finally, annoying and depressing. In the Pantheon of those demi-gods who enacted the proudest scenes in the drama of history, we are brought face to face with man in his glory, and are elated by the exhibition of what man can be, and we feel that he was properly called " Creation's Lord," who exclaims " The world, the world is mine."

All the stars are not equal in magnitude and brilliancy, nor are all great men equally great. Some are suns, others planets, and others again are satellites. The suns, it appears, are more distant from us. In art we utilize antique models; in architecture we copy ancient monuments; in prose or poetry, we imitate classical forms of by-gone days. We do precisely the same in philosophy and jurisprudence, in ethics and æsthetics, in religion and

theology.   We abstract the spirit of men and works
of the past, and systematize that essence into standards by which to measure the events and demands
of the age.   It is that which we call learning and
practical wisdom, science and art.

However humiliating the confession may be, it is
nevertheless true that, with the exception of the
natural sciences and the mechanical arts of experience, experiment and observation, we are the pupils
of the men of gray antiquity.

Not only that those ancient men lived more
closely to the lap of mother nature than we do,
but the themes of their thoughts also were more
sublime than ours.   They concentrated their energies upon themselves, sought to solve the
mysteries of human nature, and elaborated the
great themes of man, conscience, right, goodness,
beauty, God, and man's relations to the Almighty.
Their minds grew under the influence of these in-
vigorating themes.   In our phase of civilization,
however, man has become objective, science is objective, invention is objective, the occupation of the
man and the text-book of the lad are objective ; the
mind is absorbed in matter and its changes ; thought
does not reach beyond that lower region, its themes
are heavy and unelevated.

An old violin upon which an artist has played,
can not be imitated by the most skillful artisan.
The mellow notes, the sweet melodies of the maes-
tro, dwell mysteriously in the instrument.   The
beautiful moral and intellectual themes too which
are played upon the chords of the mind, leave their
sweet echoes in human character.   The violin does

not improve in tone because it records no vivifying melodies. We have no Moses, Solomon and Isaiah, Plato and Aristotle, Homer and Virgil, Cæsar and Marcus Aurelius. We can merely convert the gold they have left to us into small change, and we distribute this among our fellowmen, that they may partake of the heritage of man. If it is admitted that in the arts we are in advance of the ancients, and that in the subjective sciences they were our superiors, it must be equally admitted that they were grander characters, men and women of a more sublime and a finer type. For it is by thought treasures that the character is formed, the will invigorated, and the energies stimulated to glorious deeds, to outpourings of immortal truth. We catch fire from their fire, and we borrow light from their light. We speak of great men, therefore, as patterns of superior humanity as we speak of distant suns.

Among the documents of ancient genius the Bible occupies a pre-eminent place on account of the sublimity of its themes, the depth of its conceptions, the simplicity of its language and the exquisite beauty of human character which it presents to us. It is certainly the most ennobling and most enlightening book we possess. It presents greatness and goodness in life-size figures. It removes the veil from heaven's dome and permits mortals to gaze into the mysteries of existence and the glory of the spirit. Again, in the Bible of the Hebrews one classical and colossal figure over-towers all others. It is a veritable giant cedar among the trees, a snow-capped Baker of the Rocky Mountains, a sun among the planets. This colossal figure is the son of Amram and Jochebed—Moses, the "servant of Jehovah," the redeemer and legislator of Israel, the man who with his stylus of iron engraved upon the rock of ages the truth as to the duties and destinies of the human family, to which, as he said, nothing should be added, from which nothing should be taken away.

I regard Moses as the grandest man in history. You must not think that I have selected this subject for this lecture because it is maintained that there was no Moses, that he is a mythical character to whom posterity ascribed deeds, laws and institutions that now pass under the sanction of his name. To assertions so unhistorical and unphilosophical, I do not care to address myself. I have determined to speak of him, because I think he is the greatest man of antiquity. I wish in the first place to say a few words of

THE MAN MOSES.

Whatever Grecian writers up to Josephus, the Rabbis and the Mohammedans reported of the life of Moses in addition to the notices found in the Pentateuch has value for the thoughtful student of history, who may learn how posterity is prone to exaggerate ; but outside of what the Pentateuch gives we know nothing as to the life or character of Moses. In fact, even what the Pentateuch says of the master is meager. Its aim is not to narrate what Moses did or suffered ; but rather what God did for Israel. Moses occupies so small a space in the Books of Moses that his authorship can hardly be doubted. If that work had been written by some one else it would have glorified the redeemer, law-giver, hero, statesman and father of his people, and would have depicted him in oriental colors.

Again, among those brief notices some are evidently of a later date. "The man Moses was very meek;" and "And Moses knew not that the skin of his face beamed;" and "There rose not in Israel again a prophet like Moses." These statements are plausible only if we suppose them to have been written after the death of Moses. Instance the phrase: "And the man Moses;" it contravenes logic to suppose that he had spoken of himself in that way; besides the two other expressions I have just quoted could not be true if the former was. Being meek, he would not speak of his countenance beaming in glory, nor of his superiority as a prophet above all men in Israel. It must be admitted that though we suspect the authenticity of some parts of the Pentateuchal account, we must accept others as authentic. The object of the Pentateuch is certainly to teach righteousness, holiness and the fear of God, and to bring about the organization of society on ethical principles. The author and compiler of such a book, having no possible or personal interest, can not be suspected of falsification; and it would be wrong to do it without irrefutable proof. It is possible that he exaggerates, amplifies and even rhapsodizes. He may canonize deeds and invest them with a halo as miraculous. He may depict subjective visions in glowing colors, but he can not be suspected of deliberate perversion. We have a legitimate canon of criticism to determine which are the authentic passages, and to these we now turn.

We are told with the utmost brevity that Moses, born to Amram and Jochebed, in the time of oppression and servitude, was doomed to die by the king's cruel mandate, and that he was rescued by an incident which at once gave him back to his mother and afforded him the golden opportunity to acquire an education at the royal court. This little chain of accidents, so necessary to transform the Hebrew infant into the man Moses, is delineated with simplicity, but the reader can not tell whether the writer intended to convey the idea that Providence so designed and executed in order to make the infant Moses the redeemer and lawgiver, or whether he merely records the natural incidents by which the waif could become a powerful man. Aside from the delicate dramatic touches of a mother's anguish and a sister's devotion, the whole story is simple and natural and can not be doubted. It is too plain and unadorned to be poetry. If it had been written at any time after Moses, hosts of stars and angels, shepherds and kings, miracles and supernatural demonstrations would have been called into requisition to furnish the frame for so important a picture as the birth of a redeemer and lawgiver.

Having thus been informed of the birth and first experiences of Moses, the records are silent as to his education. We imagine that he was well instructed in all the arts and sciences of Egypt; and we imagine this by inference alone, for we have no direct information. It is certainly false to maintain that Moses was an Egyptian priest, for besides the king, none, unless born of priestly parents, was ever eligible for such a position.

Moses appears again on the stage of life, not as an Egyptian commander and the conqueror of Ethiopia, as the ancient legend had it, but after he had reached maturity and was in the habit of going among his brethren while they were in abject servitude. Then he slew a taskmaster who had smitten a Hebrew slave. Moralists may cry out in horror at that rash act, though they would hardly feel as indignant at John Brown for having killed a Virginia taskmaster under similar circumstances. It was a rash act, perhaps unworthy of the lawgiver Moses, though the text leaves it uncertain whether the Egyptian taskmaster had not killed the Hebrew slave (in both instances the same term is used). But it certainly was not unworthy of the youthful patriot to descend from the height of the royal court to his brethren in distress, and to feel outraged by the taskmaster's brutal conduct. It was certainly a case of strong provocation, which, in the hands of a capable pleader, would constitute an acceptable plea before any criminal court, to clear an ordinary defendant.

This incident, however, shows that Moses could tolerate no wrong ; nor could he be an idle spectator while wrong was being perpetrated, as another incident shows. When a fugitive in the wilderness, he witnessed how rude shepherds took advantage of some girl shepherdesses at the well of water. He protected those shepherdesses, one of whom afterward became his wife Zipporah. Here we have the trait of the lawgiver : Courage and love of justice. The man of stern justice resents every wrong done to his fellow-creatures ; and only such a man can be a lawgiver. Whoever commits a wrong, or sees others commit it with impunity, cannot become an apostle of justice. Now, I think this chivalric conduct of Moses toward Zipporah in the wilderness ought to contribute somewhat toward conciliating his opponents and lead them to condone the "mistakes" he is alleged to have made. At any rate it is certain that Moses was a living reality, for he went to the house of Jethro, married Zipporah, begat children and became a shepherd ; all this is decidedly unusual in the hero of a myth. And the critics might feel assured that these incidents were not penned by an admirer of a later date ; he would certainly not have passed unchallenged the statement that the distinguished "Servant of the Lord" had married the daughter of an Arabian sheikh, not of the house of Israel, and that he did not circumcise his sons until his wife reminded him of this duty, in rather an unkind manner, by the way, and that he heeded the advice of his heathen father-in-law in the important matter of organization. A later writer, priest or prophet, would certainly have improved upon these incidents, especially one of the days of Ezra and Nehemiah, to whom intermarriage with Gentiles was an abomination. The fact that Moses, setting out on a foreign mission, took his wife and children with him, although she was but a plain shepherdess, and returned with them to Egypt, is proof positive that he was a good husband and father.

It is unjust, to say the least, to judge the character of a statesman and legislator of the eminence of Moses, by ordinary standards. The worst "mistake" made by the fault-finders is, that they can not see that emergencies and circumstances, and the solution of extraordinary problems, such as the lawgiver was called upon to grapple with in the wilderness, require prudence, firmness and forbearance, and that great and good men alone possess these. In Moses, however, all alleged "mistakes" are outbalanced by his

UNSELFISHNESS AND HONESTY OF PURPOSE.

In the whole of his record Moses is almost totally impersonal. He assumes no titles and prerogatives and seeks for no emoluments for himself. He. was able to face his enemies in the Korah rebellion, and declare before God, "Not one ass of theirs have I taken." His sons were no officers, and inherited nothing, not even an extra portion of land in Canaan. His brother was given the priesthood, because he stood at the head of the people in Egypt as his collaborator in their redemption. His tribe, the Levites, were distinguished not on his account, but because they proved faithful to the cause, while the mob danced about the golden calf. He asked nothing for himself, not even a sepulcher, nothing in life and nothing after death. The plain and meek "Servant of Jehovah" who might have been a king and a god, the founder of a dynasty and the builder of gorgeous temples, died on Mount Nebo, "And no man knoweth his grave to this day." His children disappear from his nation's chronicle,

and a man of another tribe is his successor in office.
Those who have made man and men their study
know how rare such unselfishness is, even among
the greatest and best of the human race. Few have
ever risen to that moral height that they would say,
as did he, "I wish all the people of Jehovah were
prophets, and Jehovah would put his spirit upon
them."

Moses lived for a cause, to which his life and
energies were devoted with the utmost honesty of
purpose, and he was entirely unselfish. He embraced it when he was a youth and a prince; he
adhered to it as a shepherd in the wilderness; he
brought it to a successful issue under great difficulties in Egypt; he never doubted its final success despite the trials of the wilderness; the rebellions of
the multitude, the frustration of his hopes, the
death of comrades and fellow-sufferers about him,
could not shake his faith in God and His promises.

You know the story of the mice that conspired
one day to undermine the rock of Gibraltar; they
gnawed and gnawed with their little teeth till they
were dead, but the rock is there still. Exactly so
do those appear whose petty business it is to find
fault with Moses. Where are men of like unselfishness and of stern honesty of purpose to be found?
There is but one standard by which to measure the
statesman's and the legislator's moral character, and
to determine how much justice is embodied in his
laws, how much unselfishness he has manifested
and how much honesty of purpose has characterized
his career. It is easier to die in a moment than
to live one hundred and twenty years for a great

cause, beset by trials and storms.   It is a momentary inspiration to die for a cause; it implies
continuous inspiration and resoluteness to live for it.
No prophet has yet risen in Israel like Moses.

But we must not forget that Moses was of a san-
guine temperament,

PASSIONATE, RASH AND IMPETUOUS.

He slew the Egyptian task-master in a passionate mood.   He shattered in a moment of wrath
the two tables of stone, the most precious gift he
had been given to bestow on his people.   Im-
petuously he smote the dumb rock that it pour
forth its water, though he had been commanded
to speak to it, and he addressed his own people
and disciples in anger, "Hear now, ye rebels."

In the most trying events recorded in the Pentateuch, which momentarily arrested the career of
Moses and threatened to end it, he proved the im-
petuosity of his character.   I refer to the incident
of the "golden calf," the uproar in the camp after
the return of the spies from Canaan, and the revolt
of Korah and his conspirators.   In the first instance Moses saw the imminent destruction of the
foundation upon which he had reared the gorgeous
structure of Israel's redemption.   He perceived the
curse of Egyptian idolatry triumphant over that
pure monotheism which was his mission, his cherished hope, his faith.   The work of a lifetime and
the hope of Israel and of mankind seemed to collapse.   He hurls from his arms the two tables of
stone and breaks them; and he hears the voice of
God, "And now let me alone, that my anger wax

hot against them, and I consume them, and make of thee a great nation." Consume—utterly annihilate at once—the deluded multitude. How passionate! In the second instance Moses perceives that his hope of organizing a people in the Holy Land and of making it real, is frustrated by the cowardice of men. The returning spies had incensed the people to revolt so that it refused to go up to Canaan and demanded to be led back into Egyptian slavery. The entire fabric of redemption was at the point of destruction. Moses was wroth—and he heard the voice of God saying, "How long shall this people provoke me? And how long yet will they not believe in me, with all the signs which I have shown in the midst of them? I will smite them with the pestilence, and root them out, and I will make of thee a nation greater and mightier than they." And the third instance was perhaps no less serious than the two former. Korah and his conspirators revolt and attempt to overthrow the polity of the growing theocracy; and also in this Moses hears God say : "Separate yourselves from the midst of this congregation, and I will make an end of them in a moment."

In his wrath and passion, Moses imagined that the utter annihilation of the rebellious would be justice. The degenerate people, he felt, was unfit to realize his sublime scheme of salvation. But in all these cases Moses prays like a father for his children, and God forgives, and the threatened evil is obviated. Take all those narratives literally, and God is represented as the angry despot, ready to crush his frail and deluded children, while Moses appears as a merciful, benign and long-suffering father of Israel, whose ardent entreaties save them. All this is contrary to the theology and moral system of Moses which he laid down in the Pentateuch. Take those narratives in their correct sense, understand the dialogues between God and Moses from the psychological standpoint as subjective and not as objective incidents, as ideal and not as real facts, and those events teach how passionate Moses was, that his first impressions were undisciplined, but that soon after they appeared to him just and quite in keeping with the justice of God. But at the same time those very events suggest what the second sober thought of Moses was. They show how stringent his conscience was. He mastered, he bridled his passion, and led it to the right and the just and the true.

Great men have great passions. One cause of their greatness is the superior grade of their passion. "He who is greater than his neighbor is of mightier passion," said an ancient sage. Great deeds rise first out of the pressure of excitement and passion. Little men may be shrewd, but they will never perform great feats, will not move and inspire large masses of men, will not rouse multitudes. While passion is unbridled and leads to cruelty, the reason and conscience of man are stronger than passion and governs it ; thus you find the great man. His passions may be mighty, but his reason and conscience are mightier, and his second sober thought corrects and is juster and

wiser. If Thomas Carlyle had written a biography
of Moses, he would have summed it up somewhat
as follows: "This man's intellect was powerful,
his moral principles were correct and his deeds
mighty." "Moses is the most exalted personality in ancient history," says L. von Ranke (Welt-
geschichte, I, page 42). Ordinary causes are inadequate to produce extraordinary effects. Neither
the gigantic intellect he had nor his passions, nor
his intense love of liberty and of justice, account
for his unique character and work. Think of a
man who was educated at a royal court, spending
the greater part of his life as an obscure shepherd
in the wilderness without relinquishing the great
object of his life, the redemption of his people from
bondage, and establishing a model nation on the
principles of monotheism, moral law, freedom, justice and equality, while all around the world was
submerged in polytheism and slavery. Had he
ever abandoned that object, he would not have be-
held the vision of the burning bush. Think of a
man who comes with a staff before a mighty king
and demands in the name of an unknown God the
liberation of hundreds of thousands of slaves,
carries his point unaided by natural means, and
even leads a people out of its land into a desert
against its will, and overcomes Pharaoh despite
his power and overwhelms him. The miracles recorded in the Pentateuch are not half as wonderful
as is this simple fact. A nation was born, a free
people was organized out of a horde of slaves,
notwithstanding the relentless opposition of the
greatest power on earth. Think furthermore of

the man's organizing talent displayed in the camp ;
masterfulness which astounded even the heathen
prophet Balaam and led him to bless where he was
called to curse.   Think of the man's patience, forbearance and resistance, though he saw his projects
blocked, his comrades perish and his end approach.
Think of all this and explain it if you can.
There is a mystery at the root of this character
without precedent or parallel in history, and we are
bound to feel that Moses was in possession of truth,
the whole truth, the deathless, everlasting truth.
He had faith in the majestic power of truth ; he
was convinced that he was the servant of God, the
messenger of the Most High, the man of destiny,
the apostle of Providence.   Whatever views people
may hold with regard to Providence, miracles, inspiration, revelation and kindred conceptions, one
thing all must admit, Moses verily trusted in the
only true God and Providence, and believed that he
was commissioned by the one and true God to say
and to do that which he did say and do.   He was
not disconcerted when Eldad and Medad prophesied
in the camp, and in the hour of distress he could
address his God thus : " Behold thou hast said unto
me, bring up this people and thou hast not made
known to me him whom thou wouldst send with
me, and thou hast said, I have distinguished thee
(known thee) by name, and thou hast also found
grace in my sight."
     This conviction and this faith make the basis of
his character and complete the sketch we are able
to draw of the man Moses, of whom it is reported
in holy writ ; God said : " My servant Moses is au-

thenticated in all my house.'' This point, however, leads us directly to another division of this essay, namely, to the consideration of

THE WORK WHICH MOSES ACCOMPLISHED.

The historian whom I have quoted, says, ''The idea of the extra-mundane and intellectual God was conceived by Moses and, as it were, embodied in the people he organized. The incarnation of an idea cannot be accomplished in purity, still it radiates from everything which the legislator ordained, and one might say that he was the teacher of his people.'' This is the judgment of impartial history. Quibbling cannot change it, cannot impair it. History is just despite quibblings. Moses left to posterity in the Five Books a five-act drama, unapproachable in grandeur, in sublimity insurpassable, in beauty incomparable, incarnating the greatest subject ever thought of by man, the birth and organization of a free and sanctified nation, the birth and triumph of Heaven's truth, Shekinah upon the earth. Moses was the greatest of all artists. Painters and sculptors have failed to portray the grand work of this creative genius. He was himself the greatest of sculptors, and he has left to posterity that imperishable statue of truth, hewn out of the solid rock tracing the weal and woe of ages and generations : its pedestal is the earth, its head reaches heaven's dome : the name of that inimitable colossus is Israel, the immortal, a nation graced by the choice of God.

MOSES AS A REFORMER.

With regard to the sacrificial polity, the Levitical priesthood and the Levitical laws of cleanliness and diet, social laws and institutions, especially marital laws, slavery, the institution of the avenger of blood, and kindred topics, Moses was a reformer. The laws and customs which the Hebrews had adopted from the Egyptians, or developed in their own social life in Goshen, the division, *e. g.*, into twelve tribes and the government by the first-born and elders, and whatever they had inherited from the patriarchs, may have been in the main adopted, and may have been assimilated to Mosaic monotheism. So far, it is correct to speak of Moses as a reformer. This, however, proves two points: in the first place, that the laws and institutions, as we find them in the Pentateuch, were given to a people which came directly from Egypt; in the second place, it proves the wisdom and impartiality, as well as the prudence of Moses. Whatever was useful in the traditions of his people and of the Egyptians, and congenial to his system, he adopted and sanctioned. Evident wrongs which he could not dispose of summarily, *e. g.*, polygamy, slavery, animal sacrifices, and similar existing evils, he modified and led to their gradual abolition. Still, everything bears the impress of his spirit and the luster of monotheism —the Living God of Israel and the Sinaitic principle.

He understood that no man can begin history anew and none can uproot evils all at once. Still Moses was more than a reformer.

A WISE AND JUST LEGISLATOR.

In the presence of the universal principles which
opened the era of man's history with the Mosaic
dispensation, the reign of the spirit of holiness
and love, it is false to call Moses a mere reformer. The Mosaic dispensation is the spiritual
creation of a genius or it is the greatest gift of revelation ; Moses was either the "Servant of the
Lord," or a divinely-gifted genius, and these terms
may be synonymous. For "to behold the simili-
tude of God," and to speak with God "face to
face," are perhaps identical with genius, engaged
with the holiest themes.

Take a cursory survey of the Mosaic dispensation, and you will find this : the ineffable Jehovah
leads you through the whole Mosaic system of doctrine and law. It is supposed, by some, that monotheism was the original form of religion, and that
it degenerated into idolatry. The Bible admits this,
and documentary evidence supports it to a certain
degree. Upon this alleged fact is based the theory
that Moses adopted the monotheism of the Egyptian
priests, and that the Jews adopted it from the eastern nations. One theory is as good as another.
The monotheism of Moses differs from that discovered under the debris of crushed idols, among the
ruins of temples and in the myths of primitive men
as much as the sun differs from the candle light.
The idea of spirit and spirituality, of freedom and
holiness, is absent from ancient mythology and
theogony. The idea of a controlling intellect in
nature (Nous, the spirit) was unknown to the

Pagan world prior to Anaxagoras, in the fifth pre-Christian century. The god of the ancient nations was an abstraction of concrete nature, and the gods were abstractions of natural energies, personified in celestial bodies by Sabians, in natural objects by fetishists, in deified men and women by Greeks and Romans, and have not the least similarity to the Living God of Israel.

The monotheism of Moses, expressed in the term Jehovah, means an all-producing, all-pervading, all-controlling, all-possessing, self-conscious, all-knowing, infinite, free and almighty spirit, revealed in the material universe, which does not encompass him, and reflected in human reason, which cannot comprehend him, omnipresent in nature and history without being absorbed by them. The Living God of Israel, Moses taught in substance, and no mere abstraction. He is life and love, reason and freedom, the will and the power, and not a symbol of concrete, dead matter under necessity. He is God, the absolute and necessary existence to whom nature has relative existence alone, and of whose wisdom, power, goodness and holiness it is the mere reflex. This is Mosaic monotheism, which, apart from the elements handed down by the patriarchs, is original and unique. Moses alone could comprehend this wonderful revelation, as genius alone comprehends its mighty creations. We understand thereof only that which laboring talent can grasp, much or little, never in its completeness and unity.

This is the key to the Mosaic dispensation and legislation. In the light of that monotheism the material universe appeared to be the work of the

Great Architect, a cosmos, with design and ultimate purpose, in which things co-ordinate and subordinate themselves.

Man is the image of God, a reflex of the universal intelligence, will and love; he rose from the insignificance to which paganism had degraded him to the lofty position of creation's ultimate end, God's representative on earth, and became a free, moral and intellectual agent. This is the first result of that sublime principle of monotheism: Man is godlike and free. This is the postulate of Moses, upon which rises his system of ethics, having freedom and equality at its base, the preservation and happiness of the human race at its apex. "Ye shall be a kingdom of priests," he announced to his people—every one a priest, every person one of the highest class and caste—none to be superior and none inferior before God and His laws—one law and one statute for all, the native and the alien. This announcement of equality was original with Moses, just as is his proclamation of liberty, of Sabbath-year and Jubilee-year. It was the attendant fact of his monotheism.

In Egypt, as in India, society was broken up into castes and classes; slavery was the lot of all, as the gods themselves were the slaves of blind and relentless fate and iron necessity. The chief of a pagan nation was a god or demi-god, whom every person had to obey under penalty of death. The chief of the Mosaic government is the prophet, to whose teachings every person was commanded to listen; but none could be punished by human authority for non-obedience to the prophet. The law

governs, man can only expound and administer it.
Theocracy is identical with democracy, and democracy
means equality before the law and the sovereignty
thereof.   The law is divine, it is from God,
who alone is king, *i. e.*, it must emanate from unadulterated
reason and the principle of absolute justice.
Therefore, it must exclude none and embrace and protect
all who live among you and seek prosperity and
happiness with you.   This is the groundwork of the
Mosaic ethics, flowing naturally from the fountain
head of his monotheism.   In it is implied the moral
law which governs the individual.   That God is
holy, is, again, an original Mosaic doctrine.   The
gods of paganism were sensual beings, to whom
neither purity nor virtue, neither righteousness nor
holiness, neither spiritual love nor intellectual enjoyment,
were attributed.   The Most Holy One,
according to the Mosaic dispensation, promised His
chosen people that they should become to Him a
peculiar treasure, "a holy nation," and he commanded
them, "Ye shall be holy men unto me;"
"Ye shall be holy, for I, Jehovah, your God, am
holy;" "And ye shall sanctify yourselves and be
holy," etc.   God must be worshiped in righteousness
and holiness.

Man's happiness and the perfection of his nature
depend on the purity of his motives and the righteousness
of his doings.   Like God, man must learn
to love the true, the good and the beautiful for
their own sake, and to abhor falsehood, wickedness
and impurity as being abominable in themselves.
Thus man becomes godlike.   Religion based
upon falsehood is superstition, and superstition is

the progenitor of fanaticism, injustice and impurity.
As you forsake God, so will He forsake you; as
you desert truth and reason, so will they abandon
you. No man can worship God and feast with the
devil. But the pagans did. Religion and morals
were with them two different factors. Morals appeared to them as a social compact and a political
necessity. The pious among them were no better
by the fact of religion than the frivolous. The
idea of holiness as a form of religious worship is of
Mosaic origin.

If you cast a glance upon the entire Mosaic legislation as the prophets understood and expounded
it, you will find these thoughts at the foundation
thereof. Dietary laws and the laws of purification are, in the first place, sanitary laws, invested
with the symbolic significance of spiritual holiness.
Take care of the exhausted and the wounded
is a splendid martial law. Care for the poor,
the needy, the stranger, the widow and the orphan, said Moses, and his poor laws are without
parallel. They stand above all similar laws and
doctrines of antiquity, inasmuch as with Moses
they are means of worship, means of atonement
and redemption, making possible the release of the
soul out of the bonds of selfishness. Learn to
make sacrifices in order to overcome your undue
attachment to the dust of earth ; but let your
sacrifices be to God for holiness and to man for
goodness, for the preservation and happiness of the
race. In peace, "Love thy neighbor as thyself;"
"And ye shall love the stranger," *i. e.*, you shall
love man, he is God's child, created in His image.

In war, slay not the defenseless, fight not with those
who offer you peace and submission, protect female
chastity against violence; destroy not property
wantonly, destroy no fruit tree when you besiege
an enemy's city, and force none of your brethren
to go to war. Let the law govern, and not the
violence of passions; let the courts decide and the
bailiffs execute, have cities of refuge to protect the
manslayer, take cognizance of the innocent blood
shed in your land and accept no ransom from the as-
sassin. Take him even from my altar to put him to
death. Be just, fair and upright in all your doings
and dealings. To what end? To be holy, to do
the will of your God, to preserve intact the human
race according to God's covenant with man, to secure happiness for man and holiness for yourselves.
So the whole Mosaic dispensation and legislation
arise out of monotheism, as heat and light emanate
from the sun. In order to correctly understand
Moses as a legislator, and to comprehend him fully
as a man, one must study, first and foremost, his
theology, his monotheism, for it is truly his, and it
is the foundation of his character and his dispensation.

No, I am not going to review the whole magnificent structure of religion, law and ethics in the
hour that is allotted to me. It is too vast, too
grand, too sublime, to be surveyed in so short a
time. Moses was the author of the great principle
that the governments and religions of nations must
be built upon the same basis of truth as is individual
character. There can be no two kinds of ethics,
one for the nation and another for the individual;

no two kinds of religion, one to please God and
another to advance prosperity and happiness among
men; no two kinds of human beings, the chosen
ones and the pariahs, before God and man; there
is but one God, one truth, one justice, and one
human family; every individual is God's own
child. You have before you the organon of revelation. For Moses informs you : Not I, but your
God, has spoken to you, and announces to you the
decrees of heaven, the duties and hopes of man.
Not I, Moses, he says, but the Almighty Himself,
has taught you the highest and surest standard of
rectitude to guide you safely to prosperity, happiness, immortality and eternal bliss; to erect upon
it government to protect you and religion to elevate you. Not I, Moses, but the Almighty Himself, has revealed to you the universal dominion of
truth and justice, of freedom and love; His benign
Providence watches over all and each of you; His
mercy and forbearance with your weakness and
shortcomings; His will that you, all of you, be holy,
immortal and forever blessed. In accordance with
all those grand precepts and principles and under the
guidance of the same God, I legislate for you and
erect for you a structure of free government and a
temple of imperishable religion; I am the mere
servant and messenger of Jehovah, who is your
God and your Father. Thus did Moses speak, and
thus did he act. He built up the chosen people, the
ideal nation, the eternal nation, which is and exists
whether it have a land or it have none, a government or none; the people which has seen the rise,
decline and fall of ancient empires, has stood at the

cradle of modern nations, has groped its way
through the darkness of the Middle Ages ; and at
the dawn of liberty and justice among the nations,
rose with energy to demonstrate its ability to co-
operate in the solution of the new problems of
resurrecting humanity.

Standing before Moses you stand before the man
who has given law and religion to the civilized
world ; whose standard of right and justice is fast
becoming the world's guiding star ; whose doctrines
of religion, God, human dignity, freedom and righteousness conquer the masses, captivate the reasoners,
enlighten and humanize the nations. Once the
mighty peals of thunder roared upon Sinai, but
mightier than the roar of the thunder, resounded
the commandments of God, shaking the wilderness
and re-echoing from Paran and Seir. Loudest
and mightiest of all sounded that one great and
powerful word of the Almighty, freedom ! freedom ! freedom ! Freedom sounded from Sinai ;
the mind is free, the spirit is free, Jehovah is the
God of freedom ; and now it re-echoes from ocean
to ocean ; the mind is free, the spirit is free, man is
free; break the yoke, break the shackles, man is free.

Standing before the records of Moses, you face
the first declaration of independence, the first proclamation of liberty, the first blast from the trumpet
of freedom, the redemption of the spirit, the elevation of reason to its sovereign rights ; you stand
before the majesty of righteousness, purity and
virtue, face to face with the sovereignty of truth,
the glory of holiness, and the divine excellence of
human nature.

Was Moses a statesman, a law-giver, a teacher of righteousness and a servant of Jehovah? The civilized world testifies that he was. Was Moses a reality, an incomparable fact? That which poets cannot imitate, loftiest genius cannot duplicate, no other nation has reproduced, must be truth and fact.

WAS MOSES A GREAT MAN?

Sometimes it appears to me as if Moses were still standing upon Mount Sinai, above the mists of this earth, within the benign light of divine truth, among the seraphs of purity, pointing heavenward and looking forward, and he appears to me then inviting the nations to ascend toward the glory-crowned heights of righteousness, purity and holiness, liberty and equality, justice and peace, in the name of the One Eternal God ; a summit, alas, which the human family, in spite of all efforts and struggles, has not yet reached ! Then all persons and things appear small and insignificant to me, and I feel as if nature's productive energy had become exhausted in the mind of that one great man, who encompassed the economy of God on earth, and opened its mysterious avenues to the gaze of man. He who legislated in the wilderness for the nations and who has established the only immortal nation among them—he who taught us about God and freedom, equality, righteousness, purity and holiness—was evidently a supreme man and the herald of God's own day.

THE WANDERING JEW.

(1877.)

INTRODUCTION.

In my historical studies I have discovered a time when Jews were not persecuted, when no missionaries were hired to convert them, when no sentimental parsons lamented the fate of the poor lost souls; this was in the time of father Abraham. The pope or bishop of that classic time, whose name was Malchizedek, was a clever man. He offered bread and wine to Abraham, and meanwhile took taxes from him in the form of tithes, and everything was pleasant. But soon the trouble began. When Isaac, the son of this same Abraham, raised good crops in the land of the Philistines, he was commanded to leave—the Jew was getting too rich. Isaac, however, began to dig wells, and was prosperous, and high-born lords of Philistia courted his acquaintance. This brought to my mind the story of the Wandering Jew, and it occurred to me that possibly this was the beginning of it. With the exception of the poisoned wells, bleeding hosts, slaughtered infants, Christian blood, witchcraft, usury and other accusations preferred against the Jews in the Middle Ages, the two stories look quite alike. I am of the conviction that the legend of the Wandering Jew has grown up on Christian soil. But among the miraculous stories in the New Testament I found no Ahasverus, no Wandering Jew, no accursed

shoemaker, before whose door Jesus, bearing the
cross, wanted to rest. I found that Jesus did not
bear the cross at all, that Simon of Cyrene bore
it. I discovered, moreover, to my surprise, that
the Jews did not crucify Jesus, and the academy
of France has confirmed my discovery. The origin
of the legend of the Wandering Jew can not be
found in the Gospels.

DER EWIGE JUDE.

A poet and journalist of the last century, Christian Frederick Daniel Schubart, who for ten long
years was supported by Christian charity in the
penitentiary at Hohenaspurg, because he had said
and written things which priests and princes did
not like—wrote also that beautiful poem Der Ewige
Jude, and pointed back to the thirteenth century,
A. C. E., for the origin of this myth. This poem is
the source from which Eugene Sue took his idea of
Le Juif Errant.

It was in the civil war between Adolph of Nassau
and Albrecht of Austria, towards the end of the
thirteenth century, that under the leadership of a
fiend called Rindfleisch, more than 100,000 Jews
were slaughtered in Southern Germany, and the
death of all was threatened who would not embrace
the cross. Then, it is supposed, the myth of the
Wandering Jew originated, because the violence
of mobs, priests and princes could not succeed in
exterminating the Jew. Der Ewige Jude, "the eternal Jew," he was called ; the indestructible Jew, indeed. This outlawed Jew could not possibly attain to felicity in God ; how could a man be happy

without believing in Jesus? He must be namelessly
wretched because unregenerate. But why does he
not die? Evidently because he is cursed with everlasting life on earth and must be miserable forever.
So the barbarous phantasy of that age depicted the
character of the Jew and called him Der ewige
Jude, the eternal or the deathless Jew. Ahasverus was supposed to be an old, feeble and broken
man, with evil eye, disheveled hair, weary of life,
unable to die and condemned to suffer forever.
People did not know that in his domestic life and
faith the Jew was much happier than his persecutors. They could not comprehend that there is
something incomparably great in the conduct of
those who suffer rather than lie, who prefer misery
to hypocrisy, who can die for the sake of an ideal.
They understood the character of the Jew as little
as Shakespeare understood it when he depicted his
Shylock.

LE JUIF ERRANT.

This, however, is the ewige Jude of the Germans.
The French Juif errant, akin to the English
Wandering Jew, is a different character. He is a
robust man with a bad conscience. His breath
poisons the atmosphere. He is the messenger of
misery, tears and death, but he feels remorse and
is a burden to himself as he is a curse to others.
This, however, is no fiction of the people; it is
metaphysical, a personification of skepticism by a
theological poet. The Jew appeared to the Christian priest as personified skepticism, and skepticism
was a crime. It destroyed the faith; it engendered

misery and death in the estimation of the Christian priest.

SKEPTICISM.

It is true that the Jew is the spirit of negation, a
protest against the dogmas of creeds; and the question is, can the human family reach civilization without some skepticism? I say, no. Without helpful
doubt, and therefore without the thoughtful Jew,
the human family cannot advance. Let us examine
the records of history; they will, I believe, sub-
stantiate my proposition.

In our days the word skepticism has lost much of
the stigma formerly attached to it. It is a legitimate
philosophical term. The old-fashioned devil has
become, in the hands of Goethe, Mephistopheles.
The bottomless pit is not as deep, hell not as hot and
sulphurous, as it was in the old days. We have not
burned any witches for a long while. Everything has
changed.

OLD TESTAMENT HEROES.

But now to the records of history. I will not
dwell long on the Old Testament heroes themselves,
who were Wandering Jews, as it were, carrying far
and wide doubt in the verity of heathenism. The
prophets carried their messages to all nations about
Palestine. Elisha appointed a king of Damascus.
Jonah preached repentance and righteousness in the
distant Nineveh. Daniel brought two mighty kings
to their knees before the God of Israel, and forced
them to worship the God of the people they had
conquered. These ancient prophets were everywhere, it appears, in Persia and Ethiopia, Armenia
and Egypt, China and the Ionian Islands, centuries

before the Christian Era. How did it come about
that the ancient Hebrews became the oracles of kings
and of nations? It was because ideas from Sinai
and Moriah had been carried by their messengers
far away and had been brought to the enlightened
Gentiles. It was made known that there is a loftier
intelligence in Israel, law, justice, freedom, righteousness, virtue, and to these kings and nations
bowed with reverence. Was not this, however, an
importation of doubt into the pagan world till it dissipated belief in the gods by the light from Sinai and
Moriah? Skepticism was carried into the pagan
world by the Jew; it was the mission of the Wandering Jew.

UNJUST CRITICISM.

It is, perhaps, proper to observe here that modern
critics are often as unjust to the ancient Hebrews as
Russia and Roumania are to modern Jews. They
are always at work to point out what the ancient
Hebrews might have learned from Egypt, Phœnicia,
Assyria, or Persia, and never tell us what those nations must have learned from the Israelites. Centuries before the Ptolemies, the Hebrews were in
friendly contact with the Egyptians. Cannot the
influence have been reciprocal? It is rarely taken
into consideration that Zoroaster may have learned
from the widely dispersed Jews, although the Jewish
element in his teachings cannot be ignored.

THE CAUCASIAN RACE.

Alexandria is the starting point. There the
Wandering Jew first began to dispose of Greco-
Roman idolatry and the civilization based upon it.

THE HEBREWS' SECOND COMMONWEALTH.

The Hebrews established their second commonwealth in Palestine in 536 B. C. E. The Book of Job
tells the story of the nation's culture and enlightenment. In the year 331, Alexander the Great conquered the Medo-Persian Empire, and died in the
city of Babylon.

After his death, however, and after twenty years
of warfare, his generals divided the empire among
themselves. Palestine was first an Egyptian and then
a Syrian province up to 165 B. C. E., when the Maccabean rebellion broke out, culminating in the independence of Palestine. The Hebrews had been in
continuous contact with Gentile nations five hundred years, and had given birth to cosmopolitan ora-
tors and writers, such as the second Isaiah, the authors of the books of Jonah, Ruth, and Job, and of a
number of Psalms like the one hundred and fourth ;
men of broad, humane and universal principles.

Previous to the conquest of Persia proper, Alexander had conquered Asia Minor, Syria, Phœnicia,
Palestine, and Egypt. In Egypt he selected the
site for a commercial metropolis of the world,
which was built and called Alexandria. He and
his successors invited to Alexandria merchants and
artisans of Greece, Macedonia and Palestine, and
guaranteed them equal rights. The Jews accordingly came into Egypt, and many of them settled
in Alexandria and other maritime cities. They
flourished there. In the second century B. C. E., they
built the gorgeous Onias Temple, in imitation of
the one at Jerusalem. Their synagogue at Alexan-

dria was one of the largest structures of that city of palaces. About the same time, the Jews came into Asia Minor from Mesopotamia, and into Greece and Italy.

The Jews had settled among the Western Gentiles long before the advent of Christianity, as warriors and as captives of war, as agriculturists, mechanics, merchants, sages and men of letters.

GREEK AND JEW.

When Greek and Jew met they could not understand one another. The Grecian mind addressed itself to matter, color, form, harmony and the like. Aryan theology is materialistic, and the Aryan Greeks are masters in the plastic arts. Beauty of form, rather than wealth of ideas, makes their literature attractive. Greek philosophy, especially that of Pythagoras, is Greek in form but Jewish in substance, as ancient writers well maintained. A disciple of Aristotle, speaking of a Jew he met on his journeys, said to his master, "We learned more from the Jew than he could learn from us." The Greek lived in nature, as did his gods ; he became the priest of the beautiful, the apostle of the arts.

The Hebrew mind took the opposite trend. The Jew looked into the spirit, the soul of nature ; he penetrated eternity. The substance of all his philosophy is Jehovah, its last word is Jehovah. The Greek grasped the present moment, and was the artist ; the Jew worshiped the timeless spirit, and was the prophet. Both were great. The Greek was a

"gay boy, the Hebrew a grave and earnest man."
The Greeks were men of the world, the Hebrews a
people of priests. Therefore when they met they
could not understand each other. Equally representing the highest intelligence, they learned from
one another. In Alexandria modern history begins, in science and criticism, as well as in ethics
and theology.

THE BEGINNING OF MODERN HISTORY.

Modern history does not begin with the advent
of Christianity, for this is itself a product. It begins with the translation of the Hebrew Bible at
Alexandria. Since then all reformations have commenced with translations of the Bible ; such as those
made by Hieronymus, Saadia, Luther and Mendelssohn. The spirit of inquiry and learning progressed
in Egypt. Palestinian Jews laid down their philosophy in the translation now called the Septuagint.
New literature in the Greek language was produced. All species of poetry, lyric, epic and dramatic, were called into requisition to produce Jewish ideas in the Grecian form ; Homer and Orpheus
were interpolated in hexameters, as if the ancient
poets had already taught the doctrine of monotheism and had heralded the praise of the Hebrew
ancestors. Jews and Gentiles were engaged in
writing Jewish history, culminating in the master
works of Josephus Flavius. Jewish philosophy, as
well as the teachings of Plato, Aristotle, Zeno and
Epicurus, was reproduced in pompous Greek ; at last
came Philo, the Alexandrian Jew. So the Wandering Jew threw the torch of skepticism, that is, of

new ideas, into the Greek literature, which was for
many centuries thereafter the medium of culture.

DISSEMINATION OF JUDAISM.

About the same time the Jews came in large
numbers to Greece and Italy, especially to Rome,
most likely also to Spain, France and Belgium, as
the successors of the ancient Phœnicians and Car-
thagenians in the world's commerce. In Rome, for
instance, they had become so numerous that thousands of them wept at the urn of Caesar when
he was slain, for he had been their friend and
patron. In the time of Augustus, when Herod's
will was read in Rome, 8,000 Roman Jews protested
against its stipulations. The Emperor Tiberius
sent 4,000 Roman Jews as soldiers to Sardinia.
Along with the Jew, Judaism also went to Rome.
He had no apostles and evangelists, and yet he made
numerous proselytes. In the East, the conversion
of Queen Helene, her husband and two sons indi-
cate how far Judaism had penetrated. Its progress
in Rome and the provinces was still more rapid. It
encompassed all classes up to the palace of the
Caesars, so that the Emperor Domitian, in protection of the state religion, enacted stringent laws
against Roman proselytes to Judaism. One of
them, Aquila, made a new Greek translation of the
Pentateuch, and another, Clemens, was of consular
dignity, and his wife a near kinswoman of the
Caesars. The Jews added to their daily prayers one
for the righteous proselytes (גרי צדק). Tacitus,
Juvenal and other writers were astonished that so
many Romans, and especially the women, believed in

the Jewish God, observed the Sabbath and Jewish
ceremonies. Paul, the actual author of Gentile
Christianity, on his journeys met everywhere devout Gentiles, who believed in the Jewish Bible as
the final authority.

ORIGIN OF CHRISTIANITY.

So the Wandering Jew traversed the Roman empire. He spread skepticism among the pagans,
aroused doubts in the reality of the gods worshiped,
the efficacy of the observances and the veracity of
priests and priestesses. Thus the soil had been prepared by the Jew's skepticism. When the Jew was
disabled by the fall of Jerusalem, the first teachers
of Christianity stepped in with their policy of conciliation and . accommodation. Whatever merits
there may be in primitive Christianity, its spread
was made possible by the preparatory work done by
the Jews in the pagan world. It was the first great
service of the Wandering Jew. He was cursed and
hated by the ancient Greco-Roman orthodoxy, because he had spread skepticism and had undermined the old state religion. The work was done
by the Jew, but Christianity reaped the fruits.

JEWS IN WESTERN EUROPE.

Democratic Palestine, after a heroic struggle of
two hundred years, was vanquished by Rome. Jerusalem was laid in ruins, its temple and palaces
were destroyed, and the Jew was buried under the
ruins of his country. The land once flowing with
milk and honey became a waste. The sycamore

groves, which once re-echoed with the melodies of the harp of Judah, resounded with the cry of the woe-stricken Jew as he went forth from his land. The flower of his youth had perished there. There were the graves of his sires, prophets, heroes and singers. There were the monuments of his glory, the reminiscences of fifteen hundred years of wonderful history; every spot told a tale of sublime deeds. He left there his independence, his freedom, his rights, his happiness. He went forth an exile to the land of the strangers.

From the time of Pompey's conquest of Jerusalem, the Hebrews migrated in large numbers westward, and went with the Romans to the Rhine and the Danube. Thither came also many of the fugitives after the fall of Jerusalem and Bethar. Up to this day the largest number of Jews is Germanic in language. The Jew impressed his civilization on the aborigines. The Jews were merchants, mechanics, physicians and agriculturists. They lived in peace with their neighbors up to the close of the sixth century; their condition was bearable even up to the time of the beginning of the Crusades.

ORIGIN OF WESTERN CHRISTIANITY.

The pagans on the Rhine and the Danube learned also the Jew's religion, which was intimately interwoven with his laws and civilization. The Jew pointed back to the distant Jerusalem as the center of the religion and hopes of man. The Jew spoke of the sacrificial polity and the Aaronic priesthood, the glory of Mount Moriah, the pomp and grandeur

of Zion, the hopes of mankind as one great family ;
and he spoke in Oriental poetry, in the language of
fire, which northern hearts had not yet learned to
understand—it was unintelligible to the sons of the
forest.   He praised a God too sublime and spoke of
ethics too humane for the worshipers of Thor and
Wodan.

The Jew had done the work but the Christian
missionary reaped the benefit.   Christianity was
planted upon Jewish culture and Jewish sentiment.
The people, though Christians, continued to live in
peace with the Jews, kept the Jewish Sabbath and
observed Jewish ceremonies.   Jews and Christians
intermarried.   But then came the councils and prohibited Christians from observing the Jewish Sabbath, and practicing Jewish observances.   They repeatedly interdicted intermarriage between Jews
and Christians.   Then came princes and dispos-
sessed the Jew of his landed property, robbed him
of his treasures, and forced him to become the
trader, merchant and physician.   Still the people in-
clined to Jewish doctrines and practices more than to
those ordained by Rome, and then the cry was raised
against the Jew : '' He crucified Jesus.''   The priests
knew it was a falsehood, but they also knew it
would succeed in making the Jew odious, and that
it would sow the seed of hatred between Jew and
Christian.   But this proved ineffectual in numerous
instances ; then refuge was sought in the myth of
the Wandering Jew.   The Wandering Jew spreads
misery and death, they cried : down with the Jew !
The Wandering Jew brings progress, reformation,
intellectual advancement ; he brought Christianity

to the East and to the West; without him you
would stagnate, responded the genius of history;
and, lo and behold! the Jew, crucified a thousand
times and always resurrected, became Der Ewige
Jude, the "eternal," and invincible Jew, the immortal principle of progress. This is the second act
of the long and spectacular drama of ignorance and
fanaticism.

ORIGIN OF ISLAM.

While thousands of the exiled Jews went westward, others went eastward to their brethren on the
Euphrates and Tigris, on the Indus and Ganges,
into Arabia and Parthia. There, between the Caspian Sea, the Indus and Western Arabia, were ancient Hebrew colonies since the days of Shalmanezer.
For nearly a thousand years they had existed there
as a separate community, under a chief of the house
of David, with the title of Resh Gelutha, "Prince
of the Captivity." There were seats of Jewish learning, the celebrated schools of Sura, Nehardea, Pum-
Baditha and Machusa. There learning was system-
atized ; the results thereof we have in the Babylonian
Talmud. Reciprocal influences were active between
Hebrews and Arabs. These latter gave currency to
many Jewish tales and traditions and adopted Jewish laws ; while the Hebrews accepted many Arabic
teachings and preserved legends concerning devout
Arabs and Arabian prophets.

Here we see the Wandering Jew perform a wonderful task, especially from the second to the end
of the sixth century. The thunders of Sinai re-echo
in Arabia, the heathen temples are shaken, their
altars are overthrown, the Wandering Jew has sown

the seeds of skepticism and cultivates progress
and reform. Again a new world grows out of the
old. As little, indeed, as you can imagine the New
Testament without the Old, so little can you think
of the Koran without Jewish lore. The one like the
other is the offspring of the Jewish mind. The Wandering Jew stood sponsor for both. He has sown
the seed and others have reaped the harvest. He
has fought the battles and others have earned the
laurels. He has received ingratitude and scorn,
where he has showered blessings with munificent
hand.

THE MIDDLE AGES.

But the drama is not yet finished, there is another
act as wonderful. Progress and reform, like evolution and thought, cannot stop ; the Wandering Jew
must proceed and I must ask you to bear with him
just a little longer.

The followers of Mohammed and the Koran first
appeared on the stage of history as irresistible war-
·riors and conquerors, forcing upon the nations the
religion of the Arabian apostle. The Orient yielded
to the crescent, and this was carried in triumph into
Constantinople, into Spain, to the very doors of
France, where the Pyrenees and Charles Martel
checked their further advance.

The Arabs settled down to civilized life and cultivated the arts of peace. Gradually they rose in
the scale of culture. They studied the Greek classics. Soon they became independent thinkers, philosophers and scientists, especially in medicine, mathematics, astronomy and physics, and their schools
became famous.

The Hebrews, who, like the Christians, at the start of the Islam suffered largely from its fierceness, gradually became a part of the Mohammedan kingdoms in Asia, Africa and Europe, and were well treated. They enjoyed privileges among the Mohammedans during the dark periods of the Middle Ages. The consequence was that the Jews produced students, prominent poets, philosophers, scientists, statesmen and financiers.

However, while half of the horizon was thus illuminated by Mohammedan and Jewish learning, research and culture, the other half was dark, ignorance was triumphant, fanaticism and intolerance dominated in Christendom from the ninth to the sixteenth century, and the effects thereof were apparent in the sixteenth, seventeenth and eighteenth centuries, and even in this nineteenth century, in such lands as Russia and Roumania. The fanaticism and ignorance of the masses demoralize and disintegrate them into factions and fractions.

The dark centuries presented the anomalous fact that the Wandering Jew, persecuted and outlawed in Christendom, was at the same time the prince of commerce, the princes' counselor, the physician of popes and emperors, the apostle of science, and the representative of ancient and modern culture. The Jew was the only human being in Christendom whose intelligence was not under the control of pope and council, and who was free from dogmatism and scholastic quibbles. The Jew, except through persecution, had no Middle Ages. While he was being robbed and persecuted, Albert the Great, Thomas Aquinas, and other lights of the church, studied carefully what the Jew Avicebron (Solomon Ibn Gabirol) or R. Moses of Egypt (Moses Maimonides), had written, and quoted and expounded them for the benefit of the church. Popes and potentates had their Jewish translators engaged to reproduce in Latin what Jews had written in Hebrew or Arabic. The Jew carried books and learning from land to land.

It was an anomalous state of society. The civilized world was broken up into two hostile factions, Christendom on the one side and Mohammedanism on the other. In Christendom ignorance and oppression increased from century to century, and freedom of thought was not permitted. The science and learning of the Mohammedans were useless to the Christian, for none dared to read the books of the infidels, none ventured to learn the language of the enemies of the cross.

ORIGIN OF THE REFORMATION.

It was again the Wandering Jew who was the mediator between the hostile factions and became the agent of progress and reform. He brought to the Christians philosophy, science, letters, arts and industries from other countries. Christians began to study Hebrew, to read and to imbibe new ideas. The Wandering Jew had sown the seed of skepticism once again. The soil was prepared, the seed was sown, and out of that soil rose Martin Luther and the Protestant Reformation. As little, indeed, as the New Testament or the Koran could have come into existence without the long and consistent labors of the Wandering Jew, so little

could the Reformation have possibly evolved out
of Christian soil without the labors of Ibn Gabirol,
Maimonides, Ibn Ezra', Kimchi, Gersonides, and
many other Jewish thinkers, whose free and un-
trammeled research and range of philosophical
thought, whose conciliation of faith and reason by
making faith philosophical and philosophy religious,
cleared the dogmatic atmosphere. If it had not
been for these Jewish thinkers, theology would have
remained a divine comedy. As is the theology of a
people so are its polity, social institutions and life.

The Jew's revenge for all this, however, was
characteristic of him. He destroyed the gods of
his persecutors. He dissipated the illusions, exposed the superstitions, battled against ignorance,
protested against slavery, demanded freedom of belief, thought and speech, and raised his voice against
prejudice and oppression. He carried skepticism
and learning from land to land, gave the impulses to
the world's progress and stood at the cradle of every
idea of light and freedom. That was the Jew's
revenge.

MODERN PHILOSOPHY.

Where is the Wandering Jew of the modern day?
Is he again hunted down by persecution, or intimi-
dated by the well-known Christian love? Yes, he
was hunted down in Germany, France, Poland, but
he wakes up in Amsterdam in the shape of Baruch
Spinoza, the most formidable of all enemies of dogmatism. He upset the whole host of gods. He broke
through the fine scholastic spider-webs of theology,
claimed freedom of research and word, and became
the father of modern philosophy. He was another

link in the chain of Jewish reasoners from the Euphrates to the North Sea, beginning with Saadia in the tenth century, and ending—where?—yes, where? All modern philosophy turns about Spinoza. Two-thirds of all modern philosophers and scientists have become Wandering Jews. Our Christian neighbors themselves have become Wandering Jews. The Puritans and Presbyterians are the Pharisees of old. The Episcopalians are the aristocratic Saducees of days gone by. Our Quakers are the Essenes of old. They are Judaized and do not know it. Little more is left for the Wandering Jew to do. Still he has no rest. He must live on until there shall be no superstition, no ignorance and no intolerance, no hatred, no self-delusion and no darkness among sects.

He must wander on till the end of woe and misery has come, till the earth shall be one holy land, every city a Jerusalem, every house a temple, every table an altar, every parent a priest, and Jehovah the only God; till light and truth shall have dominion over all, every land be a home of the free, every government the guardian of liberty, and mankind one family of equal rights and duties. Then the curtain will drop on the drama of the Wandering Jew. Then a good morning will have risen upon the world.

THE SOURCES OF THE THEOLOGY OF JUDAISM.

(1887.)

Theology is the science of the conceptions of Deity in the human mind. All hopes and expectations, as well as all duties of man and the human race, originate from and are colored by man's conceptions of Deity, and are as true or false, right or wrong, as those conceptions are in the person or the community of which he is a member. God is the source of conscience. Every hope and expectation of happiness here or hereafter, every fear of misery in this or another world, as well as every conception of duty and every dictum of conscience, is directly dependent on man's conception of Deity.

Philosophy is not creative, it does not produce facts. Its office is to distinguish between the possible and the impossible, the probable and the improbable, the true and the false, by the discursive method ; and to unite the true, possible and probable into an organic system of a comprehensive conception of the world by the constructive method. Still in either case it must deal in given facts, the existence of which reason presupposes, because it is not creative and cannot produce facts. It is evident, therefore, that the facts of theology, viz., the conceptions of Deity, must be present in the mind before reason can work upon them analytically or synthetically'; hence they are revelations, or, in other words, intuitive knowledge. If we admit that some or all of those conceptions are conveyed into the mind by other men, then, as an infinite regression of cause and effect is unreasonable, we must admit that at some time or other they were originally conceived by some man or some men, and were then and there revelations. Well did Maimonides say, " With his reason man can distinguish between truth and falsehood," and adds to it, "And this existed also in Adam in its completeness and entirety." (Moreh, i, 2.)

It is no less evident, however, that theology must subject its material to constructive philosophy, in order to be a science. Again, as all human conceptions consist of thesis and antithesis, there are possible true and also false conceptions of the Deity. There are also possible false conclusions from true premises, false or even true conclusions from false premises, which in the case of theology affect the truth or error of the hopes, expectations and fears of man, and his conceptions of duty. Therefore, it is also evident that theology must subject its material to discursive philosophy. So far and no farther theology depends on philosophy. The material or the facts of theology are received from the direct revelations, the intuitive knowledge of the human mind, as man discovers them in himself. It makes no difference by what inner or outer influence those conceptions were raised from the sphere of the unconscious to that of the conscious in the mind—as recorded in the books which are believed to contain those revelations conceived by persons in former days. That which was revealed could not be revealed again, and words recording this revealed truth are only the agent which raises that truth from the sphere of the unconscious to that of the conscious. The same is the case with verbal instruction. It must always be borne in mind that the intellect will accept nothing for which it does not possess an innate capacity, that is, similar though unconscious idea-types. Education and instruction mean development of those types, or raising them from the unconscious to the conscious sphere.

Judaism relies for its material upon the revelations in the threefold covenant recorded in the Torah of Moses. Judaism constructs its theology by accepting that material and subjecting it to the process of discursive and constructive reasoning. Therefore we define thus : *The Theology of Judaism is the science of the conceptions of Deity in the human mind and their logical sequences, in conformity with the postulate of reason, as laid down in the Torah of Moses, expounded, expanded and reduced to practice in different forms, at different times, by Moses, the prophets, the hagiographists, the sages and the lawful bodies in the congregation of Israel.*

The " teaching and commandment " (תורה ומצוה) of the threefold covenant is the immovable center of Judaism as the positive and universal religion. Doctrines and precepts, which are the logical sequences from any principle laid down in the "teaching and commandment" of the covenant, are naturally of equal value and authority with the principle of which they are logical sequences. Instances thereof occur in Exodus, xxxiv; Leviticus, xix; Numbers, xv, 14–16; Deuteronomy, vi, x, 12–22; xiii, 1–6; xvii, 1–13; xviii, 9–22, and many more passages in the Pentateuch which are either taken directly from the "Book of the Covenant," or expound and expand the "teaching and commandment" of the covenant. All laws of Moses which define and reduce to practice the law of the covenant are special, national and temporary ; they are the law of the land of Israel as long as such circumstances or emergencies prevail, to regulate or counteract which the laws were originally intended. Their positive value and authority lie in the doctrine or precept which the law embodies, and not in the letter thereof. Inasmuch as such doctrine or precept is naturally contained or implied in the "teaching and commandment" of the covenant, it is of equal value and authority with the provisions of the Covenant. Instances thereof are all laws of Moses defining the right of possession and inheritance, the laws regulating the mutual relations of servant and master, the provisions for the protection and support of the poor and other weak and unprotected parties, the laws of traffic ; also the laws regulating marriage and divorce and protecting the rights of the family and the purity of the race, the sanitary laws in all their ramifications, the laws regulating the culte, and the entire penal code ; all of these contain eternal and universal doctrines or precepts, and are in letter national, temporary and transitory, hence Moses himself provided for necessary amendments and substitutes. (Deuteronomy, xvii, 8–13.) Again, all dictatorial ordinances of Moses regulating momentary affairs, such as those in reference to the seven nations of Canaan and the conquered nations east of the Jordan, also Amalek, Midian, Ammon, Moab and Edom, the stoning of the Sabbath-breaker, the treatment of Korah and his followers, the massacre of the worshipers of the golden calf, have no connection whatever either with the teaching of the covenant or the laws of Moses. They were war measures, recorded most likely in the "Book of the Wars of Jehovah," and embodied in the Pentateuch as a matter of history.

The Torah of Moses, containing the records of the covenant, together with the commentaries thereof in the legislation and speeches of Moses, is, and always has been accepted as the source of Judaism, hence also as containing the main material for the theology of Judaism. As for the laws of Judaism, it is the standpoint of the Talmud that its six hundred and thirteen commandatory and prohibitory laws, with the exception of the two rabbinical laws, are in the Torah of Moses. Whatever is not prohibited there, is not prohibited, and whatever is not commanded there, it is not the duty of an Israelite to do. The whole rabbinical law is built on these laws and a few traditional laws. Historical Judaism acknowledges no authority besides the sacred book of the Hebrews, called the Bible, which was known as far back as the second century B. C., to consist of the three divisions of Torah or Pentateuch, Former and Latter Prophets, and Hagiography. This division was known to the Greek translator of Ecclesiasticus, who mentions it in his introduction. Josephus (Contra Apion, i, 8) mentions it and gives the number of the sacred books to be twenty-two. The Tanaim frequently mention it in the Talmudic and pre-Talmudic books, and give the names of the books belonging to each part in Talmud *Babli*, Baba Bathra, 14 and 15. The books have retained the same names precisely, except that I and II Samuel, I and II Kings, I and II Chronicles, Ezra and Nehemiah were each but one book, hence there would have been altogether twenty books; but the five Megilloth, Ruth, Song of Solomon, Ecclesiastes, Lamentations and Esther, now counted one book, were then counted five; thus the Scriptures ever since the final compilation of these books consisted of twenty-four books, divided into five books of Torah, eight books of Prophets (the twelve minor prophets were always considered one book) and eleven books of Hagiography. Josephus, it appears, included Ruth in Samuel and Lamentations in Jeremiah, therefore he speaks of twenty-two books of Sacred Scriptures. The subdivision of Samuel, Kings and Chronicles was made by the Greek and Latin translators, and like the prevailing division into chapters, was imposed upon the Hebrew Bible at a later date.

These three divisions of Scriptures were not considered of equal holiness and authority by the ancient expounders of the laws; the Christians and the Karaites accept the whole Bible as the word of God. In the synagogues and the academies, as far back as the records reach, to and beyond the time of the Maccabees, the Torah of Moses was read four times every week as well as on the national feast and fast days. The congregation was not to remain three days without reading from the Torah. The duty of the Israelites, it was held, was to read some portion from the Torah every day, and it was the special duty of every one to write a copy of the Torah for himself, and of the kings to write two copies thereof. (Maimonides, *Hilchoth Tephilin*, etc., vii. 1 and 2.) Neither of these duties was prescribed in regard to the other books of the Bible. Sections from prophets were read in the synagogues and academies on Sabbaths, on feast and fast days; divine service was closed with them and they served as texts for the preachers and translators (Rappaport, Erech Millin, Art. אגדה) ; but this could be done only after reading from the Torah. The prophets were considered inferior to the Torah, and the Hagiographa inferior to the prophets in holiness and authority. Those of the ancient Rabbis who believed in plenary inspiration claimed it only for Moses, and not for any other prophet. God said what was before the mind of Moses ; to this society is to be trained by practical legislation. Also in this very rational department of his legislation Moses claimed no perpetual authority for his laws ; only the underlying principles are divine. Laws are expressed words, and words must be expounded. They change in significance from time to time, the circumstances and emergencies which made such laws necessary and beneficial change and pass away, and the law becomes a dead letter. Moses established a high court of law in Israel (Deuter., xvii, 8–13) with the prerogatives of the legislative and judiciary sovereignty, viz.: to ex-

pound the eternal law in particular cases or emergencies and thus to meet the demands of every age ;
he told his people "according to the Torah which
they will teach thee," if it be or be not written in
the Torah in your possession, "and according to
the judgment which they will tell thee, thou shalt
do," whether it be or be not according to your
judgment ; and whoever rebels against that decision
may be punished with death. No death penalty for
any political offense is threatened in the Mosaic
laws, not even for non-obedience to the prophet,
the highest authority of the theocracy (Ibid., verse
19). This solemn injunction tells forcibly that only
the divine principles are eternal, the letter of the
law embodying any of them is subject to change by
the authority established under the law. The post-
biblical legislation among the Hebrews is based upon
this provision of the law. Any law embodying a
divine principle, enacted by lawful authority, has
the sanction of Moses.

The difference then between the laws of the covenant and the laws of Moses is that the former are
eternal in letter and spirit, the law of universal
empire ; and the latter are eternal in spirit only
where they embody an eternal principle. The
prophets, as well as the later expounders of the law,
guarded this doctrine.

Whether all the laws of Moses were written by
him in various scrolls, or some of them were preserved traditionally and written down at some later
date, is in fact of no vital importance. However,
we have the authority of the book itself to the effect

that Moses wrote it (Deuteronomy, xxxi, 9, 11, 24, 26), although some matter may have been added at a late date, like Deuteronomy, xvii, 14–20 which is not in the spirit of Moses, and ibid., xviii, 3–8 which refers to the time of Solomon (cf. Rashi), and Samuel may have added his "royal constitution" to the laws of Moses (1 Samuel, x,. 25). All a priori arguments amount to nothing in face of the plain and undeniable records which state ויכתב משה "and Moses wrote." The idea of pseudonymous writings and pious frauds was foreign to those generations, and especially to earnest and god-inspired men, whose purposes are so purely humane and divine. We have before us, however, all the original sources of the Thorah with the indorsement of "and Moses wrote;" still those various Mosaic books and scrolls may have been put together later in the five books of the Pentateuch in the lifetime of Joshua or the elders after him, or even in the days of Samuel, at any rate before the latter days of David. But whenever or by whomever the compilation was completed, it was certainly believed that Mosaic writings only were included within the Torah of Moses. Whatever came into it at a later date is very unimportant in quality and quantity, and must have been added to the MSS. as marginal notes first, which then, by mistake, crept into the text.

As a source of theology, however, the remainder of the Torah is no less important than the Book of the Covenant, viz., as a commentary on the covenants. Whenever or by whomever it may have

been written, it still remains the most ancient commentary on the covenant in our possession. The
expression "and Moses repeated (every word) and
wrote (it)," is used of Moses only. The ancients
went so far in this distinction between Moses and
all others that they ordained, "Prophets and Hagiographa must not be placed upon the Thorah."
Up to the time of Rabbi Judah Hannassi it was
held that Torah, Prophets and Hagiographa must
not be written in one scroll, lest they appear of
equal holiness. (Mas. Sopherim, iii.) This is still
the case in the synagogue.

The higher authority of Moses is evident from
the Torah itself; as is written, "He is authenti-
cated in all my house" (Numb. xii, 7); and the
Torah closes with the words, "And no prophet rose
in Israel like Moses" (Deut. xxxiv, 10), a statement which none of the prophets ever contradicted.
On the contrary, the last of the prophets admonished his people, "Remember the Torah of Moses,
my servant" (Mal. iii, 22).

The Judaism of history never deviates from the
principle that its authority is based upon Moses,
whose authority is founded on the Sinaitic revelation, and that all prophets and hagiographists after
Moses expounded and expanded the words of God
laid down in the Thorah, admonished the people to
know, understand and observe the laws of God,
predicted evil to the rebellious and happiness to the
obedient person or nation in the spirit and according
to the words of Moses. Moses Maimonides, in his
compendium of the Talmudical law and doctrine

known as Mishneh Torah, otherwise called Yad Hachazakah, formulates this historical belief. He points out the superiority of Moses over all other prophets in inspiration and authority (Yesode Torah, vii, 6; viii, 1, 2), in support of the article of faith that the Torah is of eternal authority, in which all ancient expounders of the law agree. (Cf. Introduction to Chelek.) In the second part of his Moreh Nebuchim, Maimonides expatiates on this subject. There (chapter xxxv) he refers to what was laid down in his code, and adds, that in this treatise he refers exclusively to the nature of prophecy as attaching to the men called prophets in Sacred Scriptures, and not to Moses, whose prophetical powers and words are of a different and of a much higher degree than those of the other prophets. The name Nabi or prophet is given, according to his opinion, to Moses, and also to others, by equivocation, i. e., they have very little if anything in common. He returns to this subject in the thirty-ninth chapter, and there he states concerning all the prophets after Moses: "But as regards the prophets that arose after Moses, thou knowest already the idea of their words (teaching); that they performed, as it were, the function of warning the people and exhorting them to observe the Torah of Moses, threatening evil to him who forsakes it, and predicting good for him who trains himself to follow and observe it." Then again, in the forty-fifth chapter, Maimonides shows that there are different degrees of prophecy, as there is a marked difference among the wise and intelligent in general; one is superior to the other, which is also the case among prophets. He counts there ten degrees of prophecy, and gives us to understand that not all passages of the Bible are of equal authority and divinity. All Spanish Arabic reasoners on the religion and theology of Judaism, grounding their opinions on the statements of Talmud and Midrash, are of the same opinion in this matter, so that it is perfectly correct to maintain :

(*a*) The Judaism of history accepts the Torah of Moses as its primary source and unalterable authority in all matters of religion, ethics and theology.

(*b*) In the Torah of Moses are the doctrines and laws of the covenant, the immovable center, and the Law of Moses is the first important commentary, eternal in spirit and subject to change in letter.

(*c*) The prophets and hagiographists are the next most important expounders of the covenant, its documents and laws, because the whole house of Israel accepts them as God-inspired messengers of truth and righteousness.

(*d*) All post-biblical expounders of the Torah or any other portion of Sacred Scriptures, be they persons or authorized bodies, no matter whether their researches and decisions are laid down in the rabbinical, philosophical or poetical literature of the Hebrews, possess authority in the degree that they justly and wisely expound, expand, or reduce to practice the doctrine and law of the covenant in harmony with the postulate of reason.

(*e*) It follows, therefore, that the sources for the

theology of Judaism must be sought in the documents of the threefold covenant ; these are also the
standard and canon of criticism of all other Biblical
and post-Biblical writings of the Hebrews, whereby
their ethical and theological value and authority are
to be judged.

It is one of the self-delusions of this and every
previous period of history, that man, owing to his
progress and achievements in the phenomenal and
speculative sciences, knows more about the one,
only and sole God, than what is laid down in the
Torah of Moses. The prophets, hagiographists,
sages and reasoners in Israel, and among other
peoples, only expound and expand what is said concerning God by Moses, more or less correctly. The
genius at once conceives and produces in its totality
the grand picture, which thousands of lesser ability
can imitate in part or wholly, but upon which they
can never improve. Moses was the inspired genius,
his mind was the focus in which all conceptions of
Deity, as revealed in the human mind, converged ;
he separated the true from the false, and named the
grand and inimitable conception, Jehovah, יהוה the
infinite and absolute being ; beyond this human
reason cannot proceed. This infinite and absolute
being, which no man can see and live, can be recognized in his works alone, said Moses. He gave a full
and exhaustive statement of what we can know of
and about God, in the passage known as the revelation upon the rock (Exodus, xxxiv, 5, 6), the most
sublime words ever spoken by man. These are the
limits of human reason, beyond which no mortal

ever penetrated.   What any or all men ever said of and about God is either false or else it merely expounds and expands the indestructible words of Moses.

Inasmuch, however, as all true teachings of religion, ethics and theology can be but logical resultants of our true conceptions of Deity ; and, furthermore, inasmuch as the Mosaic knowledge of God is the highest and holiest, beyond which human reason cannot go, it necessarily follows that the Mosaic ethics for the individual, the human family and society, as well as the theology of Moses, must be the highest and holiest which man can expound, expand, apply, or reduce to practice in constitutions, laws and institutions.   No religion after Moses has added an iota to the Mosaic ethics, nor in the nature of things can anything be added to the Decalogue as expounded, expanded and reduced to practice by Moses himself.   The entire object of philosophical ethics is to systematize and, of late, to build up a system independent of God, an effort doomed to failure.

The greatness and glory of the prophets in Israel consist chiefly in the following points :

(*a*) Their unshaken and invincible faith in the teachings and predictions of Moses, and their incomparable devotion to and patriotism for Israel and its cause, which they knew to be the most sacred cause of the human family.

(*b*) The brilliancy of their minds and their moral fortitude, guided by the firm purpose to see and judge correctly the errors and misdeeds of their respective generations, kings, priests or people, to

point out the inevitable consequences according to
the predictions of Moses, and yet not lose their
faith in the future triumph of truth and righteousness, the indestructibility of Israel and the threefold covenant, and the final redemption and fraternization of mankind, exactly as Moses had pointed
this out before them.   They expounded, expanded
and illumined the divine revelation ; but for all that,
"all prophets received their prophecy from Mount
Sinai."

THE OUTLINES OF JUDAISM.

AN ARGUMENT BEFORE THE CONVENTION OF THE "FREE RELIGIOUS ASSOCIATION," BOSTON, MASS. (1869.)

What is Judaism? This is the question I am to expound before this venerable body. The time is short, the subject vast; I must limit my remarks to meager outlines. I represent this cause here on my own responsibility, and am delegated by none. Twenty-five years in the pulpit, and twenty years' connection with the Jewish press, are my credentials, the diffusion of truth the purpose of my presence on this platform.

I will expound Judaism in its essence; that which is called orthodox or rabbinical Judaism involves matter additional and accessory. I speak of the substance.

Judaism is the doctrine and the law; it is theocracy, or the kingdom of heaven. It comprises three sciences, viz.; theology, based on Jehovah; ethics, derivative from this, "Man is the image of God;" and politics, "God is the King." These form the integral facts of Judaism.

Law is the incarnation of doctrine; it is theory reduced to terms of practice. Doctrine is the soul, and law the body of Judaism. Doctrine is advisory. Liberty of conscience is the birthright of man. Belief and conscience are beyond the control of any authority. Knowledge of and belief in doctrine are the basis of correct faith and the motives of just action. Again, valid action within the scope of doctrine, without motive, is hypocrisy, a restraint of the natural passions, a conventional compliance for selfish ends, and is not virtue. Judaism requires both, but it lays stress upon obedience to the law, and prescribes a line of conduct for one who is to enter the kingdom of heaven. Law is obligatory. Man's actions are governed by law for the benefit of himself and society. Doctrine and law are given in the Bible, the Decalogue is the groundwork of both. The ten commandments contain, by express statement or implication, doctrine and law. Moses enlarged upon them in accordance with the needs of his age and country ; the prophets expounded and the sages applied them to meet emergencies.

Verities once uttered are the property of all men. Religion announces verities, which are implied in the Decalogue. Laws are subject to change, principles are not ; the Decalogue contains the unchangeable principles of law, but all other biblical laws are subject to modification by proper authority. With these premises to guide us, it will be easy to sketch the outlines of Jewish theology, ethics and politics.

THEOLOGY.

The outlines of Jewish theology are suggested in the word Jehovah. It is a compound of three forms of hayah, "to be." An English word expressing at once, "he was, he is, and he will be," would be an equivalent for Jehovah, but it would

have to convey the meaning not only of passive being, but also of causation. There is no such term
in the English nor in any other language, except
the Hebrew, so far as I know. The Jehovah conception is uniquely and characteristically Hebrew.

Jehovah is an absolute and infinite being, and
the cause of all finite beings and of their modifications. He is the first cause, without which no
effect is conceivable. The universe is the effect,
depending forever on the divine cause for its existence. God is independent, the universe is not.
All effects are regulated by laws which are the
manifestation of sovereign wisdom and power.

This definition of Godhead makes it *eo ipso* impossible to concieve the essence of the Deity. "No
man can see me and live." The human mind cannot form an adequate conception of eternity or of
endless space. It has no exhaustive knowledge of
substance, force or matter. How can the indi-
vidualized understanding encompass the cause of
the universe and the nature of that cause? The
Deity, the substance of being, is beyond the horizon of human understanding. All speculations
on the essence of Deity, theological or metaphysical, dualistic, trinitarian or polytheistic, spiritual-
istic or materialistic, are not only as absurd as is
atheism itself, but they are also blasphemy. They
attempt to press the infinite Deity into narrow in-
dividualized understanding. They attempt the impossible. Please, ye doctors of all ages and zones,
confess your inability ; you cannot add one iota to
the word of the Decalogue, "I Jehovah am thy

God." He is, and therefore all things are. The
things are, and therefore he must have been first.
This is the limit of human reason.

We know not the essence, but we know some of
the manifestations of the Deity in the physical
universe and in the history of mankind, in the
reason and conscience of man. In all these departments the perpetual revelations of God are observable. This is the cleft of the rock in which
we stand, hidden by the hand of the Almighty,
till he has passed. We behold Him as He reveals
Himself in facts, in the finished creations, in the
universal harmony of the world. We can see and
admire, perceive and worship. This is the basis
of theology, and the Decalogue points it out clearly.
The precept, " Ye shall walk after Jehovah your
God," means, search first, and then emulate.

The observable manifestations of the Deity show
that He is omnipotence, sovereign wisdom, supreme
justice, and incomparable goodness. God reveals
himself as the ideal of perfection. Religion is that
innate and divine impulse which prompts man to
search after God, to think His ideas, and to imitate
His perfections ; " to walk after Jehovah your God,"
as Moses expresses it. The prophets and psalmists
have embellished this idea with poetical imagery and
sublime enthusiasm. Moses, however, like a legislator, spoke in clear terms : " Ye shall walk after
Jehovah your God." " Thou shalt be perfect with
Jehovah thy God." " Ye shall be holy, for Jehovah
your God is holy." " Thou shalt love Jehovah thy
God with all thy heart, with all thy soul, and all
thy might." Such expressions point to God as the

ideal of perfection, as also do the words of the Decalogue, "To those who love me and keep my commandments." These are the three fundamental principles of Jewish theology: God is, God manifests himself, God is the ideal of perfection.

ETHICS.

The last paragraph leads us to ethics and its first principle. If man is required to try to realize the ideal of perfaction in himself, he must possess the requisite capacities. These capacities are, indeed, the characteristics of human nature, to which scripture alludes in the words, "He made man in the image of God," *i. e.*, man is gifted with God-like capacities, free will, understanding, consciousness of duty, and hope of immortality. These capacities are characteristic of human nature; because no other creature possesses them. They are God-like, because apart from man, they are discoverable in God alone.

The Decalogue starts from this principle of ethics: All men, women and children met at the foot of Mount Sinai. This is in itself proclamation of equality. All heard and understood the word of God; this vindicates understanding for every individual. All, without exception, were required to perform the four duties of man, and this points to the consciousness of duty as being innate in every human being. Rewards are promised and punishment threatened—an acknowledgment of man's free will. God speaks and man listens and understands. God is near to man, man's nature is heaven-born and immortal. God could address his words to such alone, and the idea of duty becomes conceivable and explicable on this assumption alone.

Ecce homo. This is the man of Jewish ethics. This is the citizen of the kingdom of heaven. This is the foundation upon which the ethical structure rises. This excluded all speculations on such subjects as original sin and depravity, unworthy of the benign Deity, contrary to fact, derogatory to human nature and human dignity, and destructive of self-respect and self-reliance. If his sin is original and he is depraved, no man is responsible for the wicked act he may perpetrate. If the devil tempt him, the devil is the criminal. In the light of Jewish thought, however, ethics rises majestically. Its base is on earth, in man and in his consciousness of duty. Man is free and able to do that which is just, good and generous. He has natural impulses which the Lord implanted within him. The apex of the pyramid reaches into heaven. The kingdom of heaven is immutably the same on earth and in heaven, in time and eternity ; God is the eternal source of salvation. It is attained on earth through the conscious practice of moral laws. The moral laws in emulation of the ideal of perfection are to man what the physical laws are to matter. They make him an immortal personality, just as physical laws individualize matter and make of them suns, planets and satellites.

What are these moral laws? They are expressed or implied in the Decalogue. "Love thy neighbor like thyself," the golden rule of a Confucius, a Hillel or a Jesus, is contained in the ten commandments, understanding is its interpreter, con-

science its expounder, and love its eloquent pleader.
A study of the Decalogue leads to the conviction
that Moses was right in saying, "Thou shalt not
add nor diminish." Neither Christianity, . Islam
nor Philosophy has been able to add to the Decalogue one principle on which human happiness,
either here or hereafter depends. The difficulty is,
that the words are brief and simple; therefore they
are not studied sufficiently, and are not quite understood. The commandments of the Decalogue are
categories of the moral code, and require patient
and exhaustive thought. The Greco-Roman phantasm of religion led the masses out upon the boundless sea of imagination, far, far away from the
realities of human nature. In theology, speculations on the essence of the Deity obscured human
reason, and led it astray. In ethics, too, imagination created a phantasm, and prescribed impracti-
cable laws, forgetting the real man. To man as he
is, to the free moral agent, the citlzen of the
kingdom of heaven, the Decalogue teaches a complete system of ethics.

POLITICS.

These outlines of theology and ethics contain the
germs of theocratic politics. If all men are born
equal, free and with the consciousness of duty, then
none is entitled to govern and none is born to obey.
The misunderstanding of human nature and trans-
cendental speculations on the essence of the Deity
brought God and man so far apart that priests and
saints had to be invented to intervene. Likewise
in politics it was held that man could not govern

and protect himself. God had to delegate tyrants and despots, "by the grace of God," to govern his helpless creatures. In Jewish ethics, however, man is the image of God, hence, as respects politics, Judaism says, God alone is the king, "Thou shalt have no others gods before me." Though the Jews placed kings over themselves, they revolted often enough. God is king; this implies not only democracy, but also the reign of absolute justice, not only as far as the earth is concerned, but also with regard to the kingdom of heaven on earth. Nobody has the right to govern another; but neither has anyone the right to legislate for others. Absolute justice is king, supreme and sovereign. The mandates of the king are incarnations of principles which have their point in absolute justice. No man, and no body of men can make them; they rest in reason and conscience; they are announced in the Decalogue. They may be expounded to meet emergencies and applied to existing circumstances; but every other kind of legislation is unwarranted and an assumption of unsanctioned authority. As long as there are rulers, men are slaves; as long as there are laws contrary to the principles of absolute justice, men will be wicked. It is the duty of a theocratic government to protect the people, that it be not misgoverned, but that it govern itself, so that true justice reign and nothing impede the free development of human nature. It is the duty of a theocratic legislature to expound the laws of eternal justice and reduce them to general formulas for practical purposes. It is the duty of the citizen in the kingdom of heaven to obey God, in strict compliance with the dicta of his reason and his conscience. " I, Jehovah, am thy God," is the first principle in theology ; the first in ethics, for he is thy God, because thou art his image ; and the ffrst in politics, for God is king. So theology, ethics and politics are in· separable in theocracy. This is Judaism. Nothing can be added, nothing be taken away without disturbing the harmony.

You expected me to set forth only the outlines of Judaism, no evidence, no application, no illustration, therefore I am done. If I add that this is the kingdom of heaven which Jesus of Nazareth preached, if I add that in the estimation of Jesus of Nazareth the Jews are the best Christians, you may not agree with me. If I should venture the assertion, of which, like the prophets of old, I am morally certain, that *this is the religion of coming generations*, my boldness might shock you. But I may say this : The happiness of mankind depends on no creed and on no book. It depends on the dominion of truth, which is the redeemer, the savior and the messiah. I understand that the attainment of truth is the object of the Free Religious Association, therefore I am a member of it and will support it as long as honest search for truth shall be its guiding star.

THE APOLOGETICS OF JUDAISM.

(1887.)

When we use the term "apology" in explanation of a neglect of etiquette, we do not employ the expression in its primary meaning. Its original signification is a word or treatise of defense and vindication. Plato and Xenophon wrote "An Apology of Socrates" without having the remotest intention of offering an excuse for what their venerated master did or said. Their object was to refute false accusations and to indorse the doctrines of Socrates. We use the term apology here in this, its primary sense.

During the early centuries the votaries of Christianity were frequently assailed by persons of other religions; its doctrines were contradicted by scriptural or philosophical arguments. That was the time when the defenders of Christianity wrote apologies, some of which are extant in the Christian patristic literature, and contain also vindications of purely Jewish tenets. After the fourth century apologetic writing became extinct in Christendom and crude attacks on Judaism, Mohammedanism, atheism, skepticism and free thought took its place till after the Reformation, when literature assumed a more scientific character. Then that kind of literature was given the general name of apologetics, and it became a branch of Christian theology. This literature increased considerably in our century, especially after David Friedrick Strauss had written his "Leben Jesu" and "Die Christliche Glaubenslehre."

The apologetics of Judaism begins with the last book of the Bible. The book of the Prophet Malachi is, perhaps, more polemical than apologetic; still it contains the main point of which the authors of the Book of Job and Koheleth (Ecclesiastes) treat. Job discussed the question of true righteousness and the justice of Providence, and Koheleth defends religion and revealed doctrines against the current skepticism of his days. In the apocrypha of the Old Testament the wisdom of Solomon might be called apologetic; it defends the doctrines of Judaism indirectly. Josephus' "Contra Apion" and Philo's report of the embassy to Caligula are historical apologies rather than polemics. In the Mishna, Talmud and Midrash quite an amount of polemic literature is preserved, but no attempt at apologetics is extant. Judaism appeared so self-evident to those ancient teachers that any apology of its tenets appeared superfluous to them.

After the revival of letters among the Arabs, classical, philosophical and scientific studies had become general, and in consequence of this intellectual revival, skeptics increased in numbers and influence. Traditionalists were compelled to write apologies in defense of the Koran. The Jews, too, began to produce apologetic literature in behalf of Judaism. The Gaon Saadia of Fayyum, who lived during the first half of the tenth century, is the oldest writer from whose pen a book of that kind is extant. His Emunoth ve-Deoth, of which we now possess also the Arabic original, is perhaps more polemical than apologetic; he argues against philosophical skeptics as well as against Christianity and Mohammedianism, still his object is apologetic; he defends Judaism, wards off attacks and establishes his own tenets. The Jewish-Arabic literature after Saadia, despite its opulence in philosophy and poetry, science and theology, has only two eminent apologists, Judah Halevi, the eminent poet, in his "al-Chazari," a book of dialogues between the King of the Chasars and a Jewish savant, and Moses Maimonides, whose Moreh Nebuchim is entirely apologetic.

After Maimonides only three Hebrew writers belong to this class, viz., Leon de Banolas (רלב״ג), author of Milchamoth Hashem; Joseph Albo, the author of Sepher Ikkarim; and Isaac Abarbanel, among whose numerous works Rosh Amanah, Atereth Zekenim, Miphaloth Elohim and Mashmia Yeshuah are purely apologetic. With them the fifteenth century closes, and the medieval time begins for the Jews. It is a long night, interrupted only by Menasseh ben Israel, Baruch Spinoza and others in Holland; Azariah dei Rossi, Judah di Modena and the Del Medigos in Italy and Candia; David Gans and a few others in Austria, and the few forerunners of Moses Mendelssohn in Germany.

Moses Mendelssohn reopened this kind of literature with three of his books, viz., Phaedon, Jerusalem and Morgenstunden. In the latter he attempts to give the evidence for the existence of Deity; in Phaedon he seeks to establish the doctrine of immortality of the soul, and in Jerusalem he defends the dogmatics of Judaism. His followers were few.

Besides S. Formstecher (Die Religion des Geistes), Samuel Hirsch (Die Religionsphilosophie der Juden), Nachman Krochmal (Moreh Nebuche Hazzeman), S. L. Steinheim (Die Glaubenslehre der Synagoge als exacte Wissenschaft), Ludwig Philipson (Die Israelitische Religionslehre), Luzzato, Benamozegh and Gruenebaum on the ethics of Judaism.

Why are there so few apologetic writers? There are several causes :

1. The Jew considered Judaism impregnable, built upon the highest philosophical and most profound ethical thoughts which man is capable of entertaining, and looked with disdain upon every attack made upon it or accusation advanced against it. They appeared to him as waging war against common sense. This needs no self-defense and no apology.

2. Apologetic writings demand systematic, philosophical study, logical or *a priori* evidence, historical and comparative researches, and the Jew, except in the Arabic-Spanish period and the modern Germanic period (Philo among the ancients and Baruch Spinoza excepted), never was a scholastic philosopher; his mind does not submit to formulas, methods and technicalities of any school philosophy. He moved energetically in the sphere of common sense, but there he stopped.

3. Ever since the fourth Christian century it was next to an impossibility for the Jew to defend his religion properly. Among all the wrongs inflicted upon him was also the humiliation imposed on his religious beliefs. It was deemed indispensably necessary and indisputable in Christendom that

Christianity is the whole religious truth, and Judaism or any other religious beliefs or philosophical conviction must be absolutely wrong. The same was the case in all Mohammedan countries, and there was no such a thing as a free country prior to 1776. There is to-day no land in the civilized world where the Jew, or any other man not holding the popular belief, dare give full and honest expression to his dissenting religious views without being punished for it. He would be ostracised and belittled by bigots and fanatics. The punishment might be corporeal—the prison—but formerly it was the torture-chamber or the funeral-pyre; these were the arguments; now it is the cry of heresy, of demoralization, that is raised at the heels of the Jew as well as of the skeptic, atheist or infidel.

The Jew could hardly think of defending his faith, as the defense would imply attack upon the faith of others. Such attack, direct or indirect, was punished with torture and pyre, and is punished still with ostracism. The best the Jew could do for his protection was to keep silent, and so he did. Only in Mohammedan countries could he speak freely of the superiority of Judaism to Christianity, and he did; in Christian countries he might have spoken freely of the superiority of Judaism to the Islam, but there was very little philosophical writing in Christendom prior to the seventeenth century. Besides, the Jew was so discouraged by oppression that he could not muster the boldness necessary to express himself on such matters.

4. In the nineteenth century the Jew is no less cautious; though he is a citizen of the world,

he does not like to offend his neighbors. He wishes consideration for himself, and feels under obligation to bestow similar considerateness upon others. Therefore, he does not yet feel quite at liberty to speak out freely. This is a kind of unmanly weakness, and perhaps even treason to his religion—surely a restraint upon his best convictions. Prudence may dictate such caution for the sake of mutual good understanding and peace ; but, after all, it is a truce.

Many of our modern Jewish scholars since the time of the scientific revival have been drawn away from Judaism and its philosophy. They seek their reputation, along with their livelihood, in science and art, in financial and commercial pursuits, and cannot reserve much attention from these for the problems of religion. Rabbis are interested in history, archeology and philology ; they preach practical sermons on current topics and cultivate as much theology and philosophy as is absolutely necessary. They are thus alienated from studies and from the zeal requisite for a thorough apologetics of Judaism.

And yet it appears that this is the time when Judaism can arise from lethargy and can establish its claim as the universal religion. It has been the mother of all religions, it has nurtured the religious ideas. This it seems to me is the opportune time and occasion for a comparison of the ideals of Judaism with the pretensions of the world. Thousands will be glad to hear the honest truth. Before the majesty of truth we may abandon all ungenerous considerations.

The only thing that may make us hesitate is the question, "Are we able to do it? Can we do justice to this important problem?" But this can be decided by an intelligent community ; and that it may be enabled to decide we must submit the matter clearly. We may begin, then, upon an "Apologetics of Judaism." It is a discipline in the theology of Judaism for us and for the public. Jointly we will be competent to solve the problem. Surely after our first effort some one will be found who can continue. He will avoid our errors, he will supply our deficiencies, and will come nearer to the truth ; but as for us, let us seek it, and announce honestly whatever is found.

APHORISMS ON ETHICS.

(1891.)

I.

That man is free and moral is presupposed by all systems of law, human and divine, for law would be ineffective if subjects were not credited with moral freedom.

It is maintained in scripture that this moral freedom is not acquired ; it is innate, for Adam and Eve obeyed and disobeyed commands of God.

Reward or punishment as the consequence of obedience or disobedience, is just only when the individual is addressed as a free moral agent. From the very beginning all nations considered it just to reward the obedient and to punish the disobedient. Scripture records a like attitude by God toward man himself. Man's moral freedom is recognized in all law, divine and human. Compulsory agencies coercing men to act contrary to law, divine or human, are contrary to the facts of human nature ; therefore, without validity.

Responsibility is the necessary consequence of this freedom. Man is responsible for his commissions and omissions toward himself, toward his fellowmen and toward his God.

Conscience is undeliberate reason, it has the intuitive discernment that the right and the good are the right and the good and ought to be done, and that the opposite of these ought to be shunned because they are wrong and evil. Conscious reason defines the right and good and their opposites. Conscience comprises the sense of duty, the satisfaction in its performance and the regret in its violation. It is man's own tribunal, which calls him to account, approves or disapproves. The first fratricide in scripture exclaimed, "My iniquity is too great to bear," and iniquity implies the effort to commit wrong, and also the consciousness of wrong as a crime.

Man is a member of society, his doings and omissions concern society, as much and more than they concern himself ; he is accountable to society. The human family is part of God's creation, the individual and society are equally accountable to the Creator. His laws preserve this world, and every violation of these laws is an attempt at destruction ; every violation of the laws of society is an attempt to destroy it. The right and good preserve whatever wrong and evil destroy.

That which is right and good in commission or omission may be called moral, and the opposite of these is immoral. All men, however, are moral by nature.

The immoral by nature is an abnormality or it is the product of corruption. This is scriptural doctrine. Adam and Eve did not violate God's commandment of their own free will ; it was the persuasion of the serpent beguiling Eve which led Adam to transgression.

Morality is a system of definitions as to the right and the good and their opposites. They are the product of reason and are, therefore, capable of instruction. The child, although moral by birth, is unconscious of morality, and it becomes consciously moral in the same progressive manner as it becomes intelligent. Morality conditions the existence of society and the life of the individual within it, it must accordingly be taught effectually. Consisting of rules of action, it ought to be taught by practice till each rule or law becomes lodged in the consciousness and becomes a habit. This, however, is impossible for the teacher in his limited sphere of influence, and it is the office of the religious educator to establish what is the moral duty of man.

It is the duty of every one to get to know himself, for self-consciousness is the supreme fact of life; to know what his relations and his duties to his fellow-man and to his Maker are. This self-knowledge embraces the recognition of our faults and shortcomings and the desire to overcome them. This is moral self-training. An earnest person must strive to become wiser and better with every passing day. The daily improvements shall grow virtuous habit. This is self-culture.

He that knows himself, his relations and duties to his fellow-man and to his Maker, and has overcome the faults and shortcomings of his nature is, in the language of scripture, holy. Holiness is the highest degree of moral life. In a holy person virtue has become constant.

The contents of the science of morality consist in definitions of what is right and good and what is otherwise. Morality will always have to be inculcated for the majority in every generation is immature, and their reason is not adequately developed.

When a definition of a moral fact has obtained the consent of the best of men, it becomes a moral law ; and when it has obtained the consent of a commnnity, it becomes public law.   Such moral laws and public laws constitute the foundation of ethics.

But this is the weak feature of ethics.   There exists no fixed and final authority for moral or public law. "The consent of the best class of men," or "the consent of a community, or of the majority in it," are indefinite conceptions.   In the early days of humanity definitions of morality were accepted as facts of superhuman reason, as revelations, as messages of inspired men.   This gave them recognizable authority.   Revelation is the only authority of ethics now, as it was then ; every other basis is inadequate for the superstructure.

We acknowledge but one revelation as genuine— the Torah.   It is the paramount duty of conscientious Israelites to learn from the Torah to know ourselves, our relations and duties to our fellow-men and to our Maker, and to teach these constantly and diligently.   If, understanding our own, and comparing it impartially with ethics constructed upon another basis, we should find ours inferior, we are obligated to learn the better from others.   But if ours is proven to be superior, the duty would devolve upon us to teach that.   This is the plan of the investigation which we would urge.

II.

The most reliable commentaries of the Torah are two books especially, viz.:

Psalms, which expounds the theology of Moses in the most beautiful and most convincing form, in more effective manner than philosophical or scientific treatises have done; and

Proverbs, which expounds the ethics of Moses clearly and directly, in a form almost childlike, addressed to "my son," *i. e.*, to intelligent youth, still not unprofound in spirit.

None can speak intelligently of the ethics of our Torah without referring to Proverbs (rules of prudence, too, are part of the moral code). Let us read but four verses of the second chapter:

"My son, if thou wouldst but accept my words, and treasure up my commandments with thee:

To let thy ear listen unto wisdom: (if) thou wouldst incline thy heart to understanding.

For if thou wilt call after intelligence; if after understanding thou wilt lift up thy voice;

If thou wilt seek her as silver, and search for her as for hidden treasures."

Here are two statements given of the moral life; the first is subjective and the other objective, and together they sum up the good which morality has in its keeping.

This is also the proper division of morality; it is ideal or subjective, and real or objective. Both these elements are laid down *eo ipso* at the very beginning of the Mosaic account; they are expanded in the book and unfold, as it were, the logical phases of the principle.

Matter and its forces, we are told in the first chapter of Genesis, were created in the beginning ("bara," create.) This matter and force produced all differentiated substances, but could not produce animal life ; and God created again the differentiated individual beings. These elementary creatures had no power of producing intellectual personality, and the third creation was necessary—human mind, soul, spirit, intellectual force (at this instance the third "bara" occurs in the text). God created not the body of man (it expressly states), but the spirit of man did he give to the body of clay (Genesis, i, 27, and ii, 7). God blessed (we are told there) only the animal (verse 22) and man (verse 28), and blessed naught else. However we may interpret these blessings—as a power, impulse, instinct, conscious or unconscious capacity—the several accounts outline fully the moral dignity of man. The sense of duty, conscience, the consciousness of the right and of the good—this impulse to do it and to shun its reverse—is innate in man, it is a capacity of the "soul of life," the צלם אלהים, the "image of God," which the Almighty himself created to transform a body of clay into a personality.

The moral principle is not something acquired, something produced by reason and experience. Kant's Categoric Imperative, we may say, was where the first man opened his eyes. When, then, we read in the same chapter (ii, 16), "God commanded" על האדם "upon Adam," we can easily interpret this "upon" as intimating that the commandment was additional to the consciousness of man. A commandment presupposes a moral significance. Commandments in their totality constitute the moral code ; they may be amended along with the progress of reason by the accumulation of experience ; the legislation of Moses itself offers the proof for that ; it owes its existence to moral truths inherent in human nature.

So much for the principle, and now a few words as to the two sides of it : the ideal or subjective, and the real or objective. The ideal morality of Moses, defined in Proverbs, was beautifully formulated by Rabbi Akiba eighteen hundred years ago. He said (Aboth, iii, 14), " Beloved is man (Adam) for he was created in the image (of God). It is superior love to have made him conscious that he was born in that image, as said (in Holy Writ) that He made man in the image of God."

In this resides ideal morality. It is the consciousness of man that he is the supreme being on this earth, the only one created in the image of God, the only moral and intellectual being on earth. He is the reflex of the eternal Deity ; little lower than God on earth, crowned with honor and glory, as David said (Psalm viii). With this consciousness, Adam found no " helpmate," not one like himself in the beautiful population of Eden ; he named the animals, but none could name him, he was alone in the primeval world.

In this sublime consciousness which distinguishes man lies the first law of nature—self-preservation. The Self, the Ego, is human ; to preserve himself, man must maintain the consciousness that he is the image of God. This Moses refers to when he speaks of the special blessing which was bestowed on man. In this preservation of the human self lies ideal or subjective morality. Upon this rock Moses builds the most complete system of ideal morality known to man.

He tells you first what God is whose image you are. He is "merciful, beneficent, long-suffering, abundant in grace and truth" (Exodus, xxxiv, 6), and these are the various elements of his sublime love. "He is holy," that is, he is the highest degree of purity and virtue, free from that which is repugnant to truth and justice. He tells you God is the highest wisdom, justice, truth and faithfulness ; the highest ideal of perfection which man can conceive.

Then he tells you that since these are the attributes of God, of whom you are the image, it follows of necessity that you possess the capacity to attain similar qualities. This is the point of self-preservation, viz.: the consciousness that you are the image of your Maker. In this development of yourself, in all the changes which you undergo from the cradle to the grave, you can preserve this consciousness only if your capacities grow by steady practice. You look to the highest ideal of which you are capable, as David says: "I have put God before my eyes continually, because he is at my right hand I cannot be moved from the right path." Therefore, Moses commands: "Ye shall be holy, for I, the Lord your God, am holy." "And ye shall sanctify yourselves and become holy, for I, the Lord your God, am holy." Then again, "Ye shall be perfect

with the Lord your God," and also, "Ye shall
walk after the Lord your God," which the Talmud
already explained, "as God is merciful so shall ye
be, as God is beneficent, so ye shall be ; emulate his
moral attributes." Thus the consciousness of the
god-likeness of man prevails ; this is the preservation of his Self, and this is the highest reach of ideal
morality. No man can do more than approximate
the ideal of perfection. No system of morality or
ethics can propose higher aims ; none ever did, none
ever will.

Thus Moses places man above the position which
was ever assigned to him by philosophy and science,
and demands equality for all human beings before
God ; demands that the self-respect of none be discouraged, not even of the needy, the helpless and
the unprotected, and puts the criminal also under
the ægis of the law. We shall discuss this under
the head of objective morality. Here we would
call attention to the character of Bible morality and
the history of Israel that verifies it. If it must be
admitted that these biblical characters are superior
to all we know of, it must also be admitted that this
moral system is the highest known to man, a powerful educator of a race.

III.

Ethics is also objective. It refers to the action
of man toward himself, toward man and toward
other animate beings. "Love thy neighbor as thyself" is the highest moral law. It was announced
not only by Moses, who uttered it first, but also by
Hillel, who formulated it as the so-called Golden

Rule. It is found also in the Analects of Confucius and in the book of Tobit, and later on it was re-stated by Rabbi Akiba, who declared it the "כלל גרול בתורה," "the fundamental principle of the law," as far, namely, as the moral law is concerned. This ethical formula also makes the "Thyself" the standard, *i. e.*, none can do more or better for his fellow-creatures than to do to them what he would under like circumstances do unto himself. As a moral agent he is subjective first, before he is in his motives purely subjective. Real morality depends on ideal morality, as the moral value of any deed is commensurate to its motive. The purity of motives in all doings and omissions of the individual, called in German "Lauterkeit der Gesinnung," and in Hebrew "Moreh Shamayim," or also "Leshem Shomayim," with us ideal or subjective morality, is the *conditio sine qua non* of all ethics and the ultimate of self-restraint, self-culture, and the preservation of self. Any person that acts from impure or selfish motives is no moral man; however useful or beneficial what he does or does not may be to others or to himself, he stands in need of moral culture and moral training. An honest man's criterion of moral motives is based upon self-knowledge. "Do I do, desire or wish, do I long, yearn or hope for this or that from pure and unselfish motives?" is the main question in the examination of self.

This ideal morality is of necessity neglected by utilitarians and evolutionists. Systems of ethics, however, which are built up geometrically or artistically (see Spinoza's Ethics), are by no means necessarily moral.

According to this aspect, Moses proceeds to lay down the fundamental principle of real or objective ethics thus : God blessed the animal creation (Genesis, 1, 22), "be fruitful and multiply," etc., which consecrates the instinct of self-preservation and therefore of the race, and man's regard for animate creatures. Then he reeords (i, 27) the superiority of man over all other creatures. He is created in the image of God. Then (i, 28) he records that God bestowed his blessing on man, and repeats this in the covenant with Noah (Genesis, ix, i). The second blessing contains much more than the first ; it contains in the briefest terms the declaration that man is moral.

The blessing bestowed on man, like that bestowed on the animals, declares, "be fruitful and multiply," but adds, "and fill the earth." Man is a cosmopolitan being, he can prosper in all zones and climes. Man, despite his weaknesses, in contrast with animals, will fill and populate the earth.

"Be fruitful and multiply" was understood already by the ancient rabbis to be the first commandment of the Law, viz.: the race was to be preserved ; every individual, being part of the race, has a part in this common obligation. We may now look upon the conditions expressed in that blessing. These are expressed in two Hebrew words, "subdue her (the earth) and have dominion" over fish, bird and beast. The preservation of the human race and the individual, the distribution over the earth, depend on certain conditions.

The prosperity and happiness of each and all, as well as life and health, will always be commensurate with the fulfillment of these conditions. In these two words is implied the fundamental principle of real morality.

In order to subdue the earth and to have dominion over animate beings, the first requisite is labor; hence it is man's duty to work, to perform such tasks as shall give man dominion over the earth, its elements and forces. This comprises useful labor, physical and mental, secular and spiritual, labor productive of the means of preservation. It is moral to work. It is immoral to do nothing, to be a parasite. Adam was placed in the Garden of Eden, not to enjoy the luxuries of *dolce far niente*, but "to till it and to keep it." God himself worked, he says (Genesis, ii, 2), and when He had finished, the earth was for man to work on. "Six days shalt thou labor and do all thy work" is a paragraph in the constitution of humanity; it is necessary for the health and happiness of the individual, the preservation and the progress of the race. The patriarchs labor, and Solomon apotheosizes labor; so does the Psalmist, who says (cxxviii, 2): "If thou wilt eat the labor of thy hands thou shalt be happy, and it shall be well with thee." The ancient rabbis say this means happiness in this life and well-being in life eternal. The Mosaic code is chiefly a regulation of labor; the very worship of God is connected with labor, and the injunction of rest is for the further effectfulness of labor (Leviticus, xxvi, 34 and 43). The Hebrews were an industrious people in a small and mountainous country ; their commerce was not extensive and their chief occupation was agriculture.

The religious documents of old, the New Testament, the Koran and the sacred books of the East give no similar law of sturdy morality. Modern literature and modern ethics do not inculcate it with equal preciseness. Moses alone gives it consecrated significance. Labor and slavery are synonymous in many places, idleness a divine boon, "Nirvana" felicity on earth and bliss in heaven.

IV.

When we speak of moral law, we designate two different subjects, and we may mean either of them, viz.: 1. The innate moral principle, the quality of the human mind known as conscience or the sense of duty. It necessitates a man to acknowledge and to do that which is good and right, and on account of its obligatory character it is called a law. 2. The definitions of reason as to what special sentiments, desires, doings and omissions are moral or immoral, are called moral laws; but on the whole, moral law as a product of reason, has no compulsory force ; therefore, men in various periods of history and under different circumstances agree as to the first, but disagree as to the second kind of moral law. Every man has a conscience, but not all agree in the interpretation of the dicta of conscience.

History furnishes numerous illustrations of this. We select from the Talmud : Two friends travel together and lose their way in the wilderness. One of them carries the scanty provisions, which are sufficient for both for but one day ; they cannot, however, reach the end of the wilderness in less than two or three days. Should they share their provisions and both perish, or shall one keep the food for himself, and abandon his friend, to save his own life? Here evidently we have a conflict between conscience and reason ; and yet the two learned and scrupulous rabbis disagree on this moral question, viz., whether self-preservation takes precedence. Yet both rabbis are equally men of exacting righteousness.

This disagreement is universal ; there exists no fixed standard of morality. However, the con- science of man and the well-being of society, the government of the state and the peaceable inter- course between nations, demand imperiously a fixed standard, defining what is right and good and what is not. The civilized world agrees, in the main at least, on the authority of revelation ; this is the basis of ethics. It is called the divine law, and is deferred to because it is divine. It is re- jected in part or in whole by those who deny the divinity of absolute law, as the anarchists, nihilists, communists, advocates of free love and common property.

We may remark here, in parenthesis, that all those who argue against inspiration and revelation forget that they argue against the moral foundation of society. This has no other common standard of right and wrong, and it accepts it only because it believes it to be divine. In fact, there exists no other reason to enforce its universal acceptance.

The common standard of morality was raised by

Moses. It is the voice of God, as it was interpreted
by Moses in the five books which we call the
Torah. It has been adopted in part or in whole
by all civilized nations. It is agreed that the
Mosaic definitions of what is right and good and
what is the reverse emanate from a reason higher
than man's, and they must, therefore, be accepted
by all men. History proves this. As the historical books of the canon record the historical evidence
that the dispersion of Israel was the consequence
of a departure from the divine standard, so the history of the modern nations offers the undoubted
evidence that all their sufferings, failures, woes and
miseries are traceable to a departure from that
standard of morality. Nay, according to the degree of the neglect of it was the misery. For instance, the miseries that came upon the French
people at the time of the French Revolution were a
retribution for the willful abandonment of the divine
law of right. Again, to speak frankly as well as
boldly, our nation had to pass through the great
ordeal of the Civil War because we had ignored and
violated the law of God—his justice, which none
can ignore or violate with impunity.

It is difficult to argue our thesis against the as-
sumptions of popular theology. Cardinal Manning
has said (Nineteenth Century, p. 876): "It is indeed true, that we are not bound by a divine enactment to give a tithe of all we possess. That wise
and expedient law was abolished by the higher law
which has created the Christian world. We are free
from the law of Israel, but we are not free from a

more perfect, searching, constraining and even temporary law, which is the law of liberty.'' This sounds like sarcasm.   There is a mass of irresponsible wealth in the world, there is the poverty and degradation among millions.   The law of liberty is not sufficient.   Dogmatists may sit at the loom and weave creeds, they may declare the law of Moses abrogated, but after all £700,000,000 are in the hands of responsible men, while next door to them are millions of miserable paupers.   The law of tithes, as ordained by Moses was never charged with the like condition.

Nations cannot be educated by abstraction, by the abstract law of liberty.   Nations consist of a majority of immature persons, the ripe and strong-minded are in the minority.   The first must be trained by concrete provisions ; institutions embody the principles of morality.   But the Mosaic dispensation represents these eminently.

The Israelites observed the law of tithe for fifteen centuries ; it became so forceful with them, that now philanthropists must admire the munificence and the efficiency of Jewish charities.   Concrete law and a forethoughtful institution has educative power and makes for virtue, the law of liberty has not.   So also the abstinence, the frugality, the energy of the Jew are deducible from the discipline of Mosaism.   The law of liberty cannot replace the law of Moses.

Take another example.   The laws of Moses, starting with the standard laid down in the first chapter of Genesis (which we have discussed above), declare emphatically for personal liberty and for equality in

civil law of all persons before God (Exodus, xii, 49 ;
Numbers, xv, 15, .16).   No privileges are granted,
not even to the priesthood, no person is exempt
from duty—the king no more than the laborer.
The educational effect of this training is visible in
the character of even the modern Israelite in all
parts of the civilized world—he is a citizen who
loves freedom and justice. For eighteen centuries
liberty has been agitated, but the majority of mankind is still enslaved and degraded ; princes, priests
and castes live on the labor of the disfranchised.
It took England and Holland many centuries to
emancipate their kin.   It took France still longer
to avail itself of the Mosaic doctrine of liberty,
fraternity and equality.   It is but a few years since
the serfs of Russia, the negro slaves of America,
the peasants of Austria and Hungary were emancipated.

Moses commanded, "Thou shalt love the stranger," extended to him the boon of charity, placed
him under the protection of the law and gave him
an equal standing with the rest ; under the law of
liberty, thousands were driven out from Protestant
Prussia during the last decade, and millions are
persecuted in Christian Russia and Roumania.
What of the vaunted doctrine of liberty ?

Moses commanded (Deuteronomy, xxiii, 16, 17),
"Thou shalt not deliver unto his master the servant which is escaped from his master unto thee ; "
and we, under the benign protection of liberty,
maintained till a few years ago the notorious fugitive slave law. Then the law continues : "He
(the fugitive slave, even) shall dwell with thee,

even among you, in that place which he shall
choose in one of the gates, where it liketh him
best; thou shalt not oppress him;'' but by the
doctrine of liberty every peasant in Germany, Austria and France, and every serf in Poland and
Russia, was restricted to his soil as a dog is held to
his chain, and the Jews of Russia and Poland are
driven from their homes and the places of their
birth. The law of liberty is a failure. Moses
commanded, '' Thou shalt love thy neighbor as thyself '' (Leviticus, xix, 18). No room is left for individual whim or passion. He first declares what
shall not be done to the neighbor (ibid, verses 11–
18), and then what shall be done to him. Hillel
understood it so, and so it is practicable.

We need go no further to prove our thesis. Miseries originated when the nations departed from the
Mosaic standard of morality. Statesmen in our
days begin to see this and to acknowledge it. This
is the universal standard ; it comes from a source
higher than the human intellect. It is acknowledged as the universal standard, because it is divine. Revelation is the foundation of mankind's
standard of morality. The answers as to what is
good and what is right Moses gives distinctly. We
shall now begin to discuss ''the moral laws'' laid
down by him.

V.

The main doctrine of ethics commands the preservation of the human race. Preservation implies
growth. The race is constituted of individuals, the
preservation of the race is achieved by the conserva-

tion of individuals. Whatever shortens the life of the individual, or deprives him of the means of sustenance, or diminishes his capacity, affects the race, and is a violation of its absolute law. On the other hand, whatever prolongs or protects the life, health and happiness of an individual, is consonant with the best interests of the race, and is obligatory by the law of social as well as personal righteousness. The rabbis maintained :

"Whoever saves (the life of) one person has done as much as though he had fulfilled the entire law;" for the maintenance of the race depends on the preservation of the individuals that constitute it. You cannot preserve the race or the individual without preserving the characteristic Self, the intellectual and spiritual quality inherent in the self, which is the mark of the man. So also the progress of the intellectual and spiritual qualities of man are the *conditio sine qua non* for the individual and for the race, according to Moses. The Creator bestowed on man the blessing " to fill the earth," *i. e.*, to increase steadily and not cease on earth. He pointed out the adequate means for perpetual existence, viz.: the subduing of the earth and holding dominion over animate beings. This dominion can be attained by labor alone. As we have maintained before, the effort to subdue the earth and to hold dominion over animate creatures, comprises the first category of man's duties. " It is moral to work, and immoral to do nothing." Inasmuch, however, as it is labor only which achieves the prescribed ultimate, it must be labor guided by the human Self, consequently the progress of the race is achieved through the advancement of individuals. This is the second category of man's duties.

Man is disposed to labor by his constitution. But he feels an aversion to forced and unremunerative labor. God punished Adam with that, "in the sweat of thy brow shalt thou eat bread."

But self-control and the zest for invention overcome the distaste for even this kind of labor. One of the sages of the Talmud speaks of this. He points out how many different kinds of work the first man must have done before be obtained a morsel of bread to eat or a garment to cover his body, "but now I find all these things prepared for me when I rise in the morning." Human ingenuity contrived instruments and implements (whatever you can lay your hand on is man's invention), but before these labor was exhausting and hard. In our century especially through steam and electricity, and mechanical inventions, discoveries in physics and chemistry, labor has been materially reduced.

The preservation of the human race involves also means for protection against the elements, against degenerate members of the race (who have their prototype in Cain), protection also against depravity, aggravated by ambition ; protection of life, property and honor. All this is done in the organization of society, by intellectual labor, by the establishment of civil order, by government, by international treaties, through courts of justice, through penal laws and the suppression of crime, and by the reformation of criminals, in short, by the various agencies of the people to enforce the law, and to maintain peace. The human race is assisted in subduing the earth and holding dominion over it, as that Rabbi of old wisely said : "Pray for the well-being of the government, for if it were not for its authority one would swallow the other alive." As a concrete example, let me cite the Constitution of the United States, and the amelioration it has afforded the millions. You will appreciate very readily the high value of intellectual effect.

The second, though not subordinate, category of ethical duty is comprised in the doctrine that we must protect, and help along the human family in its intellectual progress.

On these two fundamental doctrines Moses, and after him the Prophets, and after them their ex- pounders, constructed Jewish ethics, viz.: *Labor and intellectual progress.* As regards labor we have quoted Moses before. In regard to intellectual pro- gress you must consider that Moses said : "Would that all the people of the Lord were prophets, and that the Lord would put his spirit upon them." "Prophet" signifies a man of the highest intellec- tual culture. So God is reported to have told him that all Israel should become a kingdom of priests, every one a priest. "Priest" signifies a man of the highest and purest moral force. The priests of Egypt were the savants. The uncompromising resistance Moses made against idolatry was based upon the idea that paganism retards intellectual progress, and history proves this to be true. Under corruptive influences man deteriorates. The Mosaic organization of state and society, its laws and insti- tutions, are the precipitate of the highest intelligence and, without any exception, obviously devised to advance the mind and bring it to the highest it can attain.

Moses, speaking of his laws and institutions, exclaims, therefore, "This is your wisdom and intelligence in the eyes of the nations." History has indeed no counterpart to such an enlightened dispensation.

VI.

Instruction, practice and experience perfect in man his natural qualifications alone. What man has established and invented in the history of civilization is no more and no less than the realization of his latent and natural capacities, a rise out of the unconscious into the sphere of consciousness. In the light of the reality of human achievement, we may judge what is natural and a gift of God.

We may maintain that the social instinct is one of these qualifications man has had from the beginning. From the beginning and all along men have been engaged in perfecting association and organization. From the very first day man felt "it is not good to be alone."

The moral principle is the *conditio sine qua non* of society. It has realized itself in laws and institutions, and without it organization would have been impossible, for man would have continued the primeval conflict and intensified it. Obedience to the moral law is necessary for the maintenance of the social equlibrium, even as it is necessary for the maintenance of human nature. Disobedience to law destroys society and manhood. This explains

the pleasure which follows the doing of the good,
and the remorse which comes after sin.

So also as to the spiritual side of human nature.
We define this as the instinct which leads man to
seek an object for veneration and worship, and in-
duces him to set up ideals. It is the religious sense,
and like the moral law and the desire for association,
it is the source out of which doctrines, dogmas and
forms of religious practice rise. In all ages of history man has been engaged in forming and reforming gods, in establishing creeds and institutions that
have their spirit. Theories as to morals and as to
religion have been made to conform to the aspiration
of society.

It must be correct, therefore, to maintain that
the moral, intellectual and spiritual qualities of the
soul—of that personality which Scripture calls
נשמת חיים "the spirit of life"—are aspects of the
same fact. The moral aspect manifests itself as will ;
the intellectual as judgment, and the spiritual as aspiration. The preservation of this self demands
that these three qualities co-operate harmoniously.
Whatever is necessary for the self-preservation of the
individual man is indispensable for the preservation
of the human family. The third category of the
moral law, therefore, directs itself to preserve the
integration of the moral, intellectual and spiritual
life of the race and the individual. These three
categories, which we have mentioned before, viz.,
labor, intellect, and the harmony of the soul qualities, constitute the foundation of the moral laws of
Moses. This is outlined in the first chapter of the

Bible : "Fill the earth and subdue it, and have dominion" over its creatures.

What do we mean by equilibrium, harmony of the soul? Man has will, and it appears as conscience—the good and right must be done because it is good and right, and evil must be eschewed because it is not good nor right. The child, as soon as it is able to conceive an abstract idea, is conscious of this law of its nature.

Reason also re-enforces, sooner or later, instruction and training. Our forefathers may have received light on moral facts by divine revelation ; but what made them accept it, and what led them to submit to it? Besides, we may ask also, what induced millions of human beings to accept the moral code, though their forefathers received no such revelation?

It is the spiritual quality of the soul, in which all human lives share, that has roused to reason and awakened the will. When the first man, in obedience to his spiritual impulse, began to conceive, however crudely, a being more perfect than he himself, reason began to vindicate itself. Man went higher and upward, he sought an ideal, he went forth to worship. It makes no difference whether fear of harm, or hope of the good, or the natural impulse of his soul moved him, he did all he did by a quality of the soul which he had in common with every other human being. The higher an individual or nation has risen in the cognition of an ideal, the loftier the ideal is ; the loftier the God-idea is, the more vigorously reason operates and the more scrupulous judgment is as to the good and right, the higher its moral standard becomes.

The intellectual and spiritual qualities are reciprocal—the more vigorous the reason, the more forceful the spirituality is. Sometimes, it must be admitted, this interaction is disturbed. The spiritual is sometimes divorced from the intellectual, and then it produces bigotry and intolerance. The wisest then degenerates. The spiritual and the intellectual must be in perfect harmony—this alone makes perfect humanity.

This harmony invigorates also the third human faculty, the will. The stronger the intellect and the more it is furthered for good by spirituality, the more competent the judgment becomes to define what is truly good and right, and the more these invigorate the will to obey what reason declares. Spiritual disposition is a power. Man without spirituality is predisposed to rebellion by the very fact of rationalism, and on the other hand, without intellectual control, he is likely to become ascetic. But " the beginning of wisdom is the fear of the Lord ;" or, as Job said, "behold, the fear of the Lord, that is wisdom, and to eschew evil, that is understanding." The spiritual lifts the soul aloft, the intellectual gives the substance, and the moral the sweetness.

VII.

The maxim *ora et labora*, " pray and work," is a transcript of the passage in Psalms (xxxvii, 3) : בטח ביהוה ועשה טוב ("Trust in the Lord and do the good "). Prayer primarily means trust in God, in His wisdom, His justice and His providence, that they encompass every human being.

What relation is there between progress in intellectuality and progress in morality? Let us consider this special point.

1. It is admitted on all hands that it is a duty of every one to contribute to the intellectual progress of the race. This duty is an important element of both subjective and objective morality. It raises man from lower to higher conditions. It moderates lower instincts and passions. It redeems humanity from many evils.

2. We have started with the axiom that conscience is an inborn quality, and we have defined it as the innate conviction that the good and right are good and right, and ought to be done simply because they are such, and that the evil must be eschewed because it is not good and not right. But reason defines and experience establishes what is good and right in any particular case, and these determinations comprise the substance of the moral law. It is, therefore, self-evident that the recognition of the moral law runs parallel with the progress of intellectuality. "The wiser the better." Examples illustrating this are numerous and plain in history, and we need not cite them. Such are the apotheosis of *Chakhmah*, "wisdom," by King Solomon, and by the author of Job, and the deified *Sophia* and *Logos* of Grecian eclectics. The word *Chakham* in Hebrew designates both one who knows clearly and one who does well.

3. It is a matter of common sense that morality depends on rationality. The ancient rabbis well maintained, "the ignorant rustic cannot be pious," simply because he does not know how. If a man commits suicide we say he was demented, that reason had lost its control over him. Rabbinical law regards the suicide as demented, unless positive evidence is produced to the contrary.

We know well enough that the maniac must be watched and protected, so as not to harm himself or others, because his reason has lost control over his passions. Crimes committed suggest lack of discretion, "the person lacks reason to comprehend the magnitude of the wrong." The ancient rabbis maintained, "No man commits a sin unless a spirit of folly overcomes him." If the lack of cognition is the cause of immorality, the increase of cognition brings progress of morality. The level of morality is equal to the level of mind. The mental states that man attains, the intellectual progress which he makes, are a contribution to man's moralization. The higher we rise intellectually, the nearer we approach the ideal of ethics.

It is true that many persons of the highest mental culture are immoral ; these, however, are the exceptions. After all, the most intellectual people are also the most virtuous, and vice and crime are prevalent among those of the lowest mental condition.

VIII.

Laws and institutions for the moral culture of the community were and always will be necessary, institutions such as the family, the church and the state. Each of these has its authoritative usages and laws, which are based either on experience, reasoning or on a divine standard. The latter alone is perfect. We claim this for the moral doctrines of Moses, as they are stated in the first chapter of Genesis. The blessing of the Creator is there bestowed on man that he will fill the earth, subdue it and have dominion over all other creatures. And this involves the duty of each and all to do that which contributes to the preservation, the growth and the moral, intellectual and spiritual development of the human race.

Inquiring into the moral system of Moses, let us ascertain the principles which underlie its institutions, of the family in the first place.

It is not only the suppression of sensuality and the sanctification of matrimony which Moses strove for, though he was the first to chasten marriage (contrast the obscene practices in vogue in ancient religions). The seventh commandment and the Pentateuchal laws allied to it are now the basis of all respectable legislation. Moses did more than this; he made the pure family the basis of the state. Fathers and mothers have authority over their children, excepting in matters involving life and death, which in all cases are referred to the legally constituted courts of justice (Deuteronomy, xxi, 18–22). Parents must support and protect their

children ; they must educate them, and further
their intellectual, moral and spiritual welfare (Exodus, xiii, 14 ; xx, 10 ; Deuteronomy, vi, 7 ; xi, 19).
Children again are in duty bound to honor (Leviticus, xix, 3) and obey their parents. Whoever
strikes or curses his parents commits a crime (Exodus, xxi, 15–17). All this is fundamental law in
Israel. Parents are the highest authority for the
child.

Upon this foundation the state is reared on the
following principles :

(a) The tribe is a family of families, and the state
is a family of tribes, obedient to the father of them
all, God ; the duties of every child to his parents
are also the duties of every person to God and the
Torah. The prophet who is the servant and messenger of God (the priest and Levite in their official capacity are messengers of the people, Leviticus, x, 8–11 ; Deuteronomy, xxxiii, 8–11) and
the interpreter of the law, and old men of learning
and probity, must be respected, because they are
the special instruments of God (Exodus, xxii, 27 ;
Leviticus, xix, 32 ; Deuteronomy, xvii, 8–13).

(b) Personal freedom is the birthright of every
person ; it extends to the family, the tribe and the
people, encompassing aliens. It follows that the
state is representative, and though it is equivalent
to centralization, it is not unlimited as to legislation, nor is its authority arbitrary. In the Mosaic
scheme of government, the tribe is a federation of
family groups, governed by a Nasi and the heads of
the families ; the state is a federation of tribes governed by the prophet and the seventy or seventy-

two elders, six from each tribe. It was "a nation and assembly of nations" whose sovereign is God. Moses found the tribes organized, and their government was indorsed by the Sinaitic legislation. It is the oldest and the most natural, a veritable *E Pluribus Unum*, the first federal government, and is surely the first that was based upon personal freedom, upon national liberty, upon equality before the law, dispensing justice to each. The Constitution of the United States is merely a modern copy of the organization of ancient Israel (even the detail which disfranchises a foreigner from the office of chief magistrate being Mosaic, Deuteronomy, xvii, 15).

(*c*) The nation is sovereign under God and under the law. "Thou shalt not add thereto nor diminish therefrom." By the decisions of the national authority, or through force of circumstances, the form of the laws may change (Deuteronomy, xvii, 8–13), but the principles remain. The nation has no power to deprive of his freedom any one except a criminal (Leviticus, xxv, 25–42). Property could not be confiscated (1 Kings, xxi), that of a rebel excepted (Numbers, xxvii, 3). The nation has no right to declare as lawful for the nation that which is interdicted for individuals. The nation may not steal, nor kill, nor violate the rights of family, it may not lie (not even in the way of diplomacy and politics), it may not enslave, nor withhold the benefits of law, just as no individual person may do it with impunity.

(*d*) None besides the lawfully constituted authorities may execute law. The flagellants, lynchers and the like are violaters of the law of God.

Judges and bailiffs are lawfully appointed and are the arms of the law.

These four points in the ethics of the Mosaic dispensation reveal the purest conceptions of justice.

While it cannot be denied that Moses admitted alien laws into his code (chiefly Egyptian), it must still be admitted that he transformed them to correspond with Mosaic principles. Wisdom dictates to a legislator that he recognize existing conditions and tolerate prevalent customs, but he must endeavor also to subordinate them to his spirit.

The Mosaic code compromised with institutions, in accommodation to existing conditions; but the Mosaic legislation had two objects in view, first to promulgate a universal religion, to establish universal ethics; and secondly to organize a nation with existing habits, customs, organization and traditions, and to train a model nation.

There are, to be sure, ordinances in the Mosaic code which would appear as contradictory to its principles—the proceedings in the conquest of Canaan, for instance, the treatment accorded to the Midianites, the slaughter in the camp after the incident of the golden calf, the punishment of the witch, and the like. Still, it must be borne in mind that contingencies require special treatment. We are speaking here of principles and not of experiences. On some other occasion we hope to treat of these apparent exceptions and contradictions to Mosaic doctrine. Here we can only point to abstract principles. These confirm our assertion that the Mosaic conception of ethics represents the highest and most universal standard of right known

to us, and that this is evidenced by the Mosaic provisions as to the family and the state.

Look upon the world's history from the standpoint of evolution, and see how far below the
Mosaic ideal legislation and morals still are, how far
below the ideal of Moses the modern world is.   We
still have autocrats, privileged and non-privileged
classes, we have barriers of separation between nation and nation, we have standing armies recruited
from the flower of youth, we have mutual distrust
among nations and men ; think of the numerous
victims of crime and of criminal passion ; there is
levity and neglect of duty.   How far behind the
humanitarian ideal of Moses the world is now !

Add to this the undoubted fact that the formation and development of character depend largely
on the influence of the state and of its institutions,
and remember how many human beings are being
neglected and crippled by the unfair conditions that
prevail.   The miseries of humanity are the consequences of the social arrangements as much as of
mischievous temper.   The sufferings and miseries
of humanity date back to man's departure from
the standard of the Mosaic revelation.   Think also
of this before you argue against inspiration and
revelation.

REFORMED JUDAISM.

(1871.)

I.

Change, universal and perpetual, is the law of laws in this universe. Still there is an element of stability, the fact of mutation itself; the law of change changes not. This law lies in the harmony of the spheres; the mystery of truth in nature's variegation; the manifestation of the wisdom of the Immutable Deity. Progress and perfectibility are the effect, and, as far as reason penetrates, the conscious aim of this cause. The geologist, as he comes away from the lowest stratum into which his researches have gone along the crust of this planet, and the historian, who returns from the study of the life of humanity from the cradle of its birth to the nineteenth century, see the chain of conscious progress in form and idea, from the lowest to the highest known to man, see the promise of perfectibility everywhere, and see permanent retrogradation nowhere. Wisdom, boundless and ineffable, and the revelations of Deity lie in this law of laws "which God hath created to do."

Therefore, Reformed Judaism, the subject of this essay, acknowledges no necessary stability of the form, but also no change of the principle. All forms change, adapting themselves to new conditions, and all changes proceed from the same principle, which is not subject to change. This is the central idea of Jewish reasoners on Judaism in the nineteenth century.

Before following this idea in its sequence, it must be understood that the term "Reformed" in connection with "Judaism," does not imply restoration to an older form ; it is intended to convey the idea of putting into a new and improved form and condition. Judaism, from this standpoint admits no retrogession, and maintains that all forms which the principle has developed and crystallized, were necessarily beneficial for each respective time or locality. But the civilization of the nineteenth century, being the sum and substance of all previout phases, has produced conditions unknown in former periods of history. Therefore, the principle of Judaism also must develop new forms corresponding to the new conditions which surround its votaries who live among the civilized nations ; forms, too, which were neither necessary nor desirable in former periods of history, and would not be such now to other Israelites, although adhering to the same principle, who live among semi-barbarous, or even less enlightened nations. Again, as civilization progresses, the principle of Judaism will always develop new forms in correspondence with every progressive state of the intelligence and consciousness, until the great day when one shepherd and one flock will unite the human family in truth, justice and love. As an illustration of this, it is to be remembered that the Israelite of the reformed school does not believe in the restoration of the ancient mode of worship by the sacrifice of animal victims and by a hereditary priesthood. He considers that phase was necessary and beneficial, in its time and locality, but that it would be void of all significance in our age when entirely different conceptions of divine worship prevail, and it would appear much more meaningless to coming generations. The divine institutions of the past are not obligatory on the present generation or on coming ages, since the conditions which rendered them necessary, desirable and beneficial have been radically changed. Therefore, Progressive Judaism would be a better designation than Reformed Judaism. But, on account of common usage, the latter term has been adopted as the caption of this essay, and should be understood in this spirit alone.

The term "principle" in this essay is intended to signify the positive truth or truths of Judaism. The "form" is the manifestation of the principle as an organism is of laws, and a mode of worship is a regulation for man's intercourse with the Deity. The sun exists apart from the light and heat it emanates. Light and heat depend on the sun's existence, but not *vice versa*. In this sense, the existence of the sun is absolute, while that of light and heat is relative. The same distinction must be made in Judaism between principle and form ; the former is considered positive, and the latter relative. That truth which depends not on man's thoughts, deeds and relations is a principle of Judaism. The principle is expressed by doctrines and the form by laws. Both terms are contained in the

Hebrew word Torah, as the law of Moses is called in the Bible.

The distinction between principle and form, doctrine and law, spirit and letter, is as old as the Bible itself (see Deut. iv, 39, 40; v, 26; vi, 13, and parallel passages; Psalm, xix, 8 to 10; Proverbs, vi, 23; Ezekiel, xliv, 24). In the biblical books which were written after the exile this distinction is also frequently expressed (II Chronicles, xiv, 3; xix, 10; xxxi, 21; and Nehemiah, ix, 13, 14). The same is the case in the post-biblical literature of the Hebrews, especially in the Talmud. But, in all those passages, we have general terms only, without logical definitions.

The ancient Hebrews were distinguished more for their inspiration and intuitive knowledge than for philosophy. The Greek philosophized on the facts of the mind, which the Hebrews uttered as self-evident truths. With the exception of the Alexandrian school, represented by the works of Philo, there is no evidence that, in the strict sense of the term, the Jews philosophized on their religious books and traditions, previous to the period of the Arabic philosophy; although it cannot be denied that the books of Ecclesiastes and Job are essays on philosophical themes.*

* For this very reason Ecclesiastes and Job appear to be post-prophetical books. As long as a people has freshness and vigor of faith and poetry, such as is exhibited in the Prophets and older Psalms, it reasons not philosophically, and has no room for skepticism. Grecian philosophy begins with the decline of mythology. The same thing precisely is the case in Christendom. Some Psalms, therefore, like xiv and liii, are also of post-prophetical origin.

The statements of Josephus against Apion (I, i, 22), and of Eusebius (Praep. Evang. i, ix, 3) concerning ancient Jewish philosophers, have not been sufficiently investigated to adopt or reject them. When the Arabs began to cultivate Grecian literature, bestowing particular attention on poetry, philosophy, mathematics and medicine, the Jews living among them also cultivated these studies. The Caraites began them and the rabbinical Jews followed. It was not till then that attempts were made to establish the principle of Judaism with logical precision. Proverbial philosophy was the favorite wit and wisdom of the ancient Hebrews, until rabbinical hermeneutics replaced it in the Occident as well as in the Orient.

The first classical figure of philosophical reflection among the dispersed Jews was Gaon Saadia ben Joseph, of Fayyum (892 to 942 A. C.). A new epoch of Jewish culture began with that man, who was master in all branches of learning known to his age, and he opened to the Jewish mind avenues of thought and research which had been closed till then. His rabbinical and liturgical works, as well as his book on the Hebrew language, cannot be mentioned here. He was the first to translate the Bible into the Arabic, with extensive notes, portions of which are extant. S. Munk published his Arabic Isaiah in Paris in 1838. Ewald and Dukes, in 1844, published Saadia's Arabic version of the Psalms and Job from an Oxford manuscript. But most important to us is Saadia as the theological philosopher, as he proved to be in his polemical books against the Caraites, in his commentary to the oldest cabalistical book, called *Sepher Yezirah*, "The Book of the Formation," and especially in his book called *Emunoth we-Deoth*, "Faith and Knowledge." He wrote this last book, and nearly all others, in Arabic. The original is in Oxford (Cod. Pococke, 148). The Hebrew translations by Juda Ibn Tibbon and Berachia ha-Nakdon, especially the former, are well known among the Jewish students, although not frequently quoted by Christian writers, because never translated into Latin or into a modern language. This is the oldest book in which the principle of Judaism is philosophically discussed and expounded. With Saadia a new ·school of Judaism begins. Rabbinical hermeneutics are no longer sole authority for the exposition of scriptures ; philology and philosophy are appealed to as the final arbiters of scriptural teachings. It may be truly maintained that the school now called Reform had its origin then and there ; because in principle, Jewish orthodoxy signifies the abiding by the results of traditional or rabbinical hermeneutics in law and doctrine, as laid down in the two Talmudim (of Jerusalem and Babylon), and especially in the latter. Again, Jewish reform signifies in principle an appeal to philosophy and science in the exposition of scriptures, especially in regard to law and doctrine.

II. From Saadia to Maimonides.

The Gaon Saadia having thrown open the gates of Judaism to scientific and philosophical studies, the combat between religion and philosophy became more general with every passing decade. A number

of philosophical books on Judaism, and critical commentaries of the Bible, partly in print and partly in
manuscript, have been handed down to posterity,
showing that repeated attempts had been made not
only to give philosophical expression to the principle
of Judaism, but also to harmonize religion and philosophy. This golden age of Jewish philosophy, beginning in Asia, migrating to Spain, and then wandering to Egypt, culminated in the great rabbinical
authority, called "*Rambam*," the famous body
physician of the Kaliph of Kairo, Moses Maimonides, called among his cotemporaries Rabbenu Moses,
son of Maimuni, the Spaniard (of Cordova). Two
centuries intervened between Saadia and Maimonides,* and these laid the foundation to Hebrew philology, Bible exegesis and to Jewish philosophy, and
on it Maimonides erected his superstructure. The
Hebrew philologists, as such, do not interest us here
especially, although they contributed to the development of Jewish theology. Whoever wishes to know
more about them, will find information in Ewald
and Dukes' "*Beitraege zur Geschichte der aeltesten
Auslegung*," etc., Stuttgart, 1844.

The two oldest philosophers after Saadia are

---

* On Saadia, see S. L. Rappoport's Biography of Saadia
in *Bikkure Ha-Ittim*, 1828; Munk, *Notice sur R. Saadia
Gaon*, Paris, 1838, and appendix to the *Commentaire de
Rabbi Tanhoum*, Paris, 1843.

The most reliable dates concerning Maimonides, quoted
in Azulai's *Maarecheth Haggedolim*, are those written by
his grandson, David, who states that Moses Maimonides was
born on the 14th day of Nissan, 1132, and died Monday
night, the 20th day of Tebeth, 1202 A. C.

Bachja ben Joseph, of Saragossa, and Solomon ben Gabirol, of Malaga, both flourishing in the eleventh century. Bachja's principal book is the *Choboth Hallebaboth* ("Duties of the Heart"), the first complete book on the ethics of Judaism. In ten main sections, each divided into an introduction and a number of chapters, Bachja gave form to the ethics of Judaism, enabling the reader to survey the field. He starts out with a treatise of the belief in one God, and closes with one on the highest virtue of man, viz., to love God. Between these two points is the compass of his system. The book was written in Arabic, translated into Hebrew, Latin, Spanish, French and German, and was published, between the years 1490 and 1856, about fifty times. No polemics and no particular leaning to any of the Grecian philosophical systems are detectable in the book. It is purely Jewish ethics, taken from Jewish sources.*

Less influential than Bachja was Solomon ben Gabirol. As a sacred poet he ranks among the princes of song. His compositions, preserved in the various liturgical collections of the Portuguese Jews, are classical. The largest poem extant is the *Kether Malchuth*, "The Royal Diadem," a metaphysical treatise on the Deity from the cosmological standpoint of that century, replete with poetical beauty, grand in sublimity of conception and simplicity of diction. Solomon ben Gabirol had a

---

* Bechai ben Asher, who wrote a commentary on the Pentateuch about 1300 A. C., was a pupil of Rabbi Solomon b. Abraham b. Adereth, of Barcelona, who was an opponent of philosophy.

mystical turn of mind, which gives a charm to his poetry and invests his philosophy with a touch of obscurity. It was this element especially which endeared him to Thomas de Aquinas and Albert the Great, who quote largely from his book, *Mekor Chayim*, "The Fountain of Life," by its Latin title, "*Fons Vitae.*" They call him Avicebron. S. Munk has established his identity with Solomon ibn Gabirol. He also wrote a book on ethics, *Tikkun Middoth Hannephesh*, "Correction of the Soul's Qualities," from which he made an abstract called *Shelosh Esreh Middoth*, "The Thirteen Rules," neither of which has become popular among Jews, although largely used by Christian theologians of the Middle Ages, and well known to his contemporaries and immediate successors.

The greatest and most important rabbi of the eleventh century was Solomon ben Isaac, of Troyes, in France, known among Jews as Rashi or Yizchaki. He wrote commentaries to the whole Bible except Chronicles (Job doubtful), and the entire Talmud, excepting a small portion, besides a number of juridical and liturgical books. No commentary has been more extensively used among Jews and Christians than that known as Rashi, or has been more frequently published and provided with more sub-commentaries. He attained the age of sixty-five (1040, to Thursday, the 29th day of Tammuz, 1105 A. c.), wrote more than any of his contemporaries, officiated as Rabbi and as head master of an academy, made extensive tours in France and Germany, and introduced rabbinical lore into those countries. He was an excellent grammarian and Hebraist, well acquainted with the works of his predecessors and contemporaries of the Asiatic-Spanish school ; but he adheres without an exception to the traditional hermeneutics, is thoroughly rabbinical, and has contributed nothing to the development of the religious idea, and he has therefore legitimately no place in this essay. His grandson (through his daughter) and disciple was Rabbi Samuel ben Mair, known among Jews as Rashbam, who, besides his rabbinical commentaries and treatises, wrote also a commentary to the Pentateuch* and sub-commentary to Rashi, called *"Keren Shemuel."* He tells us that he desired his grandfather to expound the Bible critically and not rabbinically, and that Rashi replied he intended to do so. But it was never done. Rashbam is of decidedly more value than Rashi as a critical and ethical expounder of the Pentateuch, and may be regarded as one of the writers who led the Jewish mind from rabbinical to critical hermeneutics.

Returning to our main subject, we meet in the twelfth century, as the most diistinguished precursors of Maimonides, three great names, viz.: Judah Halevi, Abraham ibn Ezra and Abraham ibn Daud. Jehudah ben Samuel Halevi, of Castile (1100 to 1175 A. C.), the most gifted of all Jewish poets, † whose hymns are the finest gems in the

---

* He is not to be mistaken for Rabbi Samuel ben David, who also wrote a commentary to the Pentateuch. See Wolf, Vol. I, No. 2053.

† See S. D. Luzzatto's *Bethulath Bath Jehuda* from

Portuguese liturgy, and is the author of the philosophical work, called *Chazzari*. In the Platonic form
of dialogue (with Socrates), and of Cicero (with
Cato) the *Chazzari* contains a series of discussions on
Judaism and philosophy ; the king in the *Chazzari*
represents philosophy, and the Chabar "Associate"
represents Judaism. The dialogue ends in the conversion of the king, in the triumph of Judaism,
therefore, over the philosophical opinions of that
age. The original title of the book was, "The
book of evidence and argumentation in support of
despised religion." Grecian philosophy had made
deep inroads into religion. Plato and Aristotle
were to the learned higher authorities than either
the Bible or the Koran. The *Chazzari* is directed
chiefly against that spirit of the age. The author
occupies the position of the rabbinical Jew, but
reasons only on the *hagada*, the ethical and theological portions of the Talmud, without attempting
a defense on any ground of reason of the *halacha*,
the law as expounded and elaborated by the rabbis.
While he affords, therefore, a deeper insight into
the ethics and theology of the rabbis, he tacitly sacrifices rabbinical casuistics to the spirit of the age.

This book, written originally in Arabic, was
translated into Hebrew, Spanish, Latin and German, and was favorably received by all classes of
Jews, because it bore at least the semblance of
orthodoxy, and was written in a pleasant and in

Jehudah Halevi's Divan, Prague, 1840. Divan des Rabbi
Jehudah Halevi, Lyck, 1864. German metrical versions by
Dr. A. Geiger (also of Solomon ibn Gabirol) and by Dr. M.
Sachs.

popular form.   As early as 1422 and 1425 A. c.,
commentaries to this book were written, showing
its early popularity.   Next to Bachya's *Chobot
Hallebaboth* it is most extensively extant also in
our days.

More important, more profound and more radical
than Judah Halevi was his contemporary Abraham
ben Meir ibn Ezra, of Granada (1092, died in Rome
1167, A. c.).   This remarkable man, who passed
through the then civilized world like a restless
vagrant, from London to Tiberias, and from Lisbon
to Rome, and Alexandria and Paris, was, nevertheless, not only the most fertile writer of his
age, but also the wittiest, most sagacious and most
liberal Jewish thinker of his century.   Maimonides,
in a letter to his son, admonishes him to read and
study well the works of Ibn Ezra, whom he compares to the patriarch Abraham, ''Who was afraid
of no man, dreaded no creature, and journeyed
incessantly up and down the land.''   The poet
Bedarshi pronounced a grand and eloquent eulogy
on Ibn Ezra.   He says of Ibn Ezra, ''He excelled
all before him in the conception of truth, and abided
at the gates of wisdom, removed superstition,'' etc.

Abraham ibn Ezra * wrote a number of distinguished works on the Hebrew language, on mathematics, on cosmogony and astrology, hymns, poems

---

* He is not to be mistaken for the poet Moses ibn Ezra, to
whom Jehudah Halevi dedicated six of his poems, and whose
death he memoralized by an elegy.   Moses excelled in sacred
poetry, especially in the '' *Selichah* '' but not as a philosopher.   His philosophical book '' *Arugath Habbosem* '' was
never printed.   See L. Dukes, Moses ben Ezra, Altona, 1839.

and riddles (also a poem on chess), which do not interest us here. His commentaries to the Bible and his book *Yesod Mora Vesod Torah*, "The principle of worship and the mystery of the law," especially the commentary, exercised a deep and lasting influence on the development of the religious idea. He was the first to write a Hebrew commentary to the whole Bible (Chronicles excepted) from the stand-point of critical exegesis without reference to tradition or authority. In his commentary, canons of criticism are laid down, which have not been further developed in our century of classical criticism. He had the boldness to oppose traditional hermeneutics, and to carve out for himself a new path for exegesis. His wit and sarcasm are as spicy as his critical discernment is acute and profound. This has made him a favorite of the student and a delight to the reader. What Saadia, Bachya, Ibn Gabirol and Jehudah Halevi have attempted to do in philosophy, viz., to harmonize faith and reason, Judaism and philosophy, Ibn Ezra has done in reconciling the words to the Bible to the advanced intelligence of his contemporaries. He was not without success in the province of pure philosophy. His "*Yesod*," was published as early as 1530 A. C., and has been frequently republished with or without commentaries. * It is extensively quoted by the best writers ; but his place in history is secure because of his matchless commentaries, which open entirely new avenues to re-

* Dr. M. Creizenach published it, with a German version, Frankfurt a. M., 1840. It was published with Stern's commentary, Prag, 1833.

ligious and to liberal reasoners. After him none
can afford to write on the Bible without referring to
Ibn Ezra. His heretical opinions (as they were
considered then) were eagerly embraced by many
prominent writers. One hundred years later Ezra
ben Solomon wrote a commentary to the Pentateuch
re-enforcing all the heresies of Ibn Ezra. (See
Wolf, Vol. III, p. 870.)

Last, though not least, the author of the *Emunah
Ramah*, "Exalted Faith," Abraham ibn Daud,
must be mentioned. In 1180 A. c., he fell a victim
of fanaticism at Toledo. Abraham ibn Daud or
David, the Levite, was the author of a considerable
number of books, all written in Arabic, with the
exception of his *Sepher Hakkabalah*, "Book on
Tradition ; " *Sichron Divre Romi*, "Abstract of
Roman History ; " and *Dibre Malche Israel*, " History of the kings of Israel."* The main work of
Abraham ibn Daud, "Exalted Faith," translated
into Hebrew from the Arabic, is remarkable for its
opposition to Ibn Gabirol and its eulogy of Aristotle and Saadya. We have before us the first outspoken peripatetic Jew of Spain. It was at a time,
when Ibn Badja, by his thorough study of Aristotle,
had converted all Arabian philosophers to the
peripatetic school, which had become the fashion of
the day.

These outlines, brief and incomplete as they are,
may afford a survey of the two centuries between

* See *Maarecheth Haggedolim; Kore Haddoroth*, Lemberg, 1845, p. 12 ; *Shebet Jehuda*, Hannover, 1855, pp. 4,
112, 113'; Dr. B. Beer's notes to Munk's *Philosophie und
philosophische Schriftsteller*, etc.

Saadia and Maimonides.   The main object of Jewish
philosophers was on the one hand to defend Judaism,
and on the other to expound Bible and Talmud in
as rational a manner as possible, in order to reconcile faith and reason.

III.   From Maimonides to Albo.

"From Moses to Moses, there was none like
Moses," his admirers said of Moses Maimonides.
In him the learning and intelligence of his generation culminated, and he laid the foundation of a
new epoch in the history of the progress of the mind.
All that had been achieved in literature, by Arab
or Jew, in philosophy, science or law, in Arabic,
Hebrew or Talmudical lore, was mastered by this
great Moses, whose mind was vast and deep.
Almost all the young Israelites of his days spent
their best time in the sixty books of the Talmud,
and neglected secular science and philosophy.
Therefore, Maimonides wrote three systematical
works comprising the main contents of the whole
Talmud. He wrote the *Perush Hammishnah*, "Commentary of the Mishna," on which foundation the
Talmudical structure is raised, in the Arabic language, to render this part of the rabbinical writings
easily understood. He wrote a general introduction
to the Mishna and a special introduction to the
various books of it. The whole work was translated into Hebrew and Spanish, some parts of it
into Latin and German. Being in Arabic, Hebrew
and Spanish, it was accessible to all Jews in the
Orient and Occident who took hold on it with a
wonderful avidity. Pococke's Latin translation of

portions of this commentary, published in Oxford, 1655, introduced it to Christian students.

Next Maimonides codified the laws of the Talmud in a systematical order, and in the popular language and style of the Mishna. He divided the codex into fourteen books, each book into chapters, and each chapter into paragraphs, as the subject required. Fourteen is represented in Hebrew by the letters *yod* (10) and *dalid* (40), which together form the word *yad*, "hand." Therefore this code was called "*Yad*," and afterward "*Yad Hachazakah*," or "The Strong Hand." Maimonides called it "*Mishne Torah*," Review of the Law, or Deuteronomy. This being also the name of the fifth book of Moses, the code was mostly called by that name. The master mind of Maimonides alone could accomplish the gigantic task of codifying the mass of laws and customs systematically and correctly. Nobody before or after him has been able to do it as well and as completely as he has done it. This code brought the rabbinical law within a compassable limit to be mastered in a few years, and under a classification which enabled the student to find particular laws or customs without roaming over the interminable mass of rabbinical sources. Thus he afforded an opportunity to students to master the rabbinical laws and to save time for other studies. Not satisfied, however, with these achievements, Maimonides wrote an Arabic text-book, with a comprehensive introduction, on the 613 commandments, as the rabbis found them in the Pentateuch, divided and subdivided them in correspondence with the code, to afford an opportunity of knowing the laws of the Talmud without studying them. The reasons of the commandments were written by him also in Arabic and appended to his *More Nebuchim*. So Maimonides thought he had relieved people of the study of the Talmud itself and had saved time for the student to turn his attention to philosophy and science.

No books have ever so rapidly become universal authorities as did the rabbinical works of Maimonides (we have not named them all) among his cotemporaries in Africa, Asia, and Europe. From the Caspian Sea to the Arabian Gulf and the Atlantic Ocean his *Mishne Torah* became the rabbinical code. Only one man, Abraham ben David (died 1198 A. C.), had the courage to attack it, in his *Has' hogoth*. The Jews of Yemen included Moses Maimonides in their daily prayers, and he was long remembered in the prayers of the last day of the feast. This had the effect that the Eastern Jews, Spain, Portugal, and Southern France, studied Talmud less and philosophy and science more; and rabbinical studies were limited mostly to Northern France, Germany, and Italy, although there were exceptions on both sides.

The medical and other scientific works of Maimonides do not concern us here. We must dwell on his theologico-philosophical activity. He wrote for his contemporaries a treatise on Psychology (*Shemone Perakim*), one on Logic (*Miloth ha-higgayon*), another on Grammar and Rhetoric (which has not reached us), and finally wrote his great theologico-philosophical book, *More Nebuchim*, "Guide of the Perplexed." All these were in Arabic, but they were soon translated into Hebrew, Latin, Spanish, German, and French, and provided with a large number of commentaries and sub-commentaries, republished in nearly every civilized country. In the rabbinical work Maimonides is the objective expounder and codifier of the Talmud. He decided disputed matter according to rabbinical rules, and with the exception of some introductory chapters to *Mishne Torah*, he expresses no opinion of his own, and is never subjective. He reproduces the Talmud in a new and systematical form. In his theologico-philosophical works he is the subjective reasoner. Moses Maimonides himself, although a peripatetic philosopher, like so many of his time, attacks and often refutes Aristotle, where he opposes Jewish doctrine. Again, although a rabbinist of the severe type, he modifies and even rejects rabbinical theories, especially in regard to hermeneutics, revelation and prophecy, resurrection of the body (which he denies absolutely), and such doctrines as are contradicted by philosophy. Of his age he is the most successful conciliator of faith and reason, and he has placed Judaism on that lofty position where the religious philosopher and the philosophical religionist of his day could occupy common ground and contest amicably for the palm with Mohammedans and Christians. He saved Judaism from the oppressive prestige of Aristotle, who had been god and oracle of the Mohammedan and Christian world.

In his introduction to a section of the *Mishna*, called, *Chelek*, Maimonides established thirteen dogmas as the principle of rabbinical Judaism. In two

different forms, as a hymn called *Yigdal* and as a
confession called "*Ani Ma' amin*," later writers introduced these thirteen dogmas into the synagogue,
and they are still retained in the orthodox prayer-
books and catechisms. Those dogmas, however,
strange to say, do not teach that an Israelite is
obligated to subscribe to rabbinical hermeneutics or
rabbinical laws; thus a main point of the orthodox
creed is rejected, and a remarkable concession is
made to reformed Judaism; though oxthodox Jews
cling to them as a test.   In the "*More Nebuchim*,"
in which he subjects the dogmas to a thorough
analysis, he modifies them considerably.   But the
orthodox Jew says Maimonides is an authority in
his *Mishne-Torah*, though his philosophical works
contain his personal views.   This is an intimation
that Maimonides considered himself not at all orthodox.   Much was written for and against him
after his death, and to-day both orthodox and
reformer equally still appeal to his authority.   No
man, since Ezra, has exercised so deep and lasting
an influence on Jews and Judaism as has Moses
Maimonides.   His theologico-philosophical works
acquired an authority among the progressive thinkers equal to his *Mishne-Torah* among rabbinical
students.   All Jewish thinkers up to date, Baruch
Spinoza, Moses Mendelssohn, and the writers of the
nineteenth century included, are more or less the
disciples of Maimonides; so that there is no Jewish
theologico-philosophical book, from and after 1200,
of which the ideas of Maimonides do not form a
prominent part.

After the death of Maimonides controversy in

Spain, Portugal and the Provence, in behalf and against the books of Maimonides, did much damage to literature. Besides this the Cabalah spread its pernicious influence among the Jews, the books Zohar and other mystical works were then written. The Jewish mind was no longer occupied with merely the solution of Talmudic polemics, and ceased to be satisfied with the rationalistic reasoning of Maimonides, Ibn Ezra, etc., the fancies of the Cabalah and its beautiful poetry and mystical obscurity. Still the numerous disciples of Maimonides adhered to the system and worked at its completion and perfection. Two great writers of that century must be named here, Rabbi Moses ben Nachman, called Ramban, and Rabbi David Kimchi, called Redak. Ramban (1194 to 1260 A. C.) was a great Talmudist and Cabalist, still a friend of Maimonides and philosophy. His numerous works, rabbinical, Cabalistical and liturgical, have been widely circulated. His commentaries on the Pentateuch and on Job offer a peculiar combination of sound wisdom and phantastic mystery, of thorough learning and research, along with wild theories on things supernatural. As a philosopher he is remarkable in "Iggereth Musar" on Morals; Iggereth Haramban, a defense of Maimonides' *More Nebuchim* against French rabbis, and Iggereth Hakkadesh on Marriage. More successful in that century was David Kimchi, of Narbonne (1170 to 1240 A. C.), the great grammarian, lexicographer and exegete, the friend and defender of Maimonides. His commentaries on the Pentateuch, Prophets, Psalms, Ruth and Chronicles are strictly independ-

ent, and have found Latin translators at an early
period. He is the only one of the great commentators who wrote against Christianity.*

The great successor of Ibn Ezra and Kimchi as
an independent expounder of the Bible, was the excellent Leon de Banolas, Rabbi Levi ben Gerson,
also called Gersonides, or Ralbag (1299 to· 1370
A. C.). His commentaries to the Pentateuch, Joshua,
Judges, Kings, Proverbs, Job, Daniel, Ecclesiastes,
Ruth and Esther, are almost entirely independent
of rabbinical hermeneutics. They are of particular
ethical value ; his notes, called *Tho-aloth*, added to
his commentaries, point out ethical verities. Since
Bachya, no one has done what Leon de Banolas did
for a proper understanding of Biblical ethics. To
the preacher and moralist these notes are of great
value. This highly esteemed sage of the fourteenth
century was the first great thinker who attempted
a systematic elaboration of the ideas of Maimonides.
In one of the largest and most complete philosophical works of that century, *Sepher Milchamoth
Hashem*, "Book of the Battles of the Lord," Leon
attempted a concilation of faith and reason, religion
and philosophy, entirely in the spirit of Maimonides. Although the progress of philosophy was
then inconsiderable, Aristotle and Maimonides
being final and irrevocable authority, holding reason in bondage, still progress of thought characterizes the philosophy of Leon de Banolas, who would

* These commentaries have added greatly to a free exegesis
and a proper understanding of the Bible. Kimchi is not as
terse, brilliant and bold as Ibn Ezra, nevertheless he is a
good grammarian, philologist and clear-headed expounder.

not give up his independence.   Battling bravely
against anti-religious theories, prevalent in the
schools, this philosophical rabbi accomplished for
his age what Maimonides had done for his, he
reconciled religion and philosophy.   (He also
wrote notes to the Logic of Ibn Roshd.)   It is
strange that, while his commentaries were widely
circulated among Bible students, and portions of it
found Latin translators early, his philosophical
work has never been published in full, and has not
been translated.

At Barcelona, a great rabbinical authority, Rabbi
Nissim ben Reuben, known as Ran, was at the
head of the academy and the congregation.   In this
academy a new school took its rise adverse to the
dogmas of Maimonides and the philosophy of
Aristotle.   Rabbi Nissim himself was not known as
a philosophical writer.   His commentary on the
Pentateuch, portion of which Don Abarbanel
adopted, contained his philosophical principles, but
it was never published.   The most prominent of
Ran's disciples, Chasdai Crescas, of Saragossa, was
the author of the book *Or Adonoi*, "The Light of
the Lord" (about 1400 B. C.), in which he attacks
Maimonides.   This book in the proper sense of the
term, is a work of dogmatics in four treatises, in
which Aristotle is so seriously attacked, that John
Francis Pico (1522), in his very careful polemics
against Aristotle, cites the best part of Crescas'
work ; and that Spinoza also used his arguments
against Aristotle, though he does not give credit to
the author.   Like his predecessor Abu-Hamed Al
Ghazzali, Crescas considered philosophy insufficient,

and, falling back on revelation as the safest foundation of society, he attacked all philosophy by means of philosophy. Chasdai Crescas was the first one known to posterity who attacked the thirteen dogmas of Maimonides. He distinguished between Ikkarim, "fundamental principles" on which Judaism rests, and without which it can not exist, and Kelalim, "general principles" which are deduced from the body of law. A religious Jew must believe in the former and may hold to the latter. Crescas wrote also a work in Spanish on Christian dogmas, which has not been printed, however; and a work on the same subject, "*Kelimath Haggoyim*," with twelve chapters against Géronimo de Santa Fé was dedicated to him, parts of which were printed in Hamburg, 1848. His epistle on the persecution in Spain, 1392 A. C. is added to the *Shebet Jehuda* by Solomon ibn Verga (Edit. Wiener, Hanover, 1855).

The objections of Crescas to the dogmas of Maimonides were taken up by a disciple of the former, Joseph Albo, who wrote a book on the subject, "*Sepher Ikkarim*," "The Book of Principles," in which he advances three cardinal principles of Judaism, God Revelation, Reward and Punishment. This Rabbi Joseph Albo (1360 to 1444 A. C.), was one of the twenty-five Jewish representatives at the celebrated Disputation of Tortosa. Pedro de Luna, known as Pope Benedict XIII, by advice of his body physician, the ex-Jew Joshua of Lorca (Géronimo de Sante Fé), convoked a congress of Christians and Jews to Tortosa, to prove to the Jews that the Messiah had come. The con-

gress opened February 7, 1413, held sixty-nine
sessions, and closed November 12, 1414. The pope
presided. Cardinals, arch-bishops, bishops and
prominent noblemen took a part in it. The Jews
were represented by twenty of their doctors. among
them also Joseph Albo. He finished his '' Book on
Principles'' in 1425 A. C., at Soria. It is not only
one of the best written treatises on cardinal principles, but also a complete exposition on Judaism,
and an acute polemic against Christology. Nevertheless it was translated into Latin twice (Paris,
1566, and Jena, 1720). Besides, he wrote in
Spanish a controversy he had with a priest, which
had never been published.

These were the principal authors of the two
centuries from Maimonides to Albo. A number of
minor writers are grouped around these literary
centers, as the poet and translator Alcharisi
Shemtob, the opponent of Maimonides, and
Maheram Alhaker, who defended Maimonides, Don
Joseph ben Tusan, Meir ibn Altaba, and many
other writers of distinction. But we can mention
here only those whose influence in the development
of the religious idea is well known. We will name
here Mordechai Nathan, who wrote the first concordance to the Bible in the year 1437 A. C., calling
it '' *Yair Nathib*,'' to which Isaac Nathan wrote
a lengthy introduction, showing how wide awake
those doctors were as to the systematic study of
the Bible.

IV.—From Albo to the Close of the Literary Period.

The fifteenth century was one of terror and persecution to the Spanish Jews. From 1392 to 1492, thousands of Jews were slaughtered and tens of thousands forced into Christianity. But the mind does not develop by oppression. It unfolds in the shade of freedom, and under the palm of peace. So culture declined in Spain, persisted only for a while longer in Portugal, the Provence and in Italy, but set finally into a long night of darkness and ignorance.

After Joseph Albo, the disciples of philosophy and criticism among the Jews were very few indeed. It was an age of retrogression. Rabbi Samuel Çarça, one of the philosophical minds of this age, of whom nothing at all is known, was condemned to end his life on the pyre of the Inquisition, because he doubted the creation of matter. Some maintain that he was delivered to the Inquisition by the court-rabbi of Castile, Rabbi Isaac Campanton,* who was a rabbinical authority in Castile, though he was not distinguished for his great learning.† Matatia Yizhari, of Saragossa, bore a great name in his day, is known to us only by his *Midrash Alpha Bethoth*, added to *Midrash*

---

* This appears to have been the title of that rabbi, as chief officer of the crown in Jewish matters.

† See Yuchasin, ed. Amsterdam 5407 A. M., p. 101 b. *Skalsheleth ha-kabalah*, p. 49 a; Fragment of Çarça's Epistle, added to *Shebet Jehuda*, Hannover, 1855, p. 131.

T'hillim. His other works, among them also a sub-commentary to Ibn Ezra's commentary, has not reached us. Elia Levita, the great grammarian and lexicographer, born in Germany in 1469, and who died in Venice, 1549, does not belong to those who directly influenced the development of the religious idea.

Three authors of the fifteenth century (reaching over to the sixteenth), must be mentioned here to show how the philosophical and scientific spirit had disciplined the minds also of the purely rabbinical authorities of that age, notwithstanding fierce opposition. These three Rabbis are Isaac Aboab, Isaac Arama and Jacob ben Solomon Ibn Chabib. Isaac Arama, one of the Spanish exiles of 1492, who died at Venice shortly after the expulsion, wrote commentaries to Proverbs and the Book of Esther. He wrote philosophical essays called *Chazoth Kashah*, of a polemical character against infidels, which was published several times. But his great and widely-spread book is, the *Akedath Yizchak*, one hundred homilies on the Pentateuch and the Megilloth, which contain many themes with reference to religion and these are discussed in a very sagacious manner; it contains also an acute polemic against infideliy in philosophy. Since its first appearance in 1522 this book has remained the guide of all philosophical preachers in Israel. Strange to say, this work was never translated into any modern language, and yet it offers more material to the preacher than all the modern sermons combined that are in circulation to-day.

Isaac Aboab,* of Castile, was a great rabbinical authority toward the end of the fifteenth century. He has become popularly known to posterity by his book *Menorath ha-Ma'or*, containing the ethics of the Talmud, in seven sections, each divided in several treatises, and each treatise subdivided in chapters. The main object of this book appears to have been to show that rabbinical ethics are more profound and more natural than both the philosophical and Christian ethics. The book is systematical and exhaustive. The author's acquaintance with the Talmud is wonderful. His choice of passages proves his refined taste and profound sensibility as a moralist. Translated into Spanish and German, it became the favorite literature of the Jewish people, and was read in almost every home of the Ghetto. This book has largely contributed to the good morals of the secluded and oppressed Jews. It has been re-published, Krotoschin, 1846, with a German translation by Fuerstenthal and Behrend.†

The third of those rabbis was Jacob ben Solomon Ibn Chabib, another exile from Spain in 1492, who

---

* Abraham Sacuto, the author of the historical record, called *Yuchasin*, was a pupil of Isaac Aboab.

† Besides this book, the *Ze'enah u-Re'enah*, a homiletic treatise in medieval German on the Pentateuch, Megilloth and section of the prophets as read in the synagogue, by Jacob ben Isaac Germanus of Prague (died 1628), was most extensively read in the Ghetto and contributed largely to the preservation of religion and good morals among the oppressed Jews. It was translated into Latin by John Saubert, and published at Helmstadt, 1660.

went to Turkey, and died at Salonichi. This student undertook the task of compiling all the Hagadah passages from the Babylonian Talmud and part of the Jerusalem, together with notes by Rashi, Ibn Aderet, Nachmani, Jomtob ben Abraham and Nissim, to which he added his own notes and treatises, beginning always, " The author says." This book is called *En Jacob*, and is found in every rabbinical library. It is a supplement to the code of Maimonides, which necessarily excludes the Hagadah, or ethical portion of the Talmud, historical notes, poetical fictions, proverbs, maxims, fables, etc. Ibn Chabib's notes and essays are especially remarkable for the author's decided standpoint against the reality of the Talmudical legends. Maimonides had already maintained that the rabbinical legends must not be taken as matter of fact ; still it was always done, more or less. Ibn Chabib cut the Gordian knot, and reasoned rationally and radically.

The great light, however, with whom this period closes, was the Portuguese Grandee, the king's confidant and minister, Don Isaac Abarbanel, who shared and described the exode of the Jews from Spain and Portugal in 1492, after which he took up his abode in Italy. This mighty prince of the mind furnished the material for a hundred Latin volumes. He was the most fertile writer of his age. Among his numerous works, two interest us here especially, viz., the commentaries and the *Rosh Amanah*. Abarbanel wrote commentaries to Pentateuch, Joshua, Judges, Samuel, Kings, Isaiah, Jeremiah, Ezekiel, the twelve

minor prophets and Daniel. His Hebrew diction
is elegant and clear. An orthodox in faith, he is
nevertheless led by his predecessors, and prefers
rational to traditional comments, especially in the
matter of miracles. He starts out in every chapter
with a number of critical queries, proceeds then to
analytical definitions of the Scriptural terms, and
arrives finally at a synthetical solution of the proposed difficulties, so that the whole retains the
charm of polemical discourse. His commentaries,
like those of Leon de Banolas, are of great importance to the preacher, although hardly less valuable
to the critic.

In his *Sepher Rosh Amanah*, "the Book on Cardinal Principles," Abarbanel reviews the thirteen
dogmas of Maimonides, the objection to the same
by Crescas and Albo, in the same style as in his
commentaries. He adds a number of his own objections to those of Crescas and Albo, analyzes
them all, finally defends those of Maimonides.
Proceeding in an argumentative style, he has ample
opportunity for the reader to exercise his own
judgment and to form his own opinion. He proposes many a query, to each of which he gives satisfactory reply, and leads the reader to independent
reflection. This book was several times re-published
in Hebrew, and also in Latin, Amsterdam, 1638.
His commentary to the *More Nebuchim* was buried
in a library at Tunis, up to the year 1831, when it
was published in Prague.

During this whole period, from Saadia to Abarbanel (900 to 1500), the Jews of Northern France,
Germany, Italy, Poland and the East, with a very

few honorable exceptions, were completely engulfed
in the Talmud and afterward in the Cabalah. Besides a considerable number of Hebrew prayers,
hymns, elegies and penitential confessions, they produced commentaries and sub-commentaries, glossa-
ries and responses, opinions and decisions on the
Talmud, and rabbinical expositions on the Bible,
in the form of sermons, homilies and commentaries.
The rabbinical laws were discussed, expounded, enlarged and spun out to a bulky and intricate mass,
governing every emotion of human nature, and this
discussion was too bulky to be known and too intricate and hair-splitting to be intelligible or practical. Their sermons and their poetry are skillful
combinations of Talmudical passages, spiced with
rabbinical wit and imagery. An almost incredible
amount of sagacity and research is displayed in
that literature, in which, besides sound ethics, we
can discover nothing of importance to anybody
(the code according to Maimonides included), except to students of history, archæology or bibliog-
raphy. Christendom suffering all that time under
the curse of ignorance and priestly arrogance, the
poor Jew crept back into his Ghetto, and buried himself in the Talmud, so that at least he himself might
not lapse into hopeless stupidity. In the countries of the Islam, however, all this time, philosophy
and science, poetry and Grecian literature were cultivated ; the Jew was active to set himself aright
with the spirit of every age ; the spirit of Judaism
produced new forms, different from the rabbinical
and traditional, it placed itself in correspondence
with the state of culture of every century. So, at the

end of the fifteenth century, we have actually three schools in Judaism, viz.: the rabbinico-traditional, based on the Talmud ; the rabbinical-cabalistical, based on the Zohar and its expounders, and the rational school, the mother of reformed Judaism as it now exists. These three schools did not exclude one another—none considered itself a sect apart from the others—still they differed widely from one another in matters of great importance in theory, though they agreed in practice.

The literature of these schools, as specified above, is the source from which modern Judaism draws its principal information. This same literature became also the theoretical cause of the Christian reformation. The theology of the reformers came from this same source, and from cabalistic books which furnished symbols, types and mysteries ; so that if the reformation had not stopped half way there would be little difference to-day between Christian and Jew. As early as the thirteenth century, Jacob Anatoli, of Naples, translated Hebrew books into Latin. Besides, the Christian priest, who would not have dared to read Arabic, was not prohibited to read Hebrew, as we shall see hereafter in this essay.

So much about the origin of the literature from which reformed Judaism issued in the nineteenth century. It remains now to be seen why the period of reform remained uninfluential for almost three centuries.

V.—From Abarbanel to Mendelssohn.

The last decade of the fifteenth century witnessed one of the greatest calamities to which the dispersed children of Israel had been subjected. They were driven from Spain, Portugal, Sicily, Naples and the adjacent islands, from the countries where their fathers lived since the day of the Cæsars, to whose culture and civilization they had contributed more extensively than the nationalities whose fanaticism had driven them from their homes, robbed them of their property and cast them out into undescribable misery. Tens of thousands became pseudo-Christians to save their families from ruin ; others perished before they had found new homes. The surviving exiles went to Northern Africa, to Palestine and Syria, to Turkey and Northern Italy and a few to other countries. It is true, the year 1492, when the Jews were expelled from Spain, was the same when America was discovered and a new world was opened to them ; but the new world was Spanish, and therefore inhospitable to the Jew, and the inquisition made a hell of it as fast almost as it was settled by Europeans.

The countries from which the Jews had been expelled lost their commerce and were soon reduced to political impotence, from which they have not been fully reclaimed even in this latter half of the nineteenth century. After the Jews were gone three was not even one physician in Spain. The Spaniards had exiled commerce, science and literature. But the Jews themselves, also, in this respect were no less the sufferers. The exile closed the period of Jewish

literature, the outlines of which we have given
here.   The doctors exiled from their homes continued their literary labors in foreign lands.   In
the next generation some prominent men make
their appearance, especially in the families of Ibn
Yachya, Sforno, Abarbanel, Ibn Tibbon, Ibn Verga,
Aboab, Arama and others ; but then the sun set.
The Cabalah, on the one hand, and casuistic rabbinism, on the other, overshadow the horizon of
Jewish genius.   The greatest, also, of this class of
writers had made the Orient their homes and especially Palestine ; few remained in Italy, and still
less in Poland and Germany.   That spirit of research and reflection which characterized the above-
named authors was not free any more, and remained
unfree to the end of the eighteenth century.   It
appears that the oppression of centuries had broken
the Jewish spirit so that printing, the revival of
letters, the reformation and subsequent conflicts,
and immigration into America, left no trace on
the Ghettos.   Here and there a brilliant mind
loomed up like a lone-star, without exercising an
influence on the masses.   The great men of the
Del Medigo family, like Leo de Modena and Nar-
boni, passed almost unnoticed.   Baruch Spinoza of
Amsterdam, who, in the time of Bachya, Maimonides or Albo, would have called forth a host
of writers, was gravely excommunicated by the
rabbis of Amsterdam, a mode of treating scrupulous thinkers, they had learned from the Church
of Portugal.   Menasseh ben Israel, a noble soul
and an energetic man, whose merits Cromwell
and Milton acknowledge, was scarcely noticed by

his Jewish contemporaries. Azariah de Rossi, the author of the *Meor Enayim*, a fine classical scholar and liberal thinker, who, at any other time, would have given an impulse to researches, was ignored in his day. The reformation which caused all classes of people to new exertions left in Jewish literature only one book of merit, namely the *Chizzuk Emunah*, by Isaac Troki, a Polish Jew, which was translated into Latin and also into German. So deeply engulfed in Cabalah and Talmud were Jewish students that they forgot all else, even the Bible, the Hebrew language and all systematic and critical studies connected therewith, and all of these went into the hands of Christian students like Bartolocci and the Buxtorfs, Edmund Castelli, Hackspan, Hottinger and Herder, Lightfoot and Lengerke, Sebastian Muenster and Michaelis, Reuchlin, Wagenseil and Wolf and some ex-Jews who wrote for the information of Christians. From 1550 to 1750, aside of Talmud and Cabalah and the few books mentioned before, the Jews did nothing for their religious literature. With every passing decade they fell deeper into the minutiæ of casuistry, the delusions of the Cabalah, which had crept into parts of the synagogue and the family, excluding finally all secular science except medicine and mathematics and all closer intercourse with the world outside of the Ghetto. The Jews of Russia, Poland, the Danubian Principalities, Hungary, Germany and Holland, in fact, had not only a music and kitchen of their own, but also a jargon of obsolete German mixed with Hebrew, Slavonic and other languages, now called Yiddish.

It is wonderful how Providence watches over the treasures intrusted to the Jewish people. Before the Jews were driven from Spain, Elias Levita, whom we have mentioned above, resided in the house of Cardinal Egidio, as teacher in Hebrew lore of the Italian magnate. Two of his disciples, Paul Fagius and Sebastian Muenster, became advocates of Jewish learning to Christian students in Italy, where the culture of the century reached a high point. At the same time, by an inexplicable impulse, Johann Reuchlin, of Wurtemberg, felt an irresistible desire to know the language and lore of the Hebrew. In 1487 he wrote to the learned Sebastian Muenster, to obtain for him a copy of the Pentateuch. But Muenster could find none, and sent him a copy of Exodus. Happily, Reuchlin was sent to the court of the Emperor Frederick III. by the Duke of Wurtemberg, where he made the acquaintance of the emperor's body physician, Jacob Jehiel Loans, a learned Israelite and favorite of the emperor, who became Reuchlin's teacher in the memorable year 1492. Reuchlin after that had other Jewish teachers, and finally he came to Rome in 1498, where he met Obadiah Sforno, one of the prominent Hebrew commentators of the Bible, physician and philosopher, who became the last teacher of Reuchlin. He returned and began to teach Hebrew at the University of Heidelberg, although the monks opposed it most fanatically. The Duke of Saxony invited him to the University of Wittenberg, as professor of the Hebrew, but he declined, and some years later he took this place at Ingolsstadt, and afterward in Tuebingen. This made the reformation possible, and from that time the Christians cultivated the Hebrew language and lore, up to Rabe, DeWette, Gesenius, Hitzig, Ewald and Delitzsch, while the Jews themselves neglected and forgot their own treasures.   So Providence watches.

We return to our main subject.   In the middle of the last century, when Moses Mendelssohn appeared on the stage of public activity, the Jews were deplorably neglected.   This neglect was most visible in the following points :

1. *The Disabilities.*   The Jews were disfranchised politically and socially, not only by unfair laws and still more ungenerous customs, but also by burdens they imposed upon themselves in the form of the religious duties they observed.   To mention some, besides the weekly Sabbath, the Israelite observed annually thirteen holidays, ten half holidays, five fast days, thirteen half days, which, by the strictness of the rules governing them, exclude him annually (with the Sabbaths) eighty-three days from business and society.   Besides, he observed in succession six weeks, and then again three weeks, of mourning, during which he would not shave his beard nor cut his hair.   Similarly, for thirty days after the death of one of seven relatives.   So he was half of his time incapacitated for society.   To this must be added the laws of diet as to every thing he ate or drank, the pots, dishes, knives, forks and spoons used, and the manner of salting the meat.   It was impossible for the religious Jew or Jewess to live in the midst of Gentiles without doing violence to these scruples.   Ignorance of sec-

ular affairs and prejudice against learning except of
Talmud and Cabalah, intensified his disabilities, so
that no government in the world could relieve them
much.

2. *Superstition.* The rabbinical laws, as they
had been spun out, affecting every emotion of the
human being, man, woman, or child, produced
naturally a vast amount of superstition. The Cabalah added to this the belief in angels, demons,
and the spirits of the departed, attended by certain
observances and formulas. Religion itself became
for the Jew, as it was for the simple peasant, and
for the burghers among whom he lived, a caricature
of superstition, some rabbis in fact sanctioned it,
in spite of the emphatic protestations of many.

3. *Public Worship.* As the seclusion continued,
public worship became more disorderly, more offensive to good taste, more ludicrous by its antiquated observances, more burdensome by its length
and monotony, and more alien to the hearts of the
worshipers. Prayers and hymns were recited without bearing upon wants or circumstances, elegies
had reference to sufferings long endured, and penitential confessions declared sins they had not committed. Public worship became ridiculous in appearance, and lifeless within. Finally the sermon
also was abolished, and what remained of worship
was meaningless and hollow.

So, while the world progressed, Judaism retro-
graded. The political and social pressure without,
and the unsatisfactory condition within, gradually
resulted in this, some adjured Judaism, and became
the enemies of their people, others rose above

the level of their former association by talent or wealth, and held their people and its religion in contempt. It became fashionable not to be a Jew. Either there was to be a remedy for these or the end of Judaism in Western Europe had to come. The remedy came by reform; without this, little would have been left of Judaism in Western Europe or in America. In the degeneration, the Jew had still retained two excellent qualities, viz.: he remained religious, and preserved, along with his common sense, his natural sagacity. He had become the creature of form, but there was religion to spare, even in the meanest Jew. He had become a slave of the Talmud, but from Talmudic study had been derived his sagacity. He had abjured the world, but made a new one for himself in the Ghetto. These qualities facilitated the advent of reform, it came for the salvation of the Hebrew people, and it came with Moses Mendelssohn.

VI.—MOSES MENDELSSOHN.

The eighteenth century was eminently humanitarian and decidedly progressive. Before the reformation Reuchlin had laid the foundation in Germany to a new system of ethics, with the happiness of man as the key note. The disciples of the humanitarian school were numerous, and counted in their ranks the most prominent scholars of the age. The fanaticism engendered on both sides by the reformation and the triumphant barbarism of the Thirty Years' War, apparently expunged that school. But those migratory effects were overcome, and the eighteenth century continued the work of the be-

ginning of the sixteenth. The eighteenth century
justly boasts of a rare phalanx of the finest classical
scholars, poets, philosophers, critics, divines and
statesmen. Humanitarian ideals and the love of
freedom exerted a mild and elevating rule. The
American and French revolutions, which swept
from the path of humanity the debris of medieval despotism and brutality, were the necessary
results of man's roused consciousness as to his
dignity, claims and rights. Bolingbroke, Voltaire
and Paine, like Washington, Jefferson and Frank-
lin cleared the thickets, that the light of the sun
may penetrate and man may walk on smooth
ground.

The nineteenth century, it appears to me, subsists
on the wealth of the eighteenth. With the exception as to natural science and mechanical arts, this
is true. Being almost exclusively engaged with
lifeless nature (if there is such a thing) as its object
for research, the man of the nineteenth century is
cold and egotistical. He is submerged in the
cosmos, in which individual lives count for little.
Man is a part of immensity, almost nothing. The
question urges itself afresh, "What is man that
thou shouldst think of him, and Adam's son that
thou shouldst remember him?" Our respect for
human nature, our love of freedom, our patriotism
and humanitarianism are the inheritance of the
eighteenth century.

It would have been marvelous if the genius of the
century had not touched also the Jew. The mild
atmosphere, genially warmed by the rays of progressive culture, melted the ice of centuries. In

the principality of Anhalt, and in the town of
Dessau, the first exponent of the new spirit among
the Jews was born September 6, and Elul 12, 1729.
In the same year when Lessing and Reimarus
were born, Sarah, the wife of Mendel, a poor
scribe (Sopher) and schoolmaster, gave birth to
her son Moses. Mother Sarah died a few years
after the birth of Moses, and father Mendel took
care of the feeble child alone. Having received the
rudiments of education from his father, he was
placed into the school of Rabbi David Fraenkel, of
Dessau, where, besides the Hebrew and the rabbinical books, nothing else was taught and nothing else
was tolerated. Still, it was not the Talmud exclusively, though chiefly, which was read in that
school ; the Bible commentaries and the theologico-
philosophical books of the Arabic-Spanish school,
and especially the *More Nebuchim* of Moses Maimonides were taught and expounded by Rabbi
Fraenkel. Before he had reached the age of
thirteen, Moses Mendelssohn was considered pro-
ficient in the Talmud and in the *More Nebuchim*.
The father was too poor to give his son further
support, and expected him to choose a trade, as
others of his age had done. But Moses Mendelssohn had only one ambition, and this was to study
on. Penniless and friendless, he arrived at Berlin
in 1743, to begin a career of poverty and of resignation for the sake of learning. His teacher, Rabbi
Fraenkel, had moved to Berlin a year before, and
admitted Mendelssohn among his students. Hei-
mann Bamberger gave him a room and a few meals
weekly. The rest of the meals were frugal, and

frequently did not come at all. Nevertheless he
would not beg support, and preferred to suffer pri-
vation in order to maintain his independence.
Polish rabbis controlled the Jews of Berlin, and opposed with a fanatical zeal the introduction of other
studies than the Talmud, so that there was little
chance for a Jewish boy to learn anything else. A
poor and forlorn Polish Jew, Israel Samoss, almost
excommunicated on account of his profane studies,
the author of commentaries to the *Ruach Chen* and
the *Chazzari*, was known as a great mathematician
and was under the doubtful reputation of being a still
greater infidel. This Israel Samosz instructed Moses
Mendelssohn in Euclid (translated in Hebrew),
which changed the talmudist to a profound mathematician. By the help of this teacher, Mendelssohn
acquired a thorough knowledge of the Arabic-
Spanish philosophy of the Jews, and became an
acute thinker and philosopher. A young physician
of Prague, Dr. Kisch, domiciled in Berlin, gave
him for a year a quarter of an hour daily instruction
in Latin. A volume of Cicero's orations having
come to his hands by accident, Mendelssohn interrupted these studies and concentrated his attention
upon Cicero so long that he could recite every sentence and had made himself master of the language
and matter. Another Jewish physician of Berlin,
Dr. Aaron Gomperz, a scholar of eminence, took
Moses Mendelssohn in charge and introduced him
into the mysteries of science and philosophy. He
also acquired a considerable familiarity in French
and English, and was thus prepared to enter public
life.

Seven years Mendelssohn had devoted to the acquirement of an education and the habit of self-restraint. He had become great in both, he could study and suffer hunger to the extent of martyrdom. In 1770, a rich silk manufacturer of Berlin, Bermann Ziltz, offered him a position in his house as tutor. This he accepted, and so the days of misery came to ar end. He instructed the children of Mr. Ziltz, and continued his studies in Talmud, languages and philosophy ; for the latter he felt a passionate craving. History he disliked, because, he said, it offered no interest to a man who had no home on earth, and the Jews had none in those days. In philosophy he drew chiefly from four sources, the Arabic-Spanish philosophy of the Jews, from Baruch Spinoza, whose errors as the great truth he knew as well advanced from the philosophy of Leibnitz-Wolf, and from the English philosophers, especially Locke, Shaftsbury, Hutchinson and Bolingbroke. He was an outspoken opponent of the French encyclopedists ; he regarded them as shallow and disdained their cheap wit, but he was favorably impressed with the common-sense philosophy and liberal sentiments of the English deists. It was Locke who had said, "I would not have so much as a Jew or a Mohammedan excluded from the civil rights of the commonwealth because of his religion." These ideas of tolerance attracted Mendelssohn.

During the four years of his tutorship in the house of Mr. Ziltz, Mendelssohn became known and highly respected, especially through his "philosophical dialogues" which Lessing published without the author's knowledge or consent ; his "*Pope, a Metaphysician,"* which he wrote in company with Lessing, and then by his translation of Rousseau's work "On the original Inequality among men," with an appendix by him in the form of an epistle addressed to Lessing. He was introduced into the highest circles of savants and also at court, and became intimate with men, especially with Lessing and Nicolai, who were his ardent friends throughout their lives. Nicolai, and afterward also Rector Damm, became Mendelssohn's teacher in Greek, which he had neglected in former years.

From the tutor's place, he went over to the bookkeeper's, and he left that to become proprietor of a silk factory. He was never wealthy, for he spent too much for others, but, after this, he was never poor. In his thirtieth year he married a poor girl at Hamburg, Fromet Guggenheim, "the blue-eyed girl," as he called her, with whom he had fallen in love. Happy in his home, in business and in the choice of friends, and respected as no Jew in Germany ever was, he led an independent existence, living for philosophy and Judaism. Mendelssohn, the philosophical and aesthetical writer, the man of whom it is said that he brought philosophy from heaven down to earth, *i. e.*, that he popularized it, who helped build up German language and literature in opposition to the servile admirers of the French, including the king of Prussia, Mendelssohn, the man and thinker, known through many biographies and encyclopedic sketches, the author of *Phaedon, Morgenstunden, Letters on Sentiment*, etc., belongs to the world. But this sketch is limited to Mendelssohn, the Jew, and what he did

for Judaism and of this we can give a brief review
only.

The most important service which Mendelssohn
rendered to Judaism was that he remained faithful
to it in letter and in spirit. He lived in an unre-
ligious time at the court of Frederick II. The
French encyclopedists were a higher authority than
the Bible, and the companions of Mendelssohn,
Lessing and Nicolai, were not noted for sectarian
zeal. Instead of yielding to the prevailing spirit,
he opposed it energetically, especially in two books,
"*Phaedon*," in which he proved the immortality of
the soul, and in the "*Morgenstunden*," in which he
proved the existence of God. In his day it was an
appreciable disadvantage to be a Jew; the law,
social prejudice, and superstition combined to make
the life of an ambitious Jew intolerable. Being
intimate with not only the most prominent authors, but also with the pretentious aristocracy of
his age and even with crowned heads, and being
continually in touch with Christians, it would have
been natural for a man less principled than Mendelssohn to be absorbed by his environment.

When Lavater had translated Bonnet's book,
"*Investigation into the Evidence of Christianity*,"
and had made a public attempt (in 1769) to convert
Mendelssohn, he replied in a calm and philosophical
tone, and refuted the man severely. A host of
minor scribes attacked him on account of this reply
of his to Lavator, but they were discomfited by the
equanimity and the conviction of the Jew, whose
fidelity they could not shake. When, in the year
1771, he was elected member of the Berlin Academy

of Science, and the king refused to give his consent to his admission, Mendelssohn remarked, it was strange the academy should have had even the notion of electing a Jew. He remained a Jew, and so he elevated his co-religionists in the estimation of the public, and roused also the self-consciousness of the oppressed of the Jews themselves. It must not be supposed that the Jews encouraged Mendelssohn. They have never encouraged any of their champions, and they did not encourage Mendelssohn. He found stern opponents among the Jews, though he lived and worked for them with the love and the energy of a great soul. He requited the Christian world by writing for it some of the most eminent books, and he educated for it Wilhelm and Alexander von Humboldt. He requited Germany by giving it the first readable prose, and by saving the German language from French domination. He requited also the Jews by elevating them socially, politically and religiously.

VI. Mendelssohn as a Reformer, Socially and Politically.

In those days it was important to the Jews, in Germany especially, to have standing in the better classes of society. There was enlightenment in the higher circles. The bulk of the people was ignorant and prejudiced, but on the whole good-natured; it was submissive to king and priest, though oppressed by noblemen and heavily taxed by state and church. Although the universities flourished, the common schools were few and inadequate; common justice was unevenly administered,

though learned jurists commented on the pandects ;
they were without a popular literature, although
Leibnitz and Wolf had profoundly demonstrated
the nature of the Almighty. Enlightenment and
a modicum of fair treatment could be gotten from
the higher classes alone. But there the Hebrews had
no representative, none at least, who, of those who attained to distinction among them, cared for any continued connection with his less favored co-religionists.
The learned orthodox Jew had no secular education,
and was, therefore, unfit for that society. The Jewish
physicians, and the few prominent scientists, mathe-
maticians and the like, who were then living in the
cities, were restricted by the customs of their co-religionists, and werè held down by these among the
rest of the plebeian Jews. The Portuguese Jews of
France, especially of Bordeaux and Paris, however,
were an exception to this rule. They were rich, educated and influential. There were some good writers among them : Isaac Pinto (1715 to 1787), the
noted critic of Voltaire ; Roderigues Pereire (1715
to 1780), the inventor—before the Abbe l'Epee—of
the method to teach the deaf and dumb, whom
d'Alembert, Buffon, Diderot and Rousseau lauded
for his humanitarian labors. But being raised as
pseudo-Christians among the aristocracy of Spain
or Portugal, they remained aristocrats also after they
had returned to Judaism, and did not mingle with
Jews of France, Germany or Poland. Isaac Pinto
speaks of this in his book against Voltaire, and this
social disparity among the Jews is evidenced in the
execrable procedure at Bordeaux, by which all except the Portuguese Jews were expelled (1761).

The Jews constituted a helpless orphan in the world of that day.

Christian scholars, however, could not afford to ignore Moses Mendelssohn and his friends, whose number increased as his reputation grew. " 'The philosophic Moses '' was a wonderful a phenomenon, no scholar and no traveler of distinction visited Berlin without seeking an interview with the marvelous Jew. Mendelssohn and some of his Jewish friends were in contact with the best element of German and French society. In a short time the Jews had many friends, aside of Lessing, Nicolai, the eccentric Hamann, Gleim, Herder and the excellent Dohm, in Germany ; Count de Mirabeau,* Abbé Grégoire and Thierry of Nancy, in France ; the Pelham cabinet and Dean Tucker in England, where the Jews were emancipated by the act of 1753 (revoked in 1754) ; the Emperor Joseph, in Austria, and many others. Berlin was at that time the intellectual center of Germany, and Moses Mendelssohn was very prominent in it. Montesquieu was probably the first great writer of that age who advocated the cause of the Jews. In his great work, *"L'ésprit des Lois"* (livre 25, chap. 13), he exposed the disadvantages which accrue to states that maltreat the Jews. While in Lisbon, he saw a Jewish girl of eighteen years of age burned alive for the crime of believing in one God. This awful incident elicited the following words from him : " You Christians complain that the Emperor of China has tortured

* Mirabeau, *Sur Moses Mendelssohn et sur la Réforme Politique des Juifs à Londres*, 1787.

Christians by fire. You treat the Jews worse, simply because they do not believe all that you believe. If any of our descendants should ever dare say that the nations of Europe were enlightened, your example will be adduced, showing you yourselves have been barbarians. The idea one will have of you will stain your reputation, and will bring contempt on your contemporaries.''

It was not only in this way that Moses Mendelssohn contributed to the amelioration of the social and political condition of the Jews; he was active, notwithstanding his natural meekness and timidity, his apathy to public controversies, and his stoic calmness. Lessing has described him for lasting fame in his '' Nathan the Wise,'' for Nathan is no product of fancy. It is the portrait of Moses Mendelssohn in the several situations. When Lessing had published his drama, *"Die Juden,"* in which we might say he rebuked the German prejudice against the Jews (it was impossible to ignore what Lessing wrote), the Goettingen professor of theology, Chevalier Michaelis, attacked him in the *"Gelehrte Anzeigen."* I may add here that the professors at Goettingen and that organ are as reactionary to-day as they were a century ago. Michaelis thought it improbable that there could be a soul among the Jewish people as noble as the one described by Lessing. No Jew in Germany then had the courage and the ability to meet Prof. Michaelis in controversy, except Mendelssohn. In the form of a letter to Mr. Gomperz, he silenced Michaelis, and left him before the public a learned, but a very small man.

While he was still tutor in the house of Mr. Ziltz, Mendelssohn made an attempt to establish a Jewish organ. He published two numbers of a weekly—in Hebrew, of course—which he called "*Koheleth Mussar;*" but the enterprise was nipped in the bud. The Jews had no appreciation of the value and influence of a public organ, edited by an able and zealous friend of the people. Pious men discouraged the reading of anything else than sacred books; in fact, they feared it.

They had no confidence in "Moses Dessau," who, while he was clerk, had had a library containing such books as Klopstock's "*Messias*" and the New Testament. Though, while in Hamburg on a visit in the Spring of 1761, the great Rabbi Jonathan Eibenschuetz had said he was glad to learn that Moses Dessau was well versed in the Talmud, and that if married he would confer the Marenu, the rabbinical degree, on him. The ultra bigoted men were still afraid of this philosopher. Mendelssohn wrote German sermons for Berlin rabbis who could not write them themselves. He wrote one in 1757, after the battle of Rossbach, which was delivered on Thanksgiving Day, and he wrote to Lessing, "It has come so far that I write sermons and praise a king."

He wrote another, delivered at the peace jubilee, and then he wrote to Lessing concerning it, "Dr. Slop might have fallen asleep over it, and Uncle Toby might have whistled his *lillabulers* twice as loud." He wrote an excellent commentary (in Hebrew) on Maimonides' Logic (*Miloth ha-higga-yon*), presented it to a Jewish beggar from Jerusa-

lem to give him a chance to make some money ; but
the beggar would not place confidence in this new
genius. The object Mendelssohn had in entrust-
ing this book to a beggar was that it might be scattered broadcast over Germany and Poland, for who
would refuse buying of a mendicant from the Holy
Land? Thus he would attract attention to philosophy and to himself. In Saxony and in Switzerland, where chicaneries had broken out against
Jews, Mendelssohn came to their defense with his
pen as well as with the influence of his numerous
Christian friends, so that even Lavater, his opponent, supported him in behalf of his co-religionists.
Still the bigoted Jews looked upon him with suspicion. But, as might naturally be supposed, the
number of his friends and of his admirers among all
classes of Jews grew rapidly, and the sparks from
his genius were fanned into beneficent and vivifying fire.

The liberating influence of Mendelssohn did for the
Jews everywhere else more than in Prussia. Frederic the Great was an enemy of God, of the Bible,
of the Jews and of Christianity. In 1752 he issued
an edict prohibiting the immigration of the Jews,
limiting the Jewish population, and arranging
for the eventual expatriation of the rest. The
number of Jewish residents in Berlin was fixed, no
stranger was allowed to settle, except he were in
the service of one of the resident Jews, Mendelssohn
himself having been such a one. Voltaire had made
of Frederic an enemy of the Jews. Voltaire could
not forget or forgive that he had lost 20,000
francs in the bankruptcy of a London Jewish bank-

ing house, and that the Jew Hirsch, of Berlin, had charged him with swindling.

The king was a philosopher, author and poet, but Moses Mendelssohn was a consummate critic, and his authority went farther than the king's. He was a bel esprit in his day, and took up the gauntlet, on the one side, against the very strong Gottsched and, on the other hand, against the king and his French deists, along with Lessing and Nicolai. He was a match for both in metaphysics and belles lettres. He was not only the philosophical Moses, but also one of the best prose writers of his day. The " *Literaturbriefe*" was the critical journal of his day in which the literature of the period was reviewed, and Mendelssohn's were the best of the " *Literaturbriefe.*" Frederick's philosophy was hard pressed by Mendelssohn. When that king denied the immortality of the soul, and turned up from old books a number of epicurean passages, the author of the "*Phaedon*" made the king feel the Jew's superiority over him. Mendelssohn closes his review thus : "It appears to me that a Frederick who doubts the immortality of the soul is a mere chimera, a squared circle." He handled the king's " *Poésies Diverses*" (Frederick hated the German language) as only the author of " The Letters on Sensation " could do it, and treated the king's book with honesty, fairness and thoroughness such as he should like to have had for his own. The Rev. Mr. Justi, whose hymns Mendelssohn had reviewed in a similar manner, took advantage of the opportunity and charged Mendelssohn with libel and blasphemy against God and the king, and the

" *Literaturbriefe* " were confiscated. The little Jew
was commanded to appear at Sansouci on a Saturday evening. In the anteroom of the king, the
courtiers could not understand how a little Jew
could be cited before the king, and Mendelssohn
was subjected to a rigid examination. Moses knew
that the fellow he had to deal with was ignorant,
and he said in sport, " I am a magician." Ushered
into the king's presence, he was asked whether he
was the author of that review. "Yes," said Mendelssohn, " whoever makes verses plays nine pins; and
whoever plays nine pins, be he king or peasant, must
allow a fellow to tell him the pins he has thrown."
This satire took well, and the continuance of the
" *Literaturbriefe* " was granted. Still, the right to
be a Jewish citizen of Berlin the king could not
confer on him. It was against the law. Marquis
d'Argens, a French philosopher and companion of
the king, at Potsdam, happened to hear of that
law. He asked, astonished, " How about notre
cher Moise? The day he resigns as bookkeeper,
if he finds no Berlin Jew to employ him, the police
will escort him out of the city." The Marquis ex-
postulated with the king for years before he agreed
to receive a petition with regard to this, and after
it had been submitted it was lost. D'Argens induced Mendelssohn to write a similar petition, and
he himself handed it to the king, and the Marquis
wrote upon it the following satire :
" Un Philosophe mauvais catholique supplie un
Philosophe mauvais protestant de donner le privi-
lège à un Philosophe mauvais juif. Il y a trop de

Philosophie dans tout ceci que la raison ne soit pas du côté de la demande.''

The king granted the privilege, made Mendelssohn a present of a thousand thalers, which by law he would have had to pay, but refused to extend the toleration to his children. Mendelssohn thus had realized that the emancipation of the Jews in Prussia was not to be achieved. Nevertheless he would not give up the task.

A man in Alsace, by the ominous name of Hell, copyist, clerk, and finally district judge, who went to the guillotine in 1794, used the execrable laws of Alsace to keep the Jews in constant dread, and to replenish his purse. When the Jews refused to comply with his extortions, he provoked excitement against them among the burghers of Strasburg and Metz, and thus endangered their property and their lives. Pamphlets were written against the Jews, and the Jews had no one to reply. The clergy agitated in the dark, and pamphleteers in public, without opposition. Finally the Jews selected Cerf Beer to go to Paris and lay their complaint before Louis XVI. At the same time Mendelssohn was requested to defend their cause in the public press. The discretion of Mendelssohn was very valuable in such emergencies. He was moderate, sagacious, and invincible in the debate. He accepted this mission. His friend, Christian William Dohm (1751 to 1820), had just received an appointment at the royal archives, with the title of Kriegsrath. This young statesman was won over for the cause by Mendelssohn, and wrote the memorable essay '' On the Political Improvement of the Jew'' (1782).

The sins which had been committed on Jews were frankly restated. From the point of view of the statesman and the humanitarian, the matter was handled in so masterly a manner that every German statesman, professor, and every man of education was impressed by it. It produced a sensation all over Germany. Emperor Joseph of Austria gave it additional force by his edicts in favor of the Jews, as to which Klopstock (Ode an den Kaiser) chanted a hymn of praise. A controversy followed. Diez, Johannes von Mueller and others, indorsed Dohm ; Hartmann and Professor Michaelis wrote venomously against it. This brought out Mendelssohn, first in an introduction to the German translation of *Menasseh ben Israel*, "Salvation of the Jews," by Marcus Herz, and then in an independent work, "Jerusalem," in which the whole question is fully discussed. (The Rev. Isaac Lesser translated this book into English.)

Mendelssohn had already startled many Christians by his opposition to excommunication. But his philosophy in "Jerusalem," based upon the idea of civil and religious liberty, his defense of freedom of conscience and of moral responsibility, was then new and offensive to German thinkers. The eyes of thousands were just then (1782) turning to the clear light in the newly-born United States of America. From this standpoint he demanded the emancipation of the Jews with irresistible argument.

This is a brief summary of Mendelssohn's labor for the social and political reform of the Jews.

His literary fame, his high position in society, his
independence and his generosity, drew to him the
respect of tens of thousands. His manly defense
of his oppressed brethren endeared him to the
masses.

VIII.—MOSES MENDELSSOHN ON RELIGIOUS RE-
FORMS.*

The center of gravity in European Judaism had
been gradually moved from Spain to Poland. It
was Poland, where Jewish lore had its home.
The young Israelites of all other countries in
Europe were obliged to frequent the Polish academies called Yeshiboth, in order to acquire that
rabbinical knowledge which was necessary not only
for the rabbi, but also for general education.
The Talmud and the rabbinical commentaries to the
Bible, constituted the literature considered worth
knowing ; everything else was excluded from the
curriculum.

Besides the Talmud, it was the Cabalah, especially the Sepher Yezirah, the books of the Zohar,
the works of rabbi Isaac Luria, Chaim Vidal and
others, which attracted the attention of students.
This study had produced in the person of Sabbathai

* In 1740, King Charles of the two Sicilies, the first king
of that country who was independent of Spain, in order to
give a fresh impulse to the sinking commerce of southern
Italy, invited the Jews to return to his country, and in an
edict (February 3, 1740) granted them important privileges. The king's edict, however, was practically annulled
by the Jesuits and priests.

Zevi, a messianic impostor, an age of miracles and prophecy, and a new sect, small but mischievous in influence. About 1740 another cabalistic impostor, Israel Baal Shem, wrought miracles and conversed with angels. He succeeded in establishing a sect of cabalists, called Chasidim, who had votaries also outside of Poland, and spread superstition and fanaticism. The rabbis receiving continually new revelations from on high, rejected the authority of the Talmud. A heated controversy arose, in which the three greatest authorities of that age, Eliah Wilna, Ezekiel Landau and Jonathan Eibenschuetz were engaged, and bans were exchanged between rabbinists and cabalists. Jonathan Eibenschuetz, successively chief rabbi of Prague, Metz and Hamburg, was charged with being one of the cabalistic impostors of Poland, a charge he did not deny. He was seriously attacked by Jacob Emden and the rabbis mentioned before. Although Rabbi Landau defended him because he admired and venerated him, he condemned the Cabalah and the imposition connected with it. But controversies and bans were ineffectual, so far as the Chasidim were concerned ; belief in the Cabalah and in holy rabbis persists to this day among nearly 200,000 Jews in Poland and Hungary, and in Jerusalem. From time to time those saints announce that they have performed some miracle and they get rich. A great number of credulous persons believed in the supernatural powers of those men called Baale Shem, the last of whom in Germany, Rabbi Seckel Loeb, of Michelstadt, died but a few

years ago. Jews and Christians from near and far
went to such a "holy man" to work miracles for
them in case of disease or special occurrences. The
cabalistic absurdities of the Jews were of the same
nature and equally tenacious as the belief of
Christians in the miracles wrought by images of
saints, to whose chapels some crawl upon their
knees for miles, leaving the spot more bewildered
and demoralized than ever.

This was the state of society when Moses Mendelssohn wrote. His philosophical works, however, did not reach the masses. Parts of his
Phaedon on the immortality of the soul were translated into Hebrew, but Jews stood in no need of
such proofs of a doctrine which was firmly believed,
nor had they any taste for the exquisite beauty of
diction which distinguishes that book. Some of the
best among the Jews of Germany and Poland were
reached by the Phaedon, but the masses and the demoralized rabbis cared nothing about it.

Honored and beloved by the most prominent
Christians of his days, as Mendelssohn was, receiving no encouragment from the Jews, his pen might
have remained inactive had not a zealous Christain
challenged the timid man to defend his religious
belief before the public. Deacon Lavater, who had
translated the book of his colleague Bonnet, "On
the Evidences of Christianity," from French into
German, sent it to the author of the Phaedon
(1769) with a dedication challenging him either
to refute the arguments of the book or to embrace Christianity. Lavater, since 1763 a personal

friend of Mendelssohn, thought he would render
a, great service to Christianity by this prose-
lyting step, and expected that Mendelssohn and
through him thousands would come into the lap of
Protestantism by this maneuver. But he was mistaken. It had a contrary effect on Mendelssohn.
It brought out the pride and the faith of the Jew
Moses. Lessing, the friend of Mendelssohn, regarded it as in bad taste on the part of Lavater to
publicly challenge a peaceable man and to force him
into a controversy. He knew Moses would tell
the truth. The good man Lessing lacked the
moral courage to do so himself, so his attacks on
Christianity were not published till after his death
(1794). It was a precarious undertaking for a Jew
in Germany at that time to attack Christianity.
Therefore, Moses Mendelssohn in his public epistle
to Lavater did not state why he would not be a
Christian, but he told him positively and firmly
why he would remain a Jew. The epistle is a
masterpiece of argument, moderation and of style.
Although Lessing was dissatisfied, the epistle
called forth a controversy which lasted two years,
and involved some of the best German and French
writers, but it led to no result. It was a philosophical controversy without personalities, and was followed by Jew and Gentile with deep interest. Remarkable in this matter is the fact that besides
Herder, also Pastor Hesse and. Prof. Semler
sided with Mendelssohn ; and that when Mendelssohn asked the Prussian censor before its publication who would review his reply to Lavater, he was
told : '' Moses Mendelssohn may publish his works

without submitting them before this consistory,
since every one is convinced of his wisdom and
humility, and that he would write nothing which
might lead to public scandal.'' The best product
of this controversy was Mendelssohn's epistle to
the Prince of Brunswick, which was not published,
however, during the lifetime of its author.

From this time on, Mendelssohn never ceased
working for the Jews, who honored him greatly.
He wrote on and translated rabbinical laws which
are still in effect, and he also translated the Pentateuch into German for the use of his children.
Solomon Dubno (born 1738), a Polish Jew of learning, instructed Mendelssohn's children in Hebrew
grammar. It was to this man that he first showed
his translation of the Pentateuch, and this one requested that it be published for the public good.
After an agreement with Dubno to assist him, both
went to work to write a Hebrew commentary in defense of Mendelssohn's translation and to preface it
with a brief exposition on Hebrew grammar, prosody and exegesis. Mendelssohn wrote the preface
and a few chapters on Genesis; the balance of the
commentary to this book Dubno wrote. In 1778 a
proof-sheet was issued in Amsterdam, and the public
was invited to subscribe for the work. From all
parts of Germany, Holland, France and England
subscriptions came. Rabbi Hirschel Lewin, of
Berlin, and his son Saul, rabbi of Frankfurt a. d.
Oder, zealously supported the enterprise, and Naphtali Hartwig Wessely, the great Hebrew poet, on
seeing the proof and advertisement, poured forth
his enthusiasm for it in beautiful lines. The rabbis

of Fuerth, Prague and Altona, however, pronounced
the ban over the work, and prohibited its circulation in Jewish families. The imperial library of
Vienna and the king of Denmark subscribed for
the work, and in 1780 the first volume (Genesis)
appeared ; the second volume (Exodus) followed in
1781. Meanwhile, the teacher of Solomon Dubno,
a pious rabbi, had come to Berlin, and had persuaded
Dubno to leave the city, and to abandon his share
in this work of Mendelssohn's. He left and Mendelssohn was obliged to write the Hebrew commentary to Exodus alone. But Naphtali Hartwig Wessely came to his rescue and wrote his matchless commentary to Leviticus. Aaron Jaroslaw furnished the
commentary to Numbers, and Herz Homberg to Deuteronomy, so that the work was finished in 1783,
and given the title *Nethib Shalom*, "Path of Peace."
In the same year Mendelssohn's version of the
Psalms appeared in print. He translated the Song
of Solomon, the Song of Deborah, wrote a Hebrew commentary to Ecclesiastes, when death made
an end to his glorious career.

No book or books reached the Jews more rapidly
and was read more thoughtfully than were those
translations and commentaries. The Bible has always been the book of the Jews. In the darkest
days the Jewess did not stop reading the *Ze-enah
u-Re-enah*, which is the Pentateuch paraphrased in
medieval German, and the Jews would read every Friday and Sabbath the weekly section of the Pentateuch
twice, and once the Aramic translation, besides the
Haphtarah, section of the Prophets. The Psalms
were recited so frequently that almost every one

knew them by heart, though they were hardly understood. When the beautiful versions of Mendelssohn reached them, the Jews learned from them German and Hebrew, grammar and prosody, exegesis and æsthetics. A treasury of knowledge was opened for them, and in a short time they learned to know many things. Especially the young Talmud students of Poland were irresistibly seized by the new spirit, and were carried into the world of culture by Mendelssohn's versions and commentaries. The Talmud was laid aside, and other books were sought and read. It was a new kind of education they craved for; they could not find it at the Polish academies, and the universities of Austria, Italy and Holland received the Talmud students, to school them for the world and the higher vocations.

The commentaries added to the versions of Mendelssohn, though very carefully written, disposed of rabbinical hermeneutics, and re-introduced to students Ibn Ezra, Gersonides, Kimchi and Abarbanel, grammar, philology and criticism. Despite all bans and denunciations, a new era set in and rabbinism and cabalism were overthrown. The Arabic-Spanish literature of the Jews was read again. The Hebrew language again found admirers and cultivators, and people began to speak German correctly. Here modern reform had its beginning.

Mendelssohn, the manufacturer of silk goods and of good books, became the reformer and benefactor of his race. He was no rabbi and no priest, no professor and no doctor (he refused all titles), no agi-

tator and no leader, but he was emphatically an
honest man and an upright Jew. His prominence
as a scholar and a writer afforded him opportunity
to do for his co-religionists more than others could.
As beautiful and calm morning follows night, and
ushers in the bright sun, ruler of the day, so Mendelssohn was the herald of a new day, a veritable
rainbow after the storm. Had he been a Christian,
he would have been canonized; Jews merely admired him; but his memory is blessed forever.

IX.—Contemporaries of Mendelssohn.

In the time of Mendelssohn, and influenced by
him, a considerable number of Israelites became
very prominent in the republic of letters. Five of
them deserve particular notice, viz.: Marcus Herz
of Berlin, Lazarus Bendavid of Berlin, Solomon
Maimon of Nieszwic, in Russia, Naphthali Hartwig
Wessely of Hamburg, and Herz Homberg of
Lieben, near Prague. Marcus Herz (1747 to 1803),
although the son of poor parents, studied philosophy
and medicine, and became distinguished as a writer
in both. He was the favorite of Immanuel Kant,
whose philosophical system he expounded in Berlin.
His lectures were attended by the highest nobility
and by the minister of state, Mr. Zedlitz. Still
more popular were his lectures on natural philosophy and on experimental physics, which
were listened to by many princes, also Frederic
William III. No less than twelve books of this
man's pen were published between the years 1771
and 1790. As Dr. Herz was distinguished among

learned men, so was his wife eminent among the
ladies of Berlin for her beauty, wit and refinement.
In her house the greatest men of Germany met at
social gatherings. The king, courtiers, professors,
soldiers, poets, authors, composers, artists, all
kinds of distinguished characters, including the
two brothers Humboldt, Boerne and Heine, were
the sattelites of that remarkable woman. Her most
favored were Dorothea Mendelssohn, daughter of
Moses, afterward the wife of Friederich von
Schlegel, and Rachel Levin, afterward the wife
of Varnhagen von Ense. Schleiermacher said of
Henrietta Herz, she was his Platonic bride, Count
Mirabeau worshipped her and Bishop Teller admired her, Boerne, when a lad, fell in love with her,
although she was older than his mother. After the
death of her husband she lost much of her prestige,
still it is due to her to say that the prejudices against
the Jews in Germany, and especially among the
higher classes, diminished, and that social intercourse between Jews and Gentiles was beginning to
be cultivated. At the same time Fanny Itzig, of
Berlin, married a Jewish baron of Vienna, Nathan
Adam Arnstein, and exercised nearly similar influence on Vienna society as Henrietta Herz exercised
in Berlin.

Lazarus Bendavid (1762–1832) was another expounder of Immanuel Kant's philosophy. He was
both a rabbinical scholar and a mathematician of
great note. As a philosophical writer he was more
eminent than Dr. Herz, but he was not as popular
as a lecturer. He began his philosophical lectures
in 1793, at the university of Vienna, much to the

chagrin of the Christian professors, who succeeded eventually in forcing him from the university. Count Harrach opened his, palace to the Jewish philosopher, and he continued his lectures in his mansion. In 1798 he returned to Berlin, and remained there to his death, as superintendent of the Jewish free school and secretary of the royal treasury for widows.

Solomon Maimon (1753–1800) was probably the most interesting of the three great expounders of Kant. Two natures appeared to unite in him, that of the coarse cynic and of the sagacious philosopher. Besides his numerous essays and treatises on philosophical themes in the "*Berliner Monatsschrift,*" and the *Magazin*, from 1789 to 1800, constituting in themselves a small library, and besides ten books on many departments of philosophy, published between 1790 and 1797, he also wrote the *Gibath ha-Moreh*, a Hebrew commentary and a remarkable introduction to three parts of Maimonides' *More Nebuchim*, published in Berlin 1791, and then again at Vienna and Sulzbach, in which he proves himself master of philosophy. This man was a beggar all his lifetime, but always found generous admirers.

At the same time another Jew, Marcus Elias Bloch of Ansbach, distinguished himself as a naturalist, and especially as an ichthyologist. Besides his numerous treatises on medical and scientific subjects, published between 1782 and 1792, he wrote ten volumes on natural history of fishes, published in German and French, in Berlin, between 1784 and 1795. He laid the foundation of this science.

These four men did much for the German people, German literature, and especially for the German

Jew. As afterward Meyerbeer, Halévy, Mendels-
sohn-Bartholdy and Offenbach proved that Jewish
genius has the brilliancy in music, to the chagrin
and discomfiture of all pedantic egotists, so those
savants broke through the inveterate stupidity of
German professors. As Paul once sat at the feet
of Gamaliel, so now princes, generals, cabinet ministers and high-born nobility, sat at the feet of
Jewish philosophers and learned from them, and
frequented Jewish homes and were refined by
Jewish women. This changed the status of the
Jew. The masses of the German people were too
much neglected to learn the lesson of tolerance
at once, but the higher classes began to look upon
the Jew with a certain degree of respect, and
despite the iniquitous laws of Frederick the Great,
enforced also by Frederick William II, the Jew had
some hope now for improvement and elevation in
society.

Naphtali Hartwig Wessely (1725–1805) was the
son of wealthy parents, and was educated in the
rabbinical schools. In every other branch of knowledge he was a self-made man. An intimate friend
of Mendelssohn, and aspiring like him to contribute to the regeneration and elevation of the
Jew and of Judaism, he lived as a merchant on a
small income at Copenhagen, and spent his leisure
hours in the acquisition of knowledge, and in turning it to practical benefit for his fellow-men. Wessely was the most prominent Hebraist of his age.
Germany, Poland and Italy owe to his Hebrew
works, in prose and poetry, the revival of Hebrew
letters. After he had published the two volumes

of his "*Libanon*," Mendelssohn obtained for him
the place of business manager in the house of
Joseph Veitel, and Wessely moved with his family,
in 1774, to Berlin, soon to taste there, after Veitel's
retirement from business, the bitter cup of poverty
and destitution. Too proud to reveal his circumstances, he and his family suffered abject
poverty. When Mendelssohn invited him to
write the commentary to Leviticus, it was a god-
send to the poor man. Mendelssohn, knowing he
was not wealthy, provided for him and his family
abundantly, so that his mind might be at ease while
doing the work. This indestructible monument of
Wessely's learning and talent was written and published within the space of one year. His commentary to Genesis, however, was not published
till 1868 and 1870, by the association called *Me-
kize Nirdamim* (L. Silbermann, Lyck). Besides
these commentaries, his epistles and his Hebrew
version of "The Wisdom of Solomon," the Hebrew of which is as if it had been written in the
classical day of King Solomon, his main work is
the *Gan Na'ul*, "Enclosed Garden," in two volumes, in which he almost exhausts the difficult
subject of Hebrew Synonyms. Unacquainted with
comparative studies in language—they did not obtain then—he still treated his subject so thoroughly
that no Hebrew lexicographer of our days can
afford to ignore it. His Hebrew poems are numerous and some are exquisitely beautiful. But he was
more successful in the sublime than in the beautiful. His grand epos, *Shire Tiphereth*, on the
exodus, has no parallel in Hebrew poetry, and its

beauty of form and elegance of diction has roused
thousands of young Hebrews to enthusiasm for
the Bible. And yet, who knows the care he had in
bringing out his work! Wealthy friends advanced
the money at last. The waste of genius was
stayed.

Herz Homberg (1748–1841) was of another turn
of mind. He was eminently practical. It appears
to us now like a vision from dreamland, when we
recollect the hoary man with the appearance of a
prince, the imperial order in his button-hole, and
scorn in his mien for all that is vulgar, mean or
small. Young students cluster about him twice a
week to listen to his story, which reaches back as
far as the year 1760, embracing the political com-
motion, changes of empires, wars, revolutions,
progress and retrogression, all stored up in his tenacious memory. We had forgiven him the wrong
he committed on the boys of his days who were
obliged to study the Hebrew text of his catechism,
"*Imre Shepher,*" a dry book of interminable prose.
We looked up to him as to an authority of an ancient day. He loved to be compared to Socrates,
though he bore not the least resemblance to him.
One of the lads pleased the old man by writing a
Hebrew dialogue, "Socrates and His Disciples,"
with marked reference to him and to his band of
young disciples. The writer of the "Dialogues"
was called Herz Plato for years after, and, if we are
not mistaken, he is still called so by some of his
earliest friends.

Herz Homberg, as narrated before, was tutor in
Mendelssohn's house, and co-laborer in the com-

mentary to the Pentateuch. When Emperor Joseph
of Austria had issued his memorable edict, Homberg returned to Austria, highly recommended
by Mendelssohn, who was his warm friend. After
some time he was appointed Schulrath, general
superintendent of the Jewish schools in Austrian
Poland, with a considerable salary. He met with
little success, partly on account of the intolerance
of the Chasidim, partly on account of the wars
which rapidly followed one another, and partly also
on account of his imprudent opposition to rabbinical
customs and Jewish observance. His *"Imre
Shepher,"* written for schools, in which he is
much more orthodox than the thirteen articles of
Maimonides require of the rabbinical Jew, and evidently relegates it to oblivion ; he makes no mention of the ceremonial law. This was too much
for the Jews of that country and age. Emperor
Francis decorated him, and a royal pension
was paid to him during his lifetime. The publication of his second catechism (German), *"Bené
Zion,"* is his least credible effort. It is dry and
tedious reading, but every boy and girl ambitious
for higher education, or desirous of marriage, had
to pass an examination in it before a rabbi and an
imperial commissioner. This became a source of
chicanery and extortion in Austria ; but the edict
was not revoked till 1848. Through his acquaintance with Elia Morpurgo, Homberg exercised considerable influence on the Jews of Italy, and in
Prague his influence on the rising generation was
quite helpful. He was a man of enlightened principles and of energy. A splendid Hebraist, ver-

satile in Scriptures and its commentaries, well acquainted with the Hebrew philosophical literature,
and possessing enough knowledge of the Talmud
to know its weak points, he was an apostle of reform to the narrow circle of his friends and disciples, many of whom he enlisted under the banner
of Progress.

Here it is proper to mention David Friedlander,
but we must reserve him for another chapter. With
this group of men the three directions which reform
took after Mendelssohn are clearly indicated. The
first group, Herz, Bendavid, Maimon, and Bloch
(also the poet, Ephraim Kuh, and the musician,
Bernard Wessely,) indicates the course which one
portion of Jews took, viz., the cultivation of science
and art. Naphtali Hartwig Wessely indicates the
course of positive reform in religion and Herz Homberg the course of negative reform. Gradual regeneration was the tendency of the former, destruction
was the parole of the latter. The succession of
these three groups up to our days is continuous.

X. Active Reform.

The new spirit promulgated among the Jews by
Mendelssohn and his contemporaries manifested
itself first in three different directions, viz., in the
literature, schools, and political emancipation. In
literature it was the association of the *Measphim*
(compilers) that made a popular and successful beginning. During the lifetime of Mendelssohn, when
the orthodox rabbis waged war against Naphthali
Hartwig Wessely, and the great question was discussed, whether the Jew must remain restricted to

rabbinical literature, and whether he may turn his attention to philosophy and science? Wessely favored the latter. Two eminent Hebraists, Isaac Araham Euchel and Mendel Bresslau, supported by Simon and Samuel Friedlander, issued a prospectus (spring, 1783) to form an association to the cultivation of the Hebrew language, and to publish a public organ. The responses were numerous and encouraging, the society was organized, and in the fall of the same year the new periodical in Hebrew, called the *Me'asseph*, "The Compiler," made its appearance. This was the central point for the men of the new spirit. Writers from all parts of Germany and Poland, from France, Holland and Italy, sent contributions, original or translated, supplying entirely new food to the Jewish mind. Among the contributors there were Joel Loewe, Aaron Wolfsohn, David Friedlander, Baruch Lindau, Mordechai Levisohn, body physician of the king of Sweden and professor of medicine at the University of Upsala ; Isaac Satanow, Juda Joel Ben Seev, Wolf Heidendeim, David Franco Mendes, Mose Ensheim, Elia Marpurgo, and a host of others. They rejuvenated the Hebrew. The main object of the *Measphim* was correctness and beauty of language, the reform of literary taste, the education of the young, and to turn the attention of the masses to secular learning for practical ends.

This was the beginning of the periodical literature among the modern Israelites. In eighty-nine years a large number of journals have grown out

of this small beginning, which have exercised a
deep influence on the Jewish affairs and learning,
and now Hebrew, English, German, French, Italian,
New Greek, Polish, Prussian and Hungarian journals reach all parts of the globe where Israelites
live, and form a bond of union and a medium of
intercourse among all of them.

With the progress of academical studies and systematical learning among the Hebrews, writers of
prominence in all branches of literature rose among
them, and especially in Germany. We must follow
the history of some branches of literature. Most
important to the Hebrew and a proper understanding of mission is the knowledge of history, so very
much neglected by the Israelites themselves. After
Josephus Flavius the Jews had not one historiographer of distinction. This was one of the main
reasons why the Jew and his literature were so long
neglected. In France, J. Basnage wrote his " *Histoire de la Religion des Juifs,*" from the beginning
of the Christian era to 1700 A. C., published in six
volumes, Rotterdam, 1707 to 1711, and then again
in fifteen volumes, Hague, 1716, besides the three
volumes of his " *La République des Hébreux,*"
Amsterdam, 1705. In England, Dr. Humphrey
Prideaux wrote his " Old and New Testament Connected in the History of the Jews," London, 1719.
In the beginning of the eighteenth century Christian Bastholm, preacher of the Danish court, wrote
a history of the Jews from Abraham to the end of
the seventeenth century, in three volumes, which
was translated into German and published in Leip-

zig in 1786. These three books, together with various Jewish works on history, and the works of Christians like John Christopher Wolf, Schudt, and Bodenschatz, would have offered sufficient material for a good history of the Jews; but there was nobody to do it. After a considerable number of historical essays had been published in various periodicals, and A. T. Hartman had published his remarkable three volumes (Amsterdam, 1809,) on the costumes of the ancient Hebrews, "*Die Hebraerin am Putztische*," Herder, Eichborn Rosenmuller, Michaelis, and a host of others, had dug up vast historical materials. The first German Israelite published in the year 1812 a history of the Jews from B. C. to 1800 A. C., in three parts, one octavo volume, very brief and very defective. David Ottensoser, of Fuerth, in Bavaria, is the name of the writer. It was published by Zirndorf, father and son, in German, in Hebrew type. One year before, in 1820, Dr. J. M. Jost had commenced his "*Geschichte der Israeliten*," etc., "History of the Israelites from Time of the Maccabees to the Present day"; but his first volume reached only to 45 A. C., and the second volume, published in 1821, formed a supplement to the first. The ninth volume, with the alphabetical index, reaching to 1815, was published in 1825. In 1847 he wrote the concluding volume, in three divisions, reaching to 1845. In 1850 he published in two volumes a complete history of Israel, and afterward again three volumes of the history of Judaism and its sect.

Dr. Jost was the restorer of Jewish history. Besides his erudition in the Hebrew, Greek and Latin classics, he was a fine German, French and English scholar, so that he had an unusual command of sources, and he studied them scrupulously. He is systematical in his arrangement and concise and clear in his diction, though cold and pedantic, without enthusiasm, without any apparent love for his subject. Sometimes he is even unjust to the Jews, the very reverse of the Christian Basnage, whose work he largely used, like all his successors in this literature. Historiography, in the earlier days of Jost, was quite imperfect in Germany, as it was in England before Hume, and the Jewish sources had been neither sufficiently known nor critically investigated. Therefore, although Jost, after Josephus, was the father of Jewish history and did gigantic work, he necessarily affords many a weak point to the impartial critic, although in the main he is a reliable and strictly objective historian. This Dr. Isaac Marcus Jost was born in Bernberg in 1793, and died in Frankfort-on-the-Main. Besides editing for three years the periodical, " *Israelitische Annalen*," 1839 to 1841, and co-editing with Creizenach the "Zion," etc., 1841 and 1842, writing a number of text-books for the school of which he was a teacher, and a number of pamphlets and contributions to various journals, he translated the Mishnah, supplying it with vowel points (Berlin, 1832), wrote an English grammar and a dictionary to Shakspeare, a guide-book of London, the German, English and French text to F. Steuber's "*Mythologische Gallerie*," and published the works of Frederick the Great.

Jost's influence on the minds of Jewish students was deeply felt, and lead a considerable number to historical researches in Jewish literature. The impulse in this direction being given, important results were soon obtained. Three men appeared first and foremost in the field, S. L. Rappaport (born 1790), L. Zunz (born 1794). In Austrian-Poland a number of talented Jews, aroused by the friends and successors of Mendelssohn, began a new literary career by writing very elegant Hebrew contributions for the periodical, "*Bikkure ha-ittim*," which, from and after 1820, appeared at Vienna, edited by Solomon Cohen, of Hamburg. Eminent among the contributors from Lemberg was S. L. Rappaport, a poor man, persecuted on account of his progressive tendencies. His contributions (1828), which are numerous, contained also a splendid Hebrew version of Racine's "Esther." In 1829 and 1830 this same writer contributed a number of biographies of Jewish literati of the tenth and eleventh centuries, and roused the interest of Jewish students. They proved not only his vast knowledge and deep research, but also his superior talent for critical researches. He was appointed rabbi of Tarnopol in 1838, and then (1840) chief rabbi of Prague, where he died. Writing in Hebrew only, his productions remained in the hands of the few who turned them to popular use. He began to publish an encyclopedia of the Talmud "*Erech Millin*," Prague, 1852; but it is of use to learned rabbis alone, there exists in print the part of Aleph only.

The fact is, that Rappaport's researches were of no great importance to general history. His method is important, his successful application of philology and archolæogy, his sagacious suggestiveness, his discovery of sources as Eliazar ben Kalir's poetry, and the like.

More important to literature because more systematical and scientific than Rappaport, is Dr. L. Zunz. Jewish literature had found in him an impartial critic, a historiographer of rare abilities, a bibliographer of incomparable industry and exactness. In the years 1822 and 1823 Zunz was before the public as a writer of eminence ; he edited the literary periodical, *"Zeitschrift fuer Wissenschaft des Judenthums."* He had made his debut in 1820 with the first volume of a book on rabbinical literature, to which he wrote a second volume in 1828. In these he proved the necessity of classical studies in order to comprehend the importance of Jewish literature aside from its theological contents. His masterpiece in this field, *"Die Gottesdienslichen Vortraege,"* etc., appeared in Berlin in 1832. In 481 pages octavo, this remarkable book places before the reader history on the sermons, homilies, prayers and hymns of the Jews from the time when the last book of the Bible, Chronicles, was written, to the year 1830 A. c., embracing over twenty-one centuries in Asia, Africa and Europe, surveying an immense library, and placing each author and each book in exact time. The notes and quotations under the text of this book are overawing to the reader, so that it is difficult to comprehend how one man could have done that amount of reading, and have compressed it in so small a compass. The vast field surveyed by Dr. Zunz contain many details upon which he could touch but slightly. A vast field of labor was opened to the inquisitive and

critic, and a host of scribes followed Zunz to re-dis-
cover, as it were, the ancient literature of the
Hebrews, and to clear it of the dust of ages which
had gathered on it. The other books of Dr. Zunz,
"History and Literature," Berlin, 1845; "The
Synagogal Poetry of the Middle Ages," Berlin,
1855; "History of the Rites in Synagogal Worship," Berlin, 1850, and his minor works are all
of the same cast. He was a living library, animated by an eminent sense of criticism and with
a rare talent for giving shape and form to chaotic
matter.

Less important than Rappaport and Zunz, although a much more elegant writer and more successful expounder of the Bible than either of the
former, was Solomon David Luzzatto, the scion of
one of the most eminent Italian families, and to the
end of his life the leading professor at the rabbinical
seminary of Padua. He wrote Hebrew, Italian,
French and German. His diction is graceful and
exceedingly pleasant. He bears a stronger resemblance to Plato than Mendelssohn did to Socrates. He
was the Jehudah Halevi of the nineteenth century.
His lectures on moral theology are so much akin to
the Chazari, as the diction and form of his Hebrew
poems always remind one of Jehudah Halevi, whose
Divan he published, Prague, 1840, containing the
best poems of the great Castilian. In his critical
labors he appears in the same field with the two
savants named, no less learned and erudite, but less
profound and suggestive than Rappaport, and less
industrious and systematical than Zunz. His essays
and treatises in his field appeared mostly in the

" *Bikkure Ha-Ittim*," and afterward (1841, etc.,)
in the " *Kerem Chemed*," published in Vienna and
then in Prague by a man of learning in Jewish
literature, Samuel L. Goldenberg of Tarnopol.
One of his best works in this field is his " Dialogues," etc., on the Cabalah, the *Zohar*, on the
antiquity of the vowel points and accents of the
Bible. This Hebrew book, published in 1852,
shows the folly of the Cabalah, proves the origin of
the *Zohar* in the thirteenth century, and of the
vowel points in the fifth, and the accents probably
in the sixth. Luzzatto's main force was the Bible,
which he knew well. He was master of Biblical
literature in all its branches. He studied the ancient versions and published his " *Oheb Ger*," on
the Aramic version of Onkelos, Vienna, 1830. His
researches are laid down in his Italian version of
Job, Livorno, 1844 ; his French notes on Isaiah in
Rosenmuller's version, Leipzig; 1834 ; his Hebrew
notes on the Pentateuch, Vienna, 1850 ; and finally
in his " Isaiah," the Italian translation and extensive Hebrew commentary, Vienna, 1850. Luzzatto was more an exegetic than historical critic ;
but also in this, and epecially in the history of
exegesis, he was very successful. Around these
original men and writers a host of others grouped
themselves. They are too numerous to be mentioned in this sketch. One, however, who worked
independently, must be mentioned here, viz., J.
Salvador of Paris. He published his " *Lois de
Moïse*," etc., Paris 1822, and in 1828 his "*Histoire
des Institutions de Moïse et du peuple Hébreu*," in
three volumes, Paris, translated into German, with

a preface by Gabriel Riesser, Hamburg, 1836. After that he published two volumes, "History of the Romans in Palestine," which is indispensable to students of that period. Salvador was a fine classical scholar and a pleasant writer, without the scholarship of the savants I have mentioned before, and he represents the Jewish mind from another standpoint, no less true and no less worth being known and fully understood.

XI.

Reggio and Krochmal, two scholars of great distinction, who also contributed largely to the historical researches, can not be classified here. We will meet them again in their proper places. So much, however, must be said here, that the critical researches of these two men exercised a considerable influence on the Hebrew historiographers of this century.

A poor man of the city of Brody, whose name has never become known, under the protection of Issachar Beer Blumenfeld, of Brody, and Rabbi Jacob, of Lissa, was the first who had the boldness to criticise the works of Zunz and Rappaport, in a book called "Rabia," supposed to be the initials of his name. The book was published a few years after it had been written, in Ofen, 1837. This poor and unknown man developed in this (Hebrew) book great knowledge of the rabbinical literature and critical sagacity, coupled with a fine sarcasm, in the academical sense of the term. He might have become one of the best critics of his day. But poor and one-sided as he was, he was known to but a few scholars, appreciated by some and ignored by

most of them. In many points, however, he has
corrected the statement of Zunz and Rappaport, so
that the honest historian can not overlook him. In
one point, especially, he is correct. He complains
that Zunz in his quotations most always marked
the page of old editions, inaccessible to men outside
of Berlin, or other large cities, instead of giving
notations which would be found in other editions.
This, he maintains, imposes an unnecessary difficulty on the reader to control Zunz's statements.
Rabbi Jacob of Lissa, the celebrated author of
"*Havvoth Daath*" and "*Nethiboth hammishpat,*"
tells us that Rabia's name was Eliakim Getzel, son
of Juda Loeb, and that he also wrote commentaries
to the *Zohar* and *Pesikta Rabathi*, neither of which
appeared in print. Fuerst gives his name Ben Jehuda
Hammilsahagi, according to the title-page, and asserts that his original name was Mehlsack and that
he was probably rabbi in Smilow.

Elijah Carmoly, of Brussels, wrote a number of
books and treatises, in French and Hebrew, between
the years 1828 and 1845, which exercised a great
influence on the development of Jewish literature.
His works are, in the main, geographical and
biographical. One of his books, "*Histoire des Mé-
decins Juifs,*" etc., has found an English translator
in John R. W. Dunbar, and the book was published
in Baltimore, 1844. Others of his works were
translated into German. Jost translated his "Maimonides and his Contemporaries," and published it
in the "*Isr. Annalen.*" His book, "*Des Khozars
au Xe siècle,*" etc., Brussels, 1845, gives a fact then
unknown, that the *Chazari* of Rabbi Jehudah Ha-

levi is no fiction, and that a dynasty which had embraced Judaism actually existed in Arabia. Carmoly
directed the attention of scholars chiefly to geogra-
phy, in which many were very deficient and therefore the localities named in Jewish sources were
often misplaced. Most of his treatises appeared in
the *Revue Orientale*, which he published from 1841
to 1844. His books appeared in Brussels, except his
"*Tour du Monde de Petachia de Ratisbonne*," etc.,
which appeared in Paris, 1831, and his "*Toledoth
Gedole Israel*," which appeared in Metz, 1828.

It must be observed here that modern Jewish
literature originated in Germany, Poland, Italy and
France. While Jost and Zunz are Germans, Rappaport, Krochmal and Rabia are Poles, Luzzatto
and Reggio Italians, Salvador and Carmoly French-
men. They, it cannot be doubted, were the origi-
nators of the historic literature among modern Jews,
which embraces the largest part of their works.

A younger contemporary of the above is Dr.
Abraham Geiger, born (1810) in Frankfurt a. M.,
Rabbi of Berlin, editor of the periodical called
"*Juedische Zeitschrift fuer Wissenschaft and Leben*."
This remarkable man was, for nearly forty years,
one of the central figures of Jewish literature and
Jewish reform. As early as 1833, he signalized his
name by a book, "What has Mahommed taken
from Judaism?" Bonn, 1833, originally a treatise
crowned by the University of Bonn. Geiger was
successively Rabbi of Wiesbaden, Breslau, Frankfurt a. M. and Berlin, always a firm champion of
reform and a fertile and original mind. Geiger

made his journal, which was continued with slight interruptions and changes from 1835, a central point to all students, developing Jewish literature and unearthing Jewish documents. He himself was the master-spirit, and his pupils published a number of valuable and instructive treatises and essays.

Another master mind, no less important to Jewish literature than Geiger, was Dr. Julius Fuerst, born 1805, at Zolkiew, professor of history at the University of Leipzig. The nine volumes of the "Orient," which he published in Leipzig from 1840 to 1848, contained in the "*Literaturblatt*," besides the editor's essays, contributions on almost all periods of Jewish history, besides linguistic and biographical essays of considerable value. So also another prince of the mind, Dr. Zacharias Frankel, born in Prague, 1801, rabbi of Toeplitz, Bohemia, then in Dresden, and director of the rabbinical seminary at Breslau, edited a monthly periodical (from 1844 to 1846 and then again from 1851 to 1868, continued by Dr. Graetz), in which another not less important direction was taken for the progress of Jewish studies. He reconstructed various episodes of Jewish history and literature. While Geiger and Fuerst worked on general subjects, Frankel exhumed, as it were, the Talmudical literature in its historical bearings, and was certainly most successful in this. In the same field the Hungarian reformer, Dr. Leopold Loew, rabbi of Papa, then Szegedin and Gross Kanischa, was active and worked with no less success in his *Ben Chananja*, a periodical, first monthly, then weekly, from 1844 to 1868.

Independent, however, of the periodicals established for the purpose of developing Jewish literature and preparing the historical material, there appeared the works of S. Munk of Paris, Hirsch Chayes of Zolkiew, Leopold Dukes of Pressburg, Moses Landau of Prague, Dr. Derenburg and Prof. Frank of Paris, and many others.

Aside of them, the following historiographers must be named : Besides Millman, Hanna Adams, Depping, Ewald, Newman and Alexander, there were written the following books :

Joseph Wertheimer, *Die Juden in Oesterreich* (The Jews in Austria), Leipzig, 1842 ; *Geschichte der Israeliten*, etc., History of the Israelites from Alexander the Great to the year 1845, by Dr. Julius H. Dessauer (later in Cincinnati), and published in Erlangen, 1846 ; republished in Breslau, 1870.

Geschichte des Israelitischen Volkes, etc., History of the Israelitish people, by Dr. Solomon Friedlander (died in Chicago about 1875), published Leipzig, 1847 ; *Greschichte des Volkes Israel*, etc., " History of the people of Israel from the destruction of the second temple to the elevation of the Maccabean Simon to the dignity of prince and high-priest," by Dr. L. Herzfeld, Rabbi of Braunschweig, Vol. I, Braunschweig, 1847, Vol. II, Nordhausen, 1857, Vol. III, Nordhausen, 1855. History of the Israelitish Nation, by Isaac M. Wise, Albany, 1854. Post Biblical History of the Jews from 420 B. C. to 70 A. C., by Dr. Morris J. Raphall of New York, in two volumes, Philadelphia, 1855. The

History of the Jews of Spain and Portugal, etc., by
E. H. Lindo, London, 1849. Also Dr. Kayserling,
Geschichte der Juden in Portugal, Leipzig, 1867 ; *Die
Juden in Navarra, den Baskenlaendern und auf den
Balearen*, Berlin, 1861 ; and Sephardim, *Romanische
Poesien der Juden in Spanien*, Leipzig, 1859.

This vast literature was widely circulated, when,
in 1870, Dr. H. Graetz, professor at Breslau, finished
the history of the Jews, in nine volumes, from the
death of Judah Maccabee to this date. With all
these sources and preparations before him, it was
not a difficult task for Dr. Graetz to write a history,
nor was it necessary for him to state, as he does on
the title-page, that he wrote according to original
sources, for many excellent critical expounders had
well prepared them for him. The reader of the
aforementioned literature finds little new matter in
Graetz's history, although he will find something
more useful, viz.: a thorough survey of the romance
of Jewish history. He understands well to write
history in a pleasant style, although he might have
conveniently written the same account of history
in five instead of ten volumes.

Nevertheless, in the field of Jewish history,
Graetz offers a finished work, a complete compendium of all previous researches. However, his
last volume, on the modern history after Mendelssohn, must be excepted. It is a well written book,
but not history. He abuses reforms and reformers
in Judaism beyond measure, and in many instances
unjustly, praises their opponents, and ignores his
own teachers on the plea that they are not yet
dead. Still he does not adhere to this rule in the

case of Crémieux, Montefiore, Rothschild and other wealthy men, although he would not mention Dr. Loewe of Brighton, the interpreter who accompanied Sir Moses. In a history of the Jews it is unjust to dwell with particular delight on Boerne and Heine, and to ignore Geiger and Fuerst, Salvador and Herzfeld, Philippson and Stein, Mayer and Herxheimer, Zunz and Frankel, the very men who made Dr. Graetz, who did not, like Minerva, spring from Jupiter's brain all armed. But, whatever one may say about Graetz's History of the Jews, it is, nevertheless, the best work of this kind which we have.

The lectures in Jewish history by Dr. Abraham Geiger, reaching from the year 500 B. C. to the end of the sixteenth century, published in Breslau, 1864, 1865 and 1871, the first part in English by Dr. Maurice Mayer, New York, 1866, point out a new course to the future historiographer, and, in our opinion, treat successfully the main point, much neglected by Graetz, viz.: the influence of the Jew and Judaism upon the general development of the human family. This must be the main object of every Jewish history. Geiger dwells on this point with success. We only regret that he did not point out the reciprocity of Parsism and Judaism, which we consider very important.

We have allotted much space in this sketch to the historiography of the modern Jews, because we wish to sound the key-note. Since the revival of letters among the Jews, historical researches formed the main point of occupation of their scholars. It is not anything new which is sought ; it is chiefly

the exact knowledge of that which has been thought
and produced by the Jewish mind, or done and
suffered by the Hebrew people, which are the object of study and inquiry. Before we have a clear
idea of the past and its mental treasures, we can
not safely build upon it for the future. In philosophy and religion also it is not the absolute which
Jewish thinkers seek ; it is much more the result
produced by the Jewish minds, as religious or
philosophical doctrine, which are reproduced in
modern garb, as we shall see in all departments of
modern Jewish literature. The opinion still prevails that we are far behind our ancestors in the
correct comprehension and appreciation of both religious and philosophical doctrine. Perhaps it
is so ; at any rate, we are not sure that we are up
to them, as long as we have not mastered the whole
literature of the past, and do not know what is the
axis around which the Judaism of all centuries re-
volves. Therefore historical criticism and historiography have become important to modern Hebrews.
Wonderful, indeed, is the progress achieved in this
branch in the last fifty years, from 1820 to 1870,
from Ottensoser to Graetz and Geiger. A complete library, worked up by hundreds of industrious
and talented scholars, lies between the two points ;
a library of Hebrew, rabbinical, German, French,
Italian, and English books, large enough to occupy
the lifetime of a man, and interesting enough to
captivate the attention of the best of readers.
Still the masses of Jews and Christians are probably
as ignorant now of Jewish history as they were
fifty years ago. The subject has not been popu-

larized. The Jewish historian of the Jewish people has yet to come.

XII.

In exegesis, commentaries, and translations of the Bible, the modern Jews are no less active than in historiography. The successors of Mendelssohn, the *Measphim*, completed the translation of the Bible, and provided each book with a Hebrew commentary. Among the latter the commentary to Psalms, by Joel Levy, and the one to Proverbs, by Isaac Euchel, are known best; the former, indeed, is an excellent treatise on the Psalms and on Jewish poetry in general.

David Ottensoser translated and commented the book of Isaiah (published, Fuerth, 1807), Shalom Cohen translated and commentated the book of Jeremiah (Fuerth, 1810), J. L. Jeiteles, of Prague, wrote German translations and Hebrew commentaries on the book of Ezekiel, Job, Samuel, Daniel, Ezra, Nehemiah, and Chronicles. The rest of the Biblical books were translated and commentated in Hebrew by Aaron Wolfsohn, Arnswald, Neuman, and others. Herz Homberg wrote a commentary to the Pentateuch, called *Hakorem*. The whole Bible, with all these commentaries and translations, was published in Fuerth and in Vienna. This was soon followed (from 1832 to 1838) by an edition of the Hebrew text, Rashi, Onkelos, German translation in Hebrew letters, and the Hebrew commentaries of Moses J. Landau (the publisher), Wolf Meyer, Solomon Sachs, Joseph Weisse, M. Benisch, and all older commentaries to the Pentateuch and the other books. Several of the Biblical books appeared in separate editions, with new translations and commentaries, of these the Pentateuch by Wolf Heidenheim, is most notable (Roedelheim, 1818).

Meanwhile the bulk of Hebrew prayers was also translated and furnished with Hebrew commentaries, especially by the learned Wolf Heidenheim and Moses J. Landau.

The German Jews began also to read German, and new editions of the Bible appeared ; one by Dr. Zunz assisted by Doctors Z. Arnheim, Julius Fuerst, and Michael Sachs ; another by Dr. Gotthold Salomon of Hamburg, and a third with the Hebrew text and numerous notes by Dr. S. Herxheimer. These three translations are still considered standard among German Israelites. The notes of Herxheimer are of special value.

In 1832, Mr. S. Cahen, of Paris, since 1840 the editor of the Jewish monthly, *"Archives Israélites de France,"* began to publish a French version of the Bible, with critical introduction and commentaries to each book. The twenty-four books were finished in 1852. The title of the work is *"La Bible, traduction nouvelle, avec l'hébreu en regard, accompagné des points voyelles et des accents toniques, avec des notes philologiques, géographiques, et littéraires, et les principales de la version des septente et la texte samaritain."* This is decidedly the most complete and critical Bible version which the Jews possess.

In Italy, Isaac Samuel Reggio (1784 to 1855), one of the most fertile writers, published, in 1821, his Italian translation of the Pentateuch with a Hebrew commentary. The Italian Jews did very little in this field, till, in 1844, S. D. Luzzatto published his Italian version of Job, followed, in 1850 to 1856, by Isaiah, Hebrew text and commentary, with Italian translation. Reggio's Pentateuch is tinctured with Cabalistic views, in which respect Benamozegh followed him in his commentary to the Pentateuch. Luzzatto's Isaiah is of great value. The introduction and commentary are important to the Bible students, and his Italian translation is sweet and lyric. The Italian Jews have no Bible in their vernacular that has become known outside of their country.

Three attempts were made to render the Pentateuch into English, one by David Levi, one by the late Drs. Raphall, De Sola and Lindo (Genesis), and another by Dr. Kalisch. Dr. Benisch succeeded in the attempt of giving a plain translation of the Pentateuch, Haphtaroth, and the First Prophets.

In America, Isaac Lesser succeeded in translating the whole Bible. He published first the Pentateuch, Hebrew and English, five volumes, with the Haphtaroth to each; Philadelphia, 1845; and then the whole Bible, English, with brief notes, in large quarto and duodecimo; Philadelphia, 1854. The editions are typographically correct. In his translation and notes he depended chiefly on Mendelssohn, Zunz and Philippson, to whom he added nothing.

Besides the above complete works, a large number of essays and treatises on Biblical books and passages were published in books, pamphlets and periodicals, by men like Luzzatto, Reggio, Rappaport, Geiger, Krochmal, and others. This class of literature which has been produced by Jews aggregate now to a library of respectable size.

The first in Germany who attempted to reproduce the result of these researches was Dr. Ludwig Philippson, since 1834 editor of the *"Predigt und Schulmagazin,"* and of the *"Allgemeine Zeitung des Judenthums."* He published, Leipzig, 1848, a magnificent edition of the Bible in four volumes, Hebrew text, German translation, exensive notes, illustrations of historical interest and critical introductions to every book. The work has had a second edition. The translation is almost literal. The commentary offers, in brief, the opinions of acknowledged authorities, and is of great value to those who do not possess the originals. A Jewish Bible society, established in Germany, adopted Phillipson's translation.

Although the work is quite conservative, much more so than Bunsen's, the hyper-orthodox of Germany were not satisfied with it, and Dr. Samson Raphael Hirsch, of Frankfurt, a. M., published the Pentateuch, with a German translation and commentary. This is strictly rabbinical, often contrary to obvious facts, as Raphael Kircheim has proven in his criticism of Hirsch's Pentateuch (*"Die neue Exegetenschule"*).

Last, though not least, Dr. Julius Fuerst entered the field (1869) with a large and magnificent edition of the Bible, in folio, giving the Hebrew text, a German translation, commentaries and introductions, illustrations, index, chronological tables, etc., representing the results of Bible studies up to date, including Egyptian, Assyrian and Arabian discoveries. This is the best equipped Bible edition of modern Jews.

In Bible criticism, outside of the commentaries and introductions, the essays and treatises in periodicals, the modern Jews have done very little. They left this field almost exclusively to Christian scholars. Dr. Zunz opened the field with a critical introduction to Chronicles, Ezra, and Nehemiah, in his "*Gottesdienstliche Vortraege*," but he found no successors of equal celebrity. S. D. Luzzatto published, Vienna, 1830, his "*Oheb Ger*," a thorough criticism on the version of Onkelos; this found a few feeble echoes in periodicals and pamphlets, but led to no standard work. Raphael Kirchheim, in his "*Karme Shomron*" (Frankfurt a. M., 1851), gave an exposition of the variations in the text of the Samaritan Bible; but up to 1868 it produced only one rather feeble continuation in Dr. Samuel Kohn's "*Samaritanische Studien*" (Breslau, 1868). Dr. Z. Frankel, in 1841, published a work on the Septuagint, which evidences considerable research, by which he attempts to prove that the Septuagint, which is in our possession, differs from the original one, now lost, but the subject has found no competent man to give it exhaustive treatment. Dr. Adolph Huebsch (Prague, 1866), published the *Peshita*, the Syriac version of the five *Megilloth*, in Hebrew letters, with vowel points, two Hebrew commentaries, and an introduction, and calls attention to the various readings of this version; still nobody has taken up the subject. Dr. A. Geiger, Breslau, 1857, pub-

lished a book on criticism of the Bible text,
"Urschrift und Uebersetzungen der Bibel," etc.,
which contains a vast amount of learning, although
replete with hasty theories. Despite its merits, it
produced feeble echoes. Not even in Hebrew
lexicography have modern Jews done much. Since
Judah Loeb Benseb published his Hebrew German
Dictionary (Vienna, 1806), nothing was done in
this field till Dr. Fuerst improved and enlarged the
Hebrew Concordance (Leipzig, 1840), and published his Hebrew German Dictionary (Leipzig,
1863). Between those two dates lexicographical
attempts on the part of the Hebrews, with the
exception of the *Etymologisch-Symbolisch-Mytholo-
gisches Real-Woerterbuch,* by F. Nork, an ex-Jew
(Stuttgart, 1845), are of very little value. Rabbinical dictionaries will be spoken of later on.

On the whole, the Jews of the nineteenth century
have made very little progress in the critical study
of the Bible, compared with Ibn Ezra, Kimchi,
Leon de Banolas, and Abarbanel, and it would appear as if these had exhausted the subject. Recent
comparative linguistical studies, initiated by Gesenius, are limited in scope, and the archeological
discoveries have not thrown much light on the subject of Semitic philology. We open our Amsterdam folio edition of the *Biblia Rabbinica,* giving the
Hebrew text, ancient paraphrases, and the above
commentaries, and we can lay aside all modern
translations, commentaries, and introductions, and
obtain a clear understanding of the original. It appears to us that the nineteenth century has done
little more than popularize this particular field.

In conclusion, it must be remarked that the Apocrypha of the Old Testament, with the exception of the Book of Enoch, were translated into German by M. Gutmann, and were published, together with his critical introduction and notes (Altona, 1841). Most of these books were also translated into Hebrew by various writers, portions of which, with the English translation, were published by Dr. H. Vidaver and J. L. Levinsky (New York, 1871), and Ben Sirach, Hebrew and German (1850), by Dr. Mayer, of Hartford, Conn.

PAUL AND THE MYSTICS.

(1870.)

Few and far apart are the brilliant stars on the horizon of history. Strike out a hundred names and their influence upon the fate of man, and you have no history.

Those brilliant men, however, did not make history out of the resources of their mind. Ideas which tens of thousands have held, are seized upon by an executive genius at the right time and under favorable circumstances and a new epoch in history is opened. The numerous minor spirits which contributed to the sum total of the creative idea disappear, the one star remains visible in history.

Paul was one of these brilliant stars on the horizon of history. He was the author of Gentile Christianity. He conceived the idea of carrying into effect what all the prophets, all pious Israelites of all ages hoped and expected, the denationalization of the Hebrew ideal and its promulgation in the form of universal religion, among the Gentiles, so that the whole human family might be united beneath the banner inscribed with the motto, "One God and one humanity." All Jews of all ages hoped and expected that the kingdom of heaven would encompass all nations and tongues; but Paul undertook to realize this hope, this is his title to greatness.

Circumstances, of course, favored his enterprise.
Græco-Roman Paganism was undermined. The
gods were in disrepute, and the augurs smiled.
Religion was organized hypocrisy. The learned
believed nothing ; the vulgar believed everything,
no matter how absurd. So great was the influence
of Jewish thought at that time that royal families
had embraced Judaism, and the Emperor Tiberius
had found it necessary to drive the Jews from Rome
because their religion had admirers in the very
palace of the Cæsars, to say nothing of priests,
nobles and plebeians. The devout Gentiles whom
Paul met on his journeys were Judaized Greeks or
Syrians ; for the Pharisees traversed land and sea
to make one proselyte. Therefore, when Paul
preached in Asia Minor, Cicero and Cato had
spoken in Rome ; Seneca and Epictetus had given
utterance to sentiments strikingly like those of Paul.

On the other hand, the corrupt sensualism and
brutal despotism of the Cæsars and their favorites,
had demoralized the masses and brought truth itself
into ill repute. At the same time the Jewish state
was on the decline. Mystics arose who claimed an
intimate acquaintance with God and his angels ;
they looked for the interposition of the Deity in
their lives and the affairs of the state. All this
was highly favorable to Paul's undertaking.

But who was Paul ? Notwithstanding all the attempts of the author of the Acts to make of him as
mythical a character as the Gospels made of Jesus,
Paul's life is an open book. We have his epistles,
in which he gives quite a full account of himself
and his exploits. In addition he have numerous

Talmudic anecdotes about Acher, as the rabbis
called Paul ; these are of value to the historian.

Paul is not a proper name. It signifies "the
little one," a term which the Jews used to place before their names, viz., הקטון. But, it appears, he
knew no more about the matter than we do, and
changed the P of Paul into an S, to make of it the
Hebrew name Saul. In his epistles he calls himself
Paul invariably and not Saul. The author of the
"We" portion of the Acts likewise calls himself
Paul. Passing under an assumed name, the rabbis
called him Acher, "another," i. e., one who passes
under another or assumed name. They maintain
that his name was Elisha ben Abujah. But this
name must be fictitious, because it has direct reference to Paul's theology. It signifies "the saving
deity, son of the father god,"* and Paul was the
author of the "son of God" doctrine. The fact
is, he was known to the world by his assumed name
alone.

Nothing is known of his youth, except a few
spurious anecdotes recorded in the Talmud. When
quite young he sat at the feet of Gamaliel in Jerusalem, among the numerous students who listened to the wisdom of that master. He states
that he was a very zealous Pharisee, and that he
persecuted the Christians. But all of a sudden he
embraced the cause of the persecuted, and became
one of its most ardent apostles. We can easily imagine the nature of that persecution, although the
Stephen story, like the Damascus story and the

* אלישע בן אבויה

vision on the way, as narrated in the Acts, are spurious, because Paul never alludes to them, and the
Jews of Jerusalem had no jurisdiction in Damascus.
But what caused his remarkable transition from
one extreme to the other? First a Pharisee, with
law and nothing but law, and then the author of
the Epistles, which reject and abrogate the entire
law. Such a change is effected by violent agencies
only.

A number of stories narrated in the Talmud, like
those told in the Acts, point to the fact that the
youthful Paul, possessing, at any rate, a vivid imagination, witnessed many an act of violence and of
injustice. Occurrences of this nature were not rare
under the military despotism of Rome in Judea.
The soil was saturated with innocent blood. The
world was dominated by the sword, and Rome
groaned under the unnatural crimes of the Cæsars.
There was depravity among the governing classes,
and unspeakable misery among the governed. The
rabbis give us to understand that this state of affairs
misled Paul into the belief that there was no justice
in heaven or on earth, no reward nor punishment,
and no hope for Israel. It is quite natural that
under such circumstances a young and sensitive
man should become disheartened.

King Saul having received no reply from the
Prophets nor from the Urim and Thumim, sought
the Witch of Endor in his despair. Likewise
Faust, for want of a reply to his eager questions
from the philosophy and the theology of his age,
sold himself to Mephistopheles. This is human
nature. Paul did the same thing. The misery of

the age was indescribable. Men took refuge in mysticism because they could get no satisfactory solution of the problems that vexed their souls. Visionary gnostics arose among the Gentiles, and kabbalistic mystics among the Jews.

The mystic art among the Hebrews at that time was of two kinds ; its purpose was either to attract an evil spirit or to transport the devotee alive into paradise or heaven. An evil spirit was attracted by fasting and he, who remained alone in burial grounds for days and nights, till his brain was maddened, might prophesy and perform miracles. The translation to heaven or paradise was more difficult. The candidate would retire to an isolated spot and fast until he became delirious. Then, in a state of trance, he would sit on the ground, draw up his knees, and murmur magic formulæ ; he would imagine that he saw heaven open, and hosts of angels pass into the diamond palaces on high. He felt himself "caught up into paradise," where he heard "unspeakable words, which it is not possible for a man to utter" (Cor. xl. 12). It requires no great stretch of the imagination to form an idea of the eccentricities to which these mystic practices led.

Among those particularly noticed in the Talmud as having been in heaven or paradise is Acher, or Paul, as he himself states in his Second Epistle to the Corinthians (xxii). That passage gave rise to the story that Jesus had appeared in person to Paul, just as the rabbinical mystics claimed to have frequent intercourse with the Prophet Elijah, who had been translated alive to heaven.

So Paul passed from the law school of the

Pharisees to the new school of mystics. In this
state of trance he discovered the central figure of
Kabbalistic speculation, the *Metathron*, the co-
regent of the Almighty, or, as he was called, the
Synadelphos, otherwise, the confrère of the Deity
or Suriel, the "Prince of the Countenance," whom
the Kabbalists imagined to be the chief marshal or
chief scribe in heaven, who had been at one time
on earth as Enoch or as Elijah, and was advanced
to that high position in heaven. It is the *Demi-
urgos*, the highest magistrate in heaven, whom the
gnostic Valentine calls a god-like angel, and of
whom the rabbis said, "His name is like unto the
name of his Master."

This central figure, blended with the Messianic
speculation of that age, and the doctrines of Peter
and the nascent Church, combined in Paul's mind
to produce the mystic conception of the "son of
God," intelligible to Pagan minds. So he went
forth and proclaimed Jesus of Nazareth the son of
God. The term means substantially the same as
Metathron and *Synadelphos*, and the office which
Paul ascribed to Jesus is precisely of the same nature as that which the Kabbalists ascribed to the
angel who was the *Sar Haolam*, the prince or ruler
of this world, who stands before God, as Paul's Jesus
stands before God, or sits at his right hand. The
names only are changed, so that it is difficult to
decide who originated the metathronic speculations,
Paul or the rabbis, especially since these two angels
have Greek names only while the names of all the
others are Hebrew or Chaldaic. Later Kabbalists

frequently put down Joshua or Jesus in the place of Metathron.

Those who believe that Acher's dualism of Deity שתי רשויות was the Persian *Ormuzd* and *Ahriman*, hence a good and an evil principle, and that Metathron never was an evil demon, are as decidedly mistaken as those who believe that Paul had more than one God. Paul's son of God and Acher's *Metathron* are the same central figure before the throne of God, and the two authors are identical.

In that world of secret thoughts, Paul discovered discordant speculations harmonized, and the remedy for all existing evils. "The world must be regenerated by a new religion," was his great ideal. The ancient religions and philosophies have produced universal corruption. They must be swept away. Society must be reconstructed on a new basis, and this basis is the theology and the ethics of Israel, freed from national limitations. There was no hope left of rescuing the Jewish nationality from omnipotent Rome, which devoured kingdoms and nations. The object of Jesus was to reconstruct the kingdom of heaven *in Israel*, and he was crucified. All Israel had the same object in view, and its dissolution was imminent. Paul's main idea was that Jesus would be resurrected and Israel would be saved as soon as the basis and principles of the kingdom of heaven became the postulate of society at large.

The Pharisean rabbis hoped that this would come to pass at some future day, לעתיד לבוא, when, they maintained, all sacrifices and all laws would be

abolished, and the nations of the earth would be one
family, acknowledging one God and one moral law.
Paul seized upon the idea, and added to it the
simple dogma of Peter, " the Messiah has come."
That hoped-for condition has been consummated.
God's promise to Abraham, "And there shall be
blessed by thee, and by thy seed, all the families of
the earth," is fulfilled. Thus he came forth from
his mystical paradise as an apostle of Jesus and a
redeemer of Israel. He argued exactly as the
Pharisean doctors did who maintained that the
Messiah would come when mankind should be all
guilty or all righteous. In the estimation of Paul
all mankind was corrupt and demoralized, at that
particular time, and therefore that was the time for
the Messiah to make his appearance.

He went to work at once. He began to preach
his new Christianity at Damascus about the year 51,
but learned that the world was not prepared for his
ideas. He had a narrow escape at Damascus,
where the governor and soldiers pursued him.
Like the spies at Jericho, he was let down in a
basket over the city walls, and made his escape.
This is his version of the occurrence. The author
of the Acts, consistent in his hostility toward the
Jew, makes them figure as the persecutors. But
Paul rarely speaks of his kinsmen and his brothers
according to the flesh in any other manner than
with the highest regard.

The failure at Damascus did not discourage Paul.
It convinced him that he was too young (he was
at that time hardly much older than twenty-one);

that he was not sufficiently prepared for the great enterprise ; that it was not an easy task to reorganize society. He retired into Arabia and remained there nearly three years, to perfect a plan of operation. In 53 or 54 we find him again at Antioch, with his new and original gospel—the Gospel for the Gentiles,—prepared for his mission and ready to wage active war upon existing systems of religion and philosophy, and to replace all of them by his gospel. He had been in Jerusalem fifteen days, had conversed with Peter and nobody else, but he tells us repeatedly that he had taken advice of none, consulted none, was appointed by nobody and learned nothing of anybody. The Gospel was his gospel and he was an apostle by the appointment of God Almighty himself, who had revealed His son to him. In Antioch he established the first congregation of Jews and Gentiles, and called them Christians. Paul therefore was the actual author of Christianity among the Gentiles.

What was Paul's gospel ? Paul, setting out on his journeys with the intention of converting the heathen, was obliged to paganize the Gospel. The heathen knew nothing of the Jewish Messiah, and he gave him a name current among them—he called him the Son of God, which was a common name in mythology. The Son of God and Mary was a term as popular among heathens as it was foreign to the Jews, among whom Jesus was to remain the Messiah, only that he became also the *Metathron*. This suggested to Jewish mystics the possibility of the second advent, and gave a metaphysical foundation to the resurrection doctrine. The kingdom of heaven, or the theocracy, was another idea unintelligible to the heathen. Israel's laws and form of government were odious to the Pagans. Paul interpreted the kingdom of heaven in a theological sense ; he declared the laws of Israel abrogated, the spirit thereof alone being obligatory in the new state of society.

The sins of all who believe in the son are forgiven, and their flesh is crucified along with him, and will resurrect with him in purity ; for his death was a vicarious atonement for all. He was the last sacrifice and he blotted out the sins of all who have faith in him.

The crucified one did not resurrect merely in the spirit ; of this the heathen could not form a satisfactory conception, because the immortality of the soul was by no means a general belief among them, and their gods were no spirits ; he resurrected in his very body, and was caught up to heaven, to sit or stand at God's right hand, to come down again in proper time. "Here, then, is your tangible proof of immortality," he said to the heathen. "Like the crucified one, all of you will resurrect from the dead, or be changed on the day of judgment." . This language was intelligible to heathens, who knew that but lately Cæsar had been caught up to heaven as Romulus had been before him, and asked no questions as to how a human body can rise in the atmosphere and become incorruptible ; none as to what above or below, up or down means, as to where God is and where he is not ; where his right hand, or as to whether the world is full of his glory.

No such questions were asked, and the ocular
demonstration of immortality was tangible and intelligible to the grossest intellect.

The Jewish nationality and the Jewish law are at
an end, and the world is the heir of the covenant
made by God with Abraham and his seed. With
the new covenant the old one ceases. It has fulfilled its destiny. It was a state of preparation for
this period of universal salvation for all who have
love, hope and faith. With Adam and the flesh
came the sin, law and death ; with Jesus the flesh
ceases ; hence, no more sin, law or death.

These are the main features of Paul's Gospel :
The Son of God, the theological kingdom of heaven,
the vicarious atonement, the bodily resurrection of
the crucified one, the abrogation of the law and the
beginning of the new covenant, was the first man
to utter these doctrines ; with him Christianity begins, and he gave it its name.

But Paul knew well that the doctrine alone would
be insufficient to rouse the heathen world from its
demoralized state, and he resorted to the most ominous of all messages. He came to the heathen
with the dread proclamation : ''The end is nigh !
The whole earth, with all the creatures thereon ; the
whole human family, with its wickedness, will be
destroyed in a moment. Oh, you men, women and
children, you will be summoned, with all your vices
and crimes, before the Eternal and All-just ; you
must appear before the omniscient God. The end
is nigh, the destruction of the human family is imminent. It may come any moment.''

The saving opportunity of Paul's Gospel had arrived. Here is your choice. On the one hand, death and damnation; on the other, life and happiness everlasting. In anticipation of the approaching catastrophe God had sent his Son to warn you, and he is appointed now to conduct the end of all flesh. Cling to him and be saved, or believe not and be damned forever. So he came to the heathen. This was his Gospel.

All passages in the Gospels and the Acts which have reference to this christology, as to the end of things (and with respect to it the Synoptics contradict one another), are the productions of writers long after Paul, who attempted to reconcile Jewish and Gentile Christianity. For with Paul begins the new form of Christianity, and the struggle with the representatives of the old form. Within ten years he traversed the land from Antioch to Athens, in three different journeys, and established his bishopric, the first Christian congregations among the Gentiles. He organized them fully, with deacons and deaconesses, preachers and prophets; and he was their bishop and their oracle. He allowed his converts to believe that they could do wonderful things, heal the sick, drive out demons, prophesy and speak in strange tongues, because it served his purpose, although he himself did none of these things. He gave them the holy ghost, *i. e.*, he regenerated their feelings and pacified their passions, and awakened in them aspirations toward higher things. He did not feel that sovereign contempt for money which the master whom he glorified felt; for he, like the other apostles, took his pay, and argued with the Corinthians, like a good Pharisean lawyer, that bishops and preachers must be paid.

Wonderful, indeed, was Paul's success among the Gentiles within ten years. Like a pillar of fire, he traversed the deserts of heathenism ; like a second Elijah, he battled against the priests and prophets of Baal, and conjured down the fire from heaven to his assistance. Within ten years he laid the foundation of a new civilization. He did not live to see it realized, but he saw the new system take root and promise golden fruit. Wonderful, we maintain, was his success ; for he was not only opposed by the entire heathen world, and by the orthodox Jews, although he proclaimed their God and their doctrines, their religion and their hopes, but was also most strenuously opposed by the apostles and the nascent congregation in Jerusalem, whose master he glorified and whose cause he made the cause of the world. The dissensions between Paul and the apostles were of a very serious character, and there was ample cause for them.

In the first place, he claimed to be the apostle, and they had their college of twelve, to which none could be added, especially not Paul, who had never seen Jesus of Nazareth. He maintained that God had appointed him, God had revealed his son and his Gospel to him ; but the apostles did not believe it, and did not acknowledge him as an apostle. At the end of his journeys, Peter, James and John, three out of twelve, acknowledged him as an apostle to the Gentiles, but not to the Jews. The rest did not at all ; this, of course, was a hindrance to Paul among his own converts.

In the second place, they could not forgive him that he had gone to the Gentiles. Peter, who had become a pious Essene and considered it unlawful to go to the house or into the company of a Gentile ; James, to whom the eating of the bread of the Gentile was detestable (and these were the heads of the church), could not condone this innovation on the part of Paul. He silenced them by taking collections for the saints of Jerusalem on Sundays. But it was too much for them that Paul went to the Gentiles.

In the third place, he changed their religion into a sort of mythology. He made of Jesus a son of God. He preached vicarious atonement, bodily resurrection, the end of the old covenant and the beginning of the new, the end of all flesh, the last judgment, doctrines altogether quite new to them ; not one word of all these had their master told them, and they knew only what he did tell them. They naturally considered him an unscrupulous innovator. They had not experience and forethought enough to understand that Paul's success among the heathen was traceable to means that he employed. They were pious men who prayed much, believed seriously, and had no knowledge of the world as it was.

In the fourth place, they could not possibly give their consent to Paul's abrogation of the whole law, knowing as they did, how their master respected every title, every iota of the law ; that he had come to fulfill the law, and to re-establish the theocracy. How could they possibly think of abolishing Sabbath and holidays, circumcision and ablutions, all

and everything, to be guided by the phantom
of hope, love and faith, against which James
argues in his epistle with all the energy of his
soul. Those inexperienced saints did not know
that the Pharisean doctors held similar theories,
and that Paul could not possibly hope to meet with
any success among the Gentiles if he came to them
with the laws of the Jews. They were Roman citizens, who contemned the laws of the barbarians.
Had Paul come with the word Judaism on his lips,
he would have surely failed. Had he come to enforce a foreign law, he would have been derided.
They did not know that Paul cared not for any
law if only the essence could be saved ; he held
that laws are local, the spirit is free ; he was determined to drop everything which might retard
his progress.

In the fifth place, and this was the worst, they
could not forgive him for preaching the theological
kingdom of heaven. A kingdom of Israel, a throne
of David, a Davidian prince, a Zion and a Jerusalem
in heaven, and slavery, misery and oppression on
earth, was so new and foreign to them, so contrary
to what they had heard from their master, that they
could not accept it. What would become of Peter's
Messiah, of the hopes and promises connected with
the second advent, if all at once the whole scheme
is transported from earth to heaven. It was too
disappointing, they could not endure it. Those
men did not understand that Paul desired to avoid
conflict with the Roman authorities. He was too
prudent to run the risk of crucifixion. They could

not comprehend that his object was not to remove
the evil at once ; he intended to sow the seed, to
give to the heathens correct notions of God, duty,
responsibility, purity, holiness, morality, justice,
humanity and freedom, which in proper time would
elevate the views and aspirations of the nations.
They could not comprehend that their Messiah and
kingdom of heaven, together with his terrible message of the end of all flesh and the last judgment
day, were means, and nothing but means, to captivate and reform the heathen.   His son of God was
crucified and resurrected from the dead to forewarn
all of the approaching end of all flesh ; to show that
in a little while all the dead should resurrect and
the living should be changed to spiritual beings.
He had been given power by the Almighty with
respect to the catastrophe of the world, and would be
present at the last judgment day.   But after all that
was over, and the earth and man had been changed
to a new state of spiritual life, then the Son of God
would return the kingdom to the Father, and God
would be again all in all.   So the son of God was a
general superintendent, the demiurge for the time
being, a doctrine of which apostles had no knowledge, and to which they could not assent.   Paul
could not make them understand that these were
but means for the conversion of the Gentiles,
and that he had quite another gospel for the enlightened portion of the community.   They could not
see that ideas had to assume tangible form if they
were to become effective among heathens accustomed
to apotheosis, man-worship and plastic gods.   They
failed to comprehend that the sensuality and cor-

ruption of the age required heroic means to rouse
and to move the masses ; hence the dissensions and
troubles between Paul and the nascent church increased with the success of Paul among the Gentiles. His epistles, one and all, are polemics, not
against heathenism, nor against Judaism, but
against his colleagues in Jerusalem, whom, together
with their doctrines, he treats in a most reckless
manner. They were not able to measure words
with Paul, in truth there were no writers of any note
among them. Therefore, only Paul's side of the
controversy is set forth fully in the New Testament ; the side of the Jewish Christians remained
mostly matter of tradition.

Messengers were sent to follow Paul to undo the
effect of his gospel and preach that of the apostles ;
to introduce the law and circumcision among the
Gentile Christians. Those messengers (in many
cases) succeeded, notwithstanding the thundering
epistles of Paul. His influence was weakened and
his progress retarded among the Gentiles, till finally,
after ten years of hard work, he concluded to go to
Jerusalem, and, if possible, effect a compromise
with the apostolic congregation. It was a dangerous time for him to go to Jerusalem ; for just then
the fanatical high priest, Ananias, had convened a
court of his willing tools, had tried James, the
brother of Jesus, and, finding him guilty—of what,
God only knows—had had him and some of his
associates executed—a bloody deed which cost him
his office, on account of the loud and emphatic protest of the Jews before Agrippa II. and the Roman
governor. Therefore Paul was cautioned by proph-

ets and friends not to go to Jerusalem. But he
was not the man to be frightened by dangers. He
was the very type of boldness and courage. He
went to Jerusalem to effect a reconciliation with the
church. A synod met in the house of James the
apostle, who had succeeded the former James as
head of the church, and Paul was told to do that
against which his conscience, his honor, his manhood must have revolted; he was required to play
the hypocrite in Jerusalem in order to pacify the
brethren who were angry with him. They said
that the thousands of Jews, who were zealous for
the law, and knew how Paul taught the people to
forsake Moses, to give up circumcision and the
ancient customs, had heard of his presence in Jerusalem; "the multitude must needs come together"
(which points to the Jewish Christians faithful to
the law); they advised him to go through the
mockery of a purification at the temple, "to be
at charges," as they called it, with some who had
vowed a vow, and make the prescribed sacrifices
after the purification.

Poor man! After so much labor, such severe
toil, such numerous perils, dangers, trials, reverses
and triumphs, after ten long years of such work
and such dangers, he is not safe in Jerusalem
among his own kinsmen and among those whose
master he glorified, whose doctrines he taught, and
whose interests he protected. How small must he
have appeared to himself when walking up the
Temple Mount in the company of the four men,
whose expenses he paid, to be purified with them:
"And all may know that those things whereof they

were informed concerning thee are nothing; but that thou thyself also walkest orderly and keepest the law." How mortifying to the man who had defied a world this submission to the humiliating dictates of his colleagues, veritable children in comparison with him! To this incident the statement of Paul or Asher, recorded in the Talmud, undoubtedly refers; he relates that on passing behind the *sanctum sanctorum* he heard the *Bath-kol* or Holy Ghost exclaim, "Return, all ye froward children; return all, except Paul, who has known me and has rebelled against me." Paul never forgot, never forgave this humiliation. It estranged him altogether from his colleagues in Jerusalem, and he embraced the first opportunity to throw off his Jewish associations altogether.

The opportunity soon offered itself. While near the Temple, some Jews from Asia Minor recognized him. A disturbance ensued. He was arrested and locked up in the castle by the Roman commander. In describing this event the author of the Acts speaks of a great tumult, speeches, trials, a Jewish mob, a noble Roman stepping forward in time to wind up dramatically—not one word of which is historical. Paul, accused as the ringleader of the new sect who expected the second advent of the Messiah, could not but appear dangerous to the zealous and vigilant Roman authorities. Nothing else was necessary to put his life in jeopardy. During the night he determined to appeal to Cæsar, because he was a Roman citizen. Therefore, he was sent to the governor of Cæsarea under the protection of soldiers. Not a sound was heard in his

favor among the Jewish Christians. Not an angel
appeared. Not a solitary miracle was wrought;
none dreamt a dream; nobody had a vision; the
holy ghost was silent as the grave; of all the
Christians in Palestine, not one showed his face,
when Paul, laden with chains, was transported
from Jerusalem to Cæsarea. This silence speaks
volumes. They did not care much about the innovator. Therefore, Paul's epistles from his prison
in Cæsarea are thunderbolts against the law, circumcision, and his colleagues in Jerusalem. It is
the offended man, the wounded lion, who retaliates
in his anger.

In Cæsarea another mock trial is described by the
author of the Acts. There can be little doubt that
Ananias, the Sadducean high-priest who had slain
James, also thirsted for the blood of ·Paul. But it is
certainly not true that Felix was governor of Judea
when Ananias was high-priest. Felix and Festus had
been removed from their offices before Ananias was
made high-priest, as the authentic sources of history
show. If tried at Cæsarea at all (which is doubtful,
because Paul had appealed to Cæsar), he was tried
before Albinus. The speeches recorded in the
Acts contain sentences of Paul, it is true, but the
greater portion emanates from the author of the
Acts himself.

It matters little, however, whether Paul was
tried before Albinus or Felix, or whether there was
a trial at all. He had appealed to Cæsar, in order
to estrange himself from his colleagues in Jerusalem and to come before the converts as an expatri-
ated man, although Agrippa had said : "This man

might have been set at liberty, had he not appealed unto Cæsar." Fortunately, however, he was detained in Cæsarea, when Nero put to death the Christians of Rome with exquisite cruelty, and added mockery and derision to their sufferings. Had he been brought to Rome then, no angels could have saved his life, and no power could have protected him for two years. He came to Rome in the year 65, when the cruelty of Nero's proceedings against the Christians filled every breast with compassion, and humanity relented in favor of the Christians. As a result, it was possible for Paul to obtain a hearing in Rome, where he lived in a rented house for two years.

Neither Paul nor Peter was bishop of Rome, nor was either of them beheaded in Rome or anywhere else. All the legends and myths concerning them are void of truth. We know that Paul, who was then about thirty-five years old, wrote from Rome epistles in defense of his Gospel and against his colleagues in Jerusalem in the same spirit as those from Cæsarea. We know, furthermore, that he went from Rome to Illyricum, where he preached his Gospel. We know that he returned to Asia, and wrote the quintessence of his Gospel in his Epistles to the Romans. We know that many passages in his epistles were written after the destruction of Jerusalem, when Paul was about forty years old, and his principal activity commenced still later, in opposition to Rabbi Akiba and his colleagues. We know from the Talmud that he married and left daughters. We know also numerous stories of Acher or Paul and his disciple, Rabbi Meir.

Paul always speaks affectionately of the Jews, whom he calls "My brethren and my kinsman according to the flesh—to whom pertaineth the adoption, the glory, the covenant, and the giving of the law." (Read also Romans xi, 11 : "I say, then, have they stumbled that they should fall? God forbid, but rather through their fall salvation is come unto the Gentiles, to provoke them to jealousy.")

Long after the death of the apostles, the Christianity of Paul and the Messianism of Peter were Platonized by the Alexandrian eclectics in a semignostic manner, which gave birth to the fourth Gospel, according to John, and the two epistles of John the Elder, not the apostle, about 160 A. C., of which the Synoptics have no knowledge. They had only the Christianity of Paul and of Peter before them. An original Petrine Gospel, Paul's epistles, and the different traditions of the various congregations, were sources, which they attempted to blend into one system. All the Gospel writers lived in the second century ; they were not acquainted with the particulars of the story ; they had an imperfect knowledge of the Jews, their laws and doctrines ; they wrote in favor of the Romans, whom they wished to convert, and against the Jews, whom they could not convert.

The third century inherited four distinct systems of Christianity : that of Jesus with the pure theocracy, that of Peter with the Messiah and his second advent, that of Paul with the Son of God and the approaching end of all flesh, and that of John with the Logos and the self-aggrandizing demi-god or man-god on earth. The difficulties and dissensions arising from the attempts to unite all the contradictory systems into one ended with the Council of Nice in the beginning of the fourth century, the formation of the orthodox creed, the ex-communication of the Jewish Christians, and the establishment of the church as a state institution. Thereupon the sword and the pyre established doctrines.

You will find upon investigation that Jesus became the savior of the Gentiles through the exertions of Paul; that the teachings which Peter and Paul formulated for temporary purposes have been turned into main dogmas; that the religion which Jesus taught and believed is partly laid aside, and the remainder of no consequence in Christology, but that he himself has been adopted in place of his religion; and finally that the entire New Testament has no knowledge of the Trinity and the orthodox creed. You will discover further that, if any of our modern congregations are Christian, the apostolic congregation of Jerusalem was heretical. If the Pope is a Christian, Paul was not. If the orthodox creed is Christian, then Jesus of Nazareth was a Jew. If the religion and the theocracy which Jesus preached are to become the universal religion, all dogmas must fall, and God alone will be all in all. Man must become his own priest, prince and prophet. Justice must govern the nations, love must construe the law, virtue and righteousness must lead to satisfaction and happiness, and man's consciousness of God, immortality, and moral responsibility must be his catechism, his guiding

star, his protecting angel in life and death. No
dogmas ; truth in the name of God !

"I see it, although it is now ; I behold it, although it is not nigh—a star will arise from Jacob"
in whose brilliancy will shine forth all the great
and redeeming truth. Freedom and humanity,
justice and love in the name of God are the true religion ; to strive for them is divine worship, to love
them is holiness.

This was the mission of Paul. The means he
employed to accomplish that mission were such as
he thought were necessary to appeal to and convert
his generation. He could not dream that the means
would obscure the mission, that the servant would
occupy the master's seat. His was a fearless,
powerful and unyielding character ; he strove with
all his might to change the old order, to create a
now heaven and a new earth, and his success,
though incomplete, was wonderful. However
widely we may differ from men like Jesus and
Paul, whose great aim was to elevate human nature,
yet they are deserving of the student's laborious
research, the philanthropist's profound admiration.
Great works bear testimony to their authors ; great
minds are the crown and the glory and pride of
humanity. The God Jesus and the supernatural
Paul appear small in the focus of reason. The patriotic and enthusiastic Jesus, and the brave, bold,
wise Paul are grand types of humanity among those
hundred that shine on the horizon of history and
illumine the records of the human family.

SELECTIONS.

UNION.

The political condition of our brethren and the influence of modern science, philosophy and art, as well as our new social relations, have completely revolutionized the province of religious conceptions and observances. The Jewish citizen of the United States cannot think and feel as did the inmate of a secluded Ghetto in a past century. The philosophy and science of the schools pervade all departments of practical life. No man, and especially no scholar, of this day can honestly entertain the same religious opinions as did Isaac Newton and his contemporaries. Much less can we now coincide in religious opinions with the talmudical rabbi of former days to whom science and philosophy, the word and its literature were strangers. And as for the changes in social life—everybody knows them. It is perfectly useless to deny that our faith to-day, cardinal principles excepted, which have been the same under all circumstances, bear the same relation to the religion of former centuries as our republican form of government does to the Germanic empire of other days. This is especially true in the United States. But we reform in the same spirit, i. e., we aim to reconcile Judaism with the age and its needs. The reformers do it openly, systematically and self-consciously; the orthodox do it slowly, unwillingly and unconsciously—but they do it. How do we reform? We do it single-handed. Every congregation has a leader who reforms as he thinks proper. We do not struggle to maintain

Judaism, we work to maintain a congregation, each
by himself. We do not consider Israel's future,
the future of a certain congregation is every leader's
object. Since when are we so narrow-minded?
Every reform congregation has its own views, its
own prayer-book, its own catechism; every congregation behaves as a distinct sect. They call this
the free development of the religious idea, we call
it anarchy. They say it is beneficial, we say it
keeps the congregations apart and gives rise to undue
rivalry. History condemns it, common sense says,
"united we stand," there is strength in union.

The reform congregation would like to see union
of action. Only the ambition of leaders, who like
Jeroboam, ask "Who shall walk before us?" (Who
shall lead?) prevents it. Is it impossible for us to
lay aside our egotism and cement a union of the
American congregations in order to reconcile Judaism with the demands of the age? Can we lay
aside personalities and whims and think of the
future of Israel and of the sacred truths we possess?
Is there none to propose ways and means for a union
of the American Hebrew congregations?

We need the following: A uniform liturgy and
the music appertaining thereto; a catechism for
schools and for confirmands; a board of examiners
to protect the congregations from pseudo ministers
and teachers; a college and a female academy. If
all the congregational leaders would work unitedly
for these objects and advocate them earnestly, we
could realize them in a very short time, and we
could say we have done our duty to GOD and
ISRAEL.

ESTABLISHMENT OF THE UNION OF AMERICAN HEBREW CONGREGATIONS.

(1873.)

"For a child was born unto us; a son was given unto us, and the dominion shall be upon his shoulder."

On the eighth, ninth, and tenth days of July in the convention held in Cincinnati, the youngest child of Israel was born. The Union of American Hebrew Congregations was organized, constituted, and established. This is now an accomplished fact. We only wish to add that the work was done with fraternal unanimity and a feeling of solidarity such as few popular assemblies have ever manifested. Not a harsh word was spoken in three days, either in the Convention or in the committee-rooms; not one delegate left the spot dissatisfied or displeased. It was a feast of harmonious co-operation and of fraternization. We record this that future generations may know how their sires laid the foundation to the Union of American Hebrew Congregations. The new chapter in our history begins with peace, and sends forth the ancient salutation to all, Shalom Alechem—"Peace to all of you."

What has been accomplished? A constitution was adopted, an instrument of sixteen brief paragraphs; a broad, liberal and thoroughly democratic platform, upon which all Hebrew congregations of the United States can meet and join hands and hearts for a great fraternity of Israel, to foster the spiritual interests of Israel, to promote institutions which shall elevate the character of our co-religionists in this country. The Union proposes by united efforts to accomplish what individuals or separate congregations cannot do, because they have neither the means nor the influence, and it invites them all to co-operate. Individual opinions or the autonomy of congregations are in no way to be disturbed. The Union invites all to unite before God and man in such work as demands the support of all. If wisdom, moderation and earnest devotion to the cause prevail in the councils, all American Hebrew congregations will join hands and hearts under the banner of freedom, and be one in all great and progressive enterprises. The work done so far is great; the foundation has been laid for a Union of Israel in peace and by wisdom. The spirit is democratic, and truly American in all its features. This Union is a child conceived of the spirit of the age. It imposes no duties on the congregation aside of two simple obligations, viz., to be represented in the annual council of this Union, and to pay into its treasury one dollar annually for each contributing member. It imposes no other obligation, there are no "ifs" and no "whens." The whole scheme is liberal and just.

The first object of the Union is the College. It proposes, first of all, to establish a seat of learning for Hebrew literature. Whenever this shall have been accomplished other institutions are to be established.

It will be seen from the official record of the Convention all congregations of Ohio except one were represented; also congregations from Texas, Louisiana, Arkansas, Mississippi, Georgia, Tennessee, Kentucky, West Virginia, Michigan, Illinois, and Indiana, so that thirteen states were represented. This is not a Union of congregations West and South only; it is a Union for all, inviting all and excluding none. It will be an amazing fact to our co-religionists all over the country and they will learn what they can accomplish by union and the proper use of their influence. There is nothing in our way to accomplish anything which is great, good and useful for our common cause, and the cause of humanity. This fact was deeply felt in the convention, and fully appreciated.

The new chapter in the history of American Israel has opened. Go to work, all faithful sons of Israel, encourage, assist and with the help of God, the wilderness shall become a Carmel, and the work of righteousness shall abound in peace. If you are true to God and to Israel, go to work in all your congregations and speak for this Union, and it will be a tree of life for you, and for generations to come. Up and labor in the name of God and Israel.

THE CONGREGATION.

(1871.)

The duties of the congregation to Israel are two-fold: first, the preservation of Israel's sacred treas-ures and Israel's union as one indivisible congre-gation; and secondly, its efficient co-operation with all other congregations for the faithful performance of Israel's Messianic duties. In our dispersion we must be united; without pope or bishop, council or synod, prince or chief, by the spirit of truth and the word of God we must remain one intimate fra-ternity; in happiness or adversity, in light or dark-ness, in freedom or oppression, one. The Jew must be no stranger wherever a fellow Jew lives; he must not be friendless or homeless where another Jew can provide for him; he should have a home and friends wherever a son of Israel lives. Let all men learn from us the lesson of unity and frater-nity.

The public expression of Israel's unity rests in its worship. Outside of the synagogue we are cit-izens of the lands of our nativity or adoption, and do not differ from our fellow-men. In public life, in business, in culture, in all worldly aspirations, we have abandoned separation, and very few if any wish to restore it. In the synagogue, in the public demonstration of our religious life, we must pre-serve our identity, we must bear Israel's badge of honor, conferred upon the congregation of Jeshurun by Moses and the prophets, by the hand of Providence manifested in three thousand years of history. In the synagogue the Israelite must hear the sacred words of his prophets and bards, the holy accents of divine revelation, and the handmaid shall not exile the mistress of the palace. The synagogue must remain Jewish, eminently Jewish, and uniform as far as the spirit of the various countries permits. No divisions, no differences; we must remain one before God, one in spirit, and, as far as practicable, one in form. This is every congregation's first duty to Israel. Reforms in separate congregations must not be such as to disturb Israel's union.

Why attach so much importance to the external, to the mere form of worship? Why accentuate the union of Israel in the United States or in other enlightened countries, if the whole world is to become one holy land, every house a temple, every table an altar, every adult a priest of the Most High? Because this is not the case as yet, either here or elsewhere; because paganism and error still obtain in church and state; because Israel's Messianic duty is not done yet. As long as the human family is not united before the one eternal, infinite and absolute God, in freedom, justice and love; as long as wrong is done in the name of justice, paganism survives in religion, truth is dreaded and thought is hampered; as long as vice holds high carnival, fanaticism parades as holy zeal, hypocrisy assumes the garb of piety, so long Israel's mission is not fulfilled; so long we must remain a unit in our religion, and so long we must preserve uniformity in our religious practices. We must be one in spirit forever. Whatever a congregation does, it must never neglect the first of all its duties—the Messianic duty of Israel. It must contribute its full share to the elevation of human nature, the redemption of mankind, the sovereignty of truth, and the supremacy of reason, freedom and virtue.

THE 'RABBI.

(1871.)

The rabbi is the teacher in Israel, no more and no less. With the destruction of the temple at Je- rusalem and the abolition of sacrifices, the priest- hood ceased ·in Israel. Judaism knows nothing of a mediating priest standing between God and man. Intelligence and conscience are the arbiter of faiths. These interpret life as inculcated in our sacred lit- erature, and the rabbi is the spokesman for them. . Formerly, when theology and law were intimately connected among Jews as among all peoples, then the rabbi was also a judge. Now, however, the rabbi is the teacher in Israel. His claim upon the respect of his brethren is based on his intellectual superiority, his wider acquaintance with Jewish lit- erature, his purity of character, and his enthusiasm for the cause which he serves. If he is lacking in any of these gifts of grace, he is no rabbi, how- ever good, pious, charitable or clever he may be. His ordination is no warrant that he possesses all the necessary qualities. It is a testimony on the part of an acknowleged authority that the candi- date possesses adequate knowledge and blameless character. The real title, however, is earned in the creditable discharge of duty. This duty is to teach in the pulpit, the school, the family. In the name of God and Israel, he must be a bearer of light and truth, of reason's choice gifts and conscience's holy lessons. He must be a man of peace and of good will; he must conciliate wherever he can, but must always be strong in the declaration of truth without fear or favor. He must never degrade the pulpit by resorting to unworthy and undignified agencies. Sensational preachers are comedians. "For the lips of the priest shall guard knowledge, and the law is to be sought from his mouth, for he is a messenger of the Lord of Hosts."

AN APPEAL FOR A COLLEGE.

(1874.)

The morning hath come, truly; glory returns to
Zion. We unfurl the banner of Judaism, as the
light of nations, the spirit of wisdom, the spirit of
council and strength, the spirit of knowledge and
the fear of the Lord. Judaism and progress, Judaism
and moral freedom, Judaism and liberality, light
and unity are identical. "Nations walk in thy
light, and kings in the luster of thy luminary."
And yet it is night. We must go begging; we
must entreat to move our own enlightened congregations to unite in one fraternity; we must invite
and coax the discordant element of our people that
they shall rally about the sacred cause; it is night!
We are weak because we are divided into congregations, small republics as it were, and have no organization. We could do great and good things
for Israel's cause and bring about the triumphs of
humanity, if we would only co-operate fraternally.
We must beg: "Please join the Union of American Hebrew Congregations; it costs only one dollar a
year! Let us have your mite, so that we can do
what should be done in the name of God and
Israel." I beg? Who called me here to beg?
No one. Why am I here? Do I want anything of
you for myself? Nothing. Why am I your servant, your beggar? I know not. Nobody knows.
I complain to myself all day and by night that I

must be a beast of burden! I am growing old, and yet I go. I cannot rebel against my God and my conscience. I cannot separate myself from my people; cannot be faithless to my religion. I have come to plead, to beg, to raise my feeble voice in a holy cause. I beg you, Brethren, come assist your aged father, help him to save our cause and to raise our people. I beg, Brethren, lay aside all other considerations; do what it is your duty to do as men and Israelites. Forty-four congregations in Israel have promised "let us go in the light of the Lord." Drop all small considerations, and ask yourselves whether you should stand in the background in this great movement to unite the forces in the American Israel for our mission. In a hundred years hence, the annals of history will be examined and posterity will tell what we have done; and will it then be to your glory that you have hesitated now? What could you urge to justify inaction? We stand before God, in this holy place; here is the Thorah, and a numerous congregation; I call you to witness before God that I have done my duty. If I should die this very moment, I have done my duty. Go, each and all, and ask yourselves the solemn question, "Have I done my duty?" You must render an account to Him whose name is ineffable, and whose glory fills the universe. You are God's messengers on earth, the anointed of the Most High. Our days are numbered, our end is certain, and God liveth forever; he judgeth every man according to his doings, and the fruits of his life. Brethren, let us be right.

HEBREW UNION COLLEGE.

ADDRESSES

AT

OPENING OF HEBREW UNION COLLEGE.

I.

Students, let us be mindful of our duties, our mission, the holy cause in which we are engaged; let us remember the prayer of Moses, "Let not, I beseech thee, the congregation of Israel, be like sheep which have no shepherd." You have volunteered to be hereafter, under the Guardian of Israel, the shepherds of his people, the banner-bearers of His Law, the expounders of His Word, the champions of truth, priests of light and apostles of humanity. Whether you will occupy the pulpit or rostrum, the teacher's chair or any other responsible position in life, you are pledged to be, אצלי בני ישראל, "Select sons of Israel," dedicated to the service of God and of His people.

Your service will be very important, for more than one reason. American Israel is now in a period of transition. The ancient spirit of devotion to Israel's cause, once so mighty among our ancestors, is declining, otherwise there would be hundreds for every ten of you; the spirit of conviction, enlightenment, and self-reflection, has not gone deep enough into the hearts and minds of our people. Be of Gideon's three hundred champions, who did not bend the knee. Be of בני נביאים, the "Sons of the Prophets," for you are called upon to-day as

they were in the days of Samuel, to assist Israel in
a crisis, and to guide it.

When you will come in contact with the world
you will perhaps be astonished to learn how rapidly
dogmatism and blind faith decline. None can ar-
rest the wheels of progress. Freedom and learning
progress in exact ratio with the retrogression of reactionary theology. As in the household of nature,
law rules; so also in the realm of mind, the fundamental principles of Judaism persevere. As long
as the intellect thinks logically and the heart beats
sympathetically, God, Providence, moral responsibility, immortality, the happiness of man and the
solidarity of mankind will be the guiding stars of
good people, and so long must Judaism last; for
these are its themes conceived from the loftiest
standpoint of philosophical thought. It will be your
task, students, to understand this thoroughly, and
to expound it adequately. Your mission will be a
holy one, and will involve a grave responsibility before God and man.

There can be no victory without combat, no triumph without a struggle, and the value of the
one is measured by the intensity of the other.
The students' combat is in his studies, and his triumphs in his learning. You are making war upon
ignorance, and the more courageously and efficiently
you do it, the more glorious will be your victory.
He who harvests in time will have plenty, but the
indolent will beg his bread. Young men, the great
mystery of success lies in your acquisition of knowledge first, and an enthusiastic persistence in your
work. Your knowledge is your capital. There is

nothing profane in learning, and what is usually called profane learning is an important department of your studies. All knowledge is sacred; it is all revelation of the same God addressed to the same human mind.

Judaism must be studied in the products of the Hebrew mind, and these are preserved in Israel's great literature. As little as one can possess an adequate knowledge of a country without surveying it, so little can one form a correct idea of Jewish history, ethics, metaphysics and theology without an intimate acquaintance with the original sources, in which the Hebrew mind has actualized itself. As for the scientists no object of nature is without interest, so for us not a line of Jewish literature is without significance. The spirit can be correctly understood by the entire sum of its manifestations. Israel's spirit is expressed in its vast literature, whose beginning is co-equal with the beginning of historical man, whose periods are the index to all phases of human culture, whose forms seem to exhaust all possibilities of dialectics, and whose contents comprise the whole of man's moral, intellectual and spiritual nature. Every line, every word is of grave importance, to you and to every student of human mind; and the part the Hebrew mind has had in that totality of the world's civilization is of so wonderful a magnitude, in quantity and quality, that without the knowledge thereof the human mind can not be properly understood.

As long as your mind is engaged in Jewish literature you stand in spiritual rapport with the greatest men of all ages, with the Patriarchs of Israel, with

Moses, the Prophets and the inspired bards of ancient times; you are in spiritual kinship with the heroic sons of Mathatia, the Asmonean, the Scribes of olden times, the teachers of Judaism, the expounders of the traditional treasures, a host of expounders, philosophers, men of high aspirations and exalted genius, men of first magnitude in human greatness; while you are engaged in the study of Jewish literature you are in the very presence of the Shekinah, the Great, Glorious and Ineffable, I AM.

"Also one alone who sits engaged in the Law has the Shekinah with him."

II

The morality of a rabbinical student, who seeks rabbinical honors from his alma mater, includes the possession of genuine religious zeal and enthusiasm. Without this he may become an actor in the pulpit, a polished elocutionist, a sensationalist, a seeker of plaudits, but no rabbi. I consider it my duty to admonish all present to leave this college, if they lack religious zeal and enthusiasm, for they never will be honest rabbis; their whole life would be immoral. If you do possess this excellent quality, you must cultivate it assiduously, so that it may become permanent in your character; you must be as conscientious in your religious practices as in your studies and in the fulfillment of all other moral duties. Whatever is not steadily and diligently cultivated is slowly but surely deadened. The rabbi furthermore must be a faithful Israelite, a true expounder and champion of Israel's religion, and this also you must learn, cultivate, and practice, during this eight years of probation, before you can expect to receive the rabbinical diploma. In connection with this, it must be borne in mind, that we know of no religion, and acknowledge none, without the Living God of Israel at its beginning, end, and center; hence we know of no authority, and acknowledge none besides that laid down in Israel's Thorah, which teaches us our God, our duty, and our hope. Whatever hagiographists, scribes, rabbis, or philosophers wrote and preached on Israel's religion, morals, and duties, is no more than a commentary to the Thorah. Judaism in its entirety, in its completion and perfection, is in this very Thorah, and that only. A faithful Israelite is he whose belief and life are regulated by the Thorah to the best of his understanding. Whoever feels no zeal and enthusiasm for the Thorah will never be a rabbi and an honest man at the same time. This is no Biuristic standpoint; it is the rock upon which the temple of Israel proudly stands and has stood these three thousand years and more. It is historical Judaism, I know of no other. There is no Judaism without the Thorah and Revelation. This college was established to teach the literature of Israel; to train, educate and license rabbis for real Judaism.

The Talmud of the nineteenth century can claim no higher authority than the Talmud of the fifth century. Biblical criticism is no more than the Talmud of this century; scientifically it does not stand as high as the old Talmud, which had its fixed rules of interpretation, while the modern Talmud has none; no fixed laws of hermeneutics; it is still in its pilpulistic state. Kuenen, Welhausen, Renan, Ewald, or Smith, are no more reliable authorities than the Jochanans, Gamaliels, Jehudas or Rabbina and Ashi. In order to be a very faithful disciple of the sciences, we may maintain the student ought to acquaint himself with them and the Talmud alike, and like Rabbi Mair of old, enjoy the kernel and reject the shell. As free born Israelites we claim this right of free choice. Where the old Talmud appears to us contrary to the spirit of the Thorah, we reject its teaching. The same thing exactly we do with the new Talmud, and we do it on general principles, not being slaves of any system. Wherever the new Talmud is contrary to the spirit and letter of the Thorah, we reject it, and we do so because we are servants of Judaism, and not of any domineering school; and there is no Judaism without this Thorah and revelation, except in the unclear minds of the latitudinarians, whose faculty of reason is bedimmed by scholastic prejudices, so that they can only think of the when, and never of the what. This Thorah is authentic, truthful, perfect, or your Judaism is a farce also before the judgment seat of reason. We are the expounders of Judaism, so must you be if you would aspire honestly to rabbinical honors.

WOMEN AS MEMBERS OF CONGREGATIONS.

(1876.)

In the Bible, woman stands very high. At the beginning of Israel's natural life, Miriam appears as a leader so that she could say: "Did God perhaps speak through Moses only, did He not also speak through us?" Rahab saved the spies at Jericho, and Achsah was a heroic woman. During the rude period of the Judges, the Bible mentions five women of exceptional caliber. The mother of Samson, wiser than her husband; Jephtha's daughter, the beloved child, nobler than her father; the inspired patriotic heroine Deborah, the poetess queen of her people; the lovable, idyllic and childlike Ruth, faithful and quietly obedient; and Hannah, the pious mother of the Prophet, who stands in a much higher place than the high-priest. The brief stories of Abigail, the Shunnamite, the wise woman of Tekoah, and the Prophetess Huldah, reveal that woman held a high position during a period of advanced civilization. Queen Esther, the daughters of the Levites who sang in the temple, Susannah and Judith, the wise and pious Queen Salome Alexandra, and the many great women of the Talmud, like Beruriah and Yaltha, all testify to the lofty position woman had in ancient Jewish society.

None of the rabbinical provisions as to law

and practice affected the high regard for women; she always remained the queen of the heart and home. But up to 1000 A. c., all Jewish laws and customs adopted in Europe were Oriental in origin. The influence of Oriental society and the Koran gradually excluded woman from public affairs of the community, so that up to our very day she was assigned to a subordinate position in the synagogue. To call a woman to the Thorah, or admit her to public honors equally with men, would have appeared preposterous, and would to-day be considered a desecration by the orthodox synagogue.

In the early days of our activity in America, we admitted females to the choir. Then we confirmed boys and girls together, and we allowed girls to read the Thorah on that occasion. Later on we introduced family pews into the temple.

With the admission of mothers and daughters to a recognized place in public worship, came order and decorum. Abuses that had crept into the synagogue disappeared as soon as woman again took her proper place in the temple. But we cannot stop here; the reform is not complete. You must enfranchise woman in your congregations, she must be a member, must have a voice and a vote in your assemblies. We need women in the congregational meetings to bring heart and piety into them. We must have women in the boards for the sake of the principle. We must have women in the school-boards to visit the Sabbath-schools, and to make their influence felt. We must have women in the choir committee, because they understand music better than men. But, all other considerations aside, the principle of justice, and the law of God inherent in every human being, demand that woman be admitted to membership in the congregation, and be given equal rights with man; that her religious feelings be allowed scope for the sacred cause of Israel.

We are ready to appear before any congregation in behalf of any woman wishing to become a member thereof, and to plead her cause. We will debate the question with anyone who will show us in what woman is less entitled to the privileges of the synagogue than man, or where her faith is less important to her salvation than man's is to him. Till then, we maintain that women must become active members of the congregation for their own sake, and for the benefit of Israel's sacred cause.

LETTER TO A GENTLEMAN WHO WITH HIS FAMILY WISHES TO EMBRACE JUDAISM.

(1860.)

Dear Sir and Brother:—You seek the Lord and you will surely find him; for those who seek truth shall not find error, and those who long after light shall not abide in darkness. The spirit of the Lord is nigh to all who yearn after it, and the words of the Most High are clear and accessible to all. They are laid down in the twenty-four books of the Bible, commonly styled the Old Testament, which contains the path of righteousness and salvation. The five books of Moses, commonly called the Pentateuch, teach you what you shall do and believe, and what you shall not do and not believe, in order to be happy here and hereafter and acceptable in the eyes of God and man.

First of all, Judaism demands of you to believe in one spiritual and invisible God, the great first cause, the source of all intellect and essence, who cannot be compared to anything or person, not limited by any space or time, not fully conceived by any human intellect; who is the Father, Maker, Governor and Preverser of all things. Hence he never was nor will be incarnated, nor shall he ever appear in a human form or shape. This our God is revealed in His works and words as a being all-mighty, all-wise, omnipresent, infinite, all-just, most merciful, most benign and most gracious. If you, dear brother, can comprehend this sublime doctrine, which most of the Gentiles cannot, and who, therefore, cling to an incarnate God or mediator— if you, with all your heart, all your soul and all your might can believe and worship the true God, trust in him in life and death, wait for him in joy and adversity, and call on him with love and confidence as a child calls on its parents, then you are in heart and spirit of the seed of Israel, and you are redeemed from all the errors that becloud the soul of the unredeemed, then we welcome you into the covenant of God and Israel.

As a son or daughter of the divine covenant, it is furthermore expected of you that you truly believe in the justice and grace of our God. You cannot and shall not for one moment believe that an original sin rests upon man, for it would be unjust for God to punish all unborn generations for the sin of the first parents of the human race. Nor shall you believe that there is a devil, and much less that the devil or unclean spirits exercise any influence on man; for God is absolutely good, He cannot have created anything absolutely evil. Nor shall you believe the doctrine of universal depravity, i. e., that evil propensities predominate in most men; for this would be an unjust charge against our Creator. On the contrary, you shall believe that man was made in the image of God, that he was gifted with all the qualities to be good, just, righteous, pious and happy. God in His infinite goodness bestowed upon us intellect, moral free-

26

dom, respect for justice, truth and magnanimity, aversion to injustice and meanness, and the desire to worship the Most High. Sin is the consequence of ignorance or error, therefore the Lord revealed to us the Law and truth. As a son or daughter of the divine covenant you are required to regard every human being as the image of God, and to love your neighbor as yourself. You are required to instruct the ignorant, enlighten the erring, pity him who goes astray, protect the weak, feed the hungry, clothe the naked and give shelter to the homeless, because each of these is the image of God. If you can look upon man from this exalted point of view and do to every one as love dictates, if thus you behold man as God's noblest work, His image, His reflex on earth, "His son," then you will do as God's redeemed ones are required to do, then you fulfill the stipulations of the divine covenant.

We must tell you, beloved brother, virtue, righteousness, goodness, piety, and the kindred terms, signify obedience to the laws of God as they are revealed in his sacred words and in our soul. Disobedience is sin, impiety is vice and crime. Therefore salvation lies in obedience. You have free will to obey; therefore salvation lies in your hands exclusively. None can pray and make atonement for you; for none can obey the laws of God for you. God judges you according to your obedience or disobedience to His laws, according to your doings you shall be judged. The Omniscient, All-just God rewards the righteous and punishes the wicked here and hereafter. You yourself must appear and do appear every moment before the judgment seat of God. Your righteousness is your advocate and your wickedness is your adversary. You are responsible to your God for all you do or omit; for to your intellect and free will the divine laws are addressed. If you are prepared to meet your God at His judgment seat, if you, the child, require no advocate before your Father, then come to us and be of the divine covenant; then with us appear as children of the house before the Father, and His paternal love will receive you.

Again, we must admonish you not to believe for a moment that God is unjust or unkind. Laws in themselves imply the possibility that they might be violated. In fact, virtue is the triumph of our good nature. God in ordaining the Law must have known that we might transgress it. Just and gracious as He is, He must have enabled the prodigal son to return to the father. So he has done. Sin does not estrange God from us, for God is not affected by our actions; but it estranges us from God, for we forget him when we disregard His laws. Cease to sin, be rebellious no more, improve your heart, obey again the laws of God; the cause of estrangement between God and yourself will then be removed, and you will have made atonement for your sins. "Return to me and I shall return to you." God punishes not out of vengeance, for He is all-good. He punishes to correct the sinner and to bring him back to the path of virtue and righteousness. But if the sinner inflicts upon himself the punishment of repentance, of remorse, of

the mortifying knowledge of guilt, ingratitude and
rebellion, and this self-inflicted punishment corrects
the sinner and brings him back to the path of
righteousness and obedience; then God need not
punish him, his sins are forgiven, atonement is
made. Sin stains our minds and not God, hence
we must wipe the stain from ourselves and not
from God. God ordained a Day of Atonement that
we remember both our sins and His grace and
mercy.

Brother, can you honestly repent your sins and
amend your conduct before God? If so, be sure of
the remission of sin by Him who said that He forgives "iniquity, transgression and sins." Sin not
that you may be always nigh to your God; but
when sin has drawn you from him, return to Him
and He will return to you. No blood of sacrifices,
no blood of a dying man, is required by God. "The
sacrifices of the Lord are a broken spirit " (broken
with penitence). God will not despise the broken
and contrite heart.

We furthermore enjoin upon you the duty to believe with the prophet that the time will come when
"God will be King over all and His name will
be one." Understand me aright, my brother. God
is absolute justice, and this must finally govern all
mankind. While love and benignity must regulate
our conduct toward our fellow-man, the laws, which
emanate from the principle of absolute justice
(God's law), must govern the nations in their
mutual intercourse, the states and commonwealths
in their very organism. When thrones and violence and self-willed depotism will be no more,

when every knee will be bent before absolute justice, then God will be King over all the earth. Remove the chains which priestcraft and statecraft, selfishness and obstinacy, forged about the neck of humanity, let all men be politically free and be governed by justice only, and mankind will awake from a long and dreary dream and cast away their idols of silver and their idols of gold, and be ashamed of the errors and fictions, and seek God in truth and light. Whoever seeks Him shall find Him. Whenever all the nations shall seek Him, all of them shall find Him in truth and light; on that day "God shall be one," truth shall gloriously triumph over error; light over night and right over might. There is but one truth and this was revealed to Israel; therefore Israel is the mountain of the Lord which all nations must finally ascend, there to learn of God's ways and to walk in His paths. As God revealed His nature and will to Israel, even so He will ultimately be known to humanity. As He revealed his name to Israel, so He shall be called the nameless great first cause of all, Jehovah, blessed forever be His glorious name. Whenever the nations will know God in truth and light, they will also know that they learned Him from Israel, and they shall call him Jehovah, as we claim him, not Allah, not Jupiter, not Jesus, not Messiah, but Jehovah, the God of all, the cause and governor of all; then "His name will be one." The knowledge and fear of God will invite all men to know and observe His laws; this is redemption, there is the fountain-head of salvation. This is our Messiah for whom we wait.

Can you, my brother, as we do, adhere firmly to these sublime doctrines, despite persecutions, scorn and misery? Can you, like us, sacrifice joy, happiness, nay, even home and life on the altar of sublime and divine truth? Can you with all your heart work for the redemption of mankind when ten thousand times you are repulsed, rejected with scorn, and lose not your confidence in God and the sacred cause? If you then come to us, you are welcome, you are a son or daughter of the divine covenant. Believe thus, hope thus, live and act as the divine laws command; before all things observe strictly the ten commandments and the laws logically connected therewith, and you are one of us, one of the covenant before God here and hereafter. If, before man, also, you wish it to be, come to me and be blessed in the name of GOD and ISRAEL.

INDEX

Abahu, Rabbi, on the Decalogue, 148.
Abarbanel, Isaac, 223, 281, 287.
Aboab, Isaac, 285.
Abraham Ben David's Has'hogoth, 276.
Abraham ibn Ezra on paganism, 131.
on the Decalogue, 149.
as author, 271.
Abraham Sabba, quoted, 151.
Academy of France on the crucifixion, 180.
Acher and Paul, 91, 356.
Adath Israel, 103.
Adereth, Solomon ben, 267.
Adler, Henry, 82.
Adler, S., 97.
Advent, second, 360.
Ahasuerus, the legendary Wandering Jew, 179.
Akedath, Yizchak, 285.
Akiba Rabbi, on hermeneutical rules, 128.
authority on halacha, 129.
quoted, 234.
on the love for others, 237.
Albany, congregation of, 27–43.
Albert the Great, student of Jewish philosophy, 194, 268.
Albo, Joseph, on the Decalogue, 151.
as apologist, 223, 282.
Alcharisi, Shemtob, 283.
Alexandria, starting point of modern culture, 184
Al Ghazzali, 281.

Alhaker, Maheram, 283.
Altaba, Meir ibn, 283.
Altar, Jonathan, rabbi of Jenikau, 7.
Alt neu schul of Prague, 4.
American Judaism, 59, 62.
American Rabbis, 86.
Anaxagoras, philosophy of, 171.
Anatoli, Jacob, 290.
Ani Ma'amin, 278.
Anshe Chesed, congregation of New York, 103, 104.
Anshe Emeth, congregation of Albany, 39.
Anti-semitism, 62.
Apocrypha of Old Testament, 351.
Apologetics of Judaism, 221–227.
Christian, 221.
Mohammedan, 222.
Aquila, proselyte to Judaism, 187.
Aquinas, Thomas de, 268.
Arabs, Jews and, 191.
culture of, 192.
Arama, Isaac, 285.
Aristotle, 273, 277.
in Graeco-Jewish literature, 186.
Armenia, Jewish prophets in, 182.
Aruch, Talmudical dictionary, 10.
Aryan theology, 185.
Asmonean, Jewish newspaper, 41, 80, 84, 108, 112.
Auerbach, Berthold, anecdote about, 15.

(407)

Sopher, Moses, Rabbi in Pressburg, 9.
Spain, Jews in, 291.
Spanier, Louis, president of congregation in Albany, 38.
Spinoza, father of modern philosophy, 195; as philosopher, 287–292; and Maimonides, 278; and Crescas, 281.
Spirit of Age, 289.
Spiritual element in man, 250.
State senatorship, 108.
State, principles on which based, 256.
Stein, Leopold, preacher in Frankfort, 15; on decalogue, 151.
Steingrub, birthplace of I. M. W., 2.
Steinheim, S. L., on decalogue, 151; as apologist, 224.
Stern, editor of Ibn Ezra's Yesod, 272.
Straus, David Friedrich, writings of, 221.
Sue, Eugene, author of "Le Juif Errant," 180.
Sulzer, Solomon, Jewish cantor, 10.
Sunday service, 76.
Sunday-school, first Jewish, in United States, 22.
Superstition, 296.
Sura, academy of, 191.
Synod, 70, 71, 73.

Tacitus on Judaism, 187.
Talmud and Einhorn, 66.
and Wise, 67.
and Cleveland Conference, 70.
and tradition, 72.
Talmud Yelodim Institute, 106.
Taylor, President Z., 36.

Ten commandments, 95.
Teweles, E. L., a rabbinical scholar in Prague, 10.
Text-book of history, 94.
Text-books, 98.
Theocracy, principles of, 173.
Theology, the science of the conception of deity, 197.
and philosophy, 198.
of Judaism, 199.
sources for, 208.
Thomas Aquinas, student of Jewish philosophers, 194.
Tiberius, Jews under, 187.
Tikkun Middath Hanephesch, 268.
Tobit, book of, Golden Rule in, 237.
Torah, source of Judaism, 201.
most important portion of scripture, 203.
the only revelation, 231.
and Judaism, 395.
Tortosa, 282.
Tribe, a family of families, 256.
Troki, Isaac, 293.
Tusan, Joseph ben, 283.

Union of American Hebrew Congregations, first movement towards, 45–54; realized, 57; see also 78, 82, 83, 380, 381, 389.
Union and democracy, 382.
Union, and the ritual, 64.
Union Prayer Book, 31, 68, 106.
United States, constitution, 257.

Verga, Solomon Ibn, 282.

Wandering Jew, 179–197.
Webster, Daniel, 36.
Weed, Thurlow, 109.
Wellhausen, 96, 396.
Wessely, Naphtali, 324.